WRITING THE REVOLUTION

WRITING THE REVOLUTION

MICHELE LANDSBERG

Second Story Press

Library and Archives Canada Cataloguing in Publication

Landsberg, Michele, 1939-
Writing the revolution / by Michele Landsberg.

A collection of columns previously published in the Toronto Star.

A project with the Feminist History Society/Société d'histoire féministe

ISBN 978-1-897187-99-9

1. Feminism–Canada–History. I. Title.

HQ1453.L36 2011   305.420971   C2011-904502-8

Edited by Sarah Swartz
Cover illustration by Louis-Martin Tremblay
Designed by Zab Design & Typography Inc.
with Melissa Kaita, Second Story Press

Printed and bound in Canada

Feminist History Society is a project of
the Women's Education and Research
Foundation of Ontario Inc.

*Second Story Press gratefully acknowledges the support of
the Ontario Arts Council and the Canada Council for the Arts
for our publishing program. We acknowledge the financial support of the
Government of Canada through the Canada Book Fund.*

Published by
Second Story Press
20 Maud Street, Suite 401
Toronto, ON M5V 2M5
www.secondstorypress.ca

For my grandsons, Zev Nachum, Yoav Sholem, and Zimri Alan

CONTENTS

viii   *Feminist History Society*

x   *La Société d'histoire féministe*

12   ABOUT MICHELE LANDSBERG
Constance Backhouse and *Lorraine Greaves*

26   Introduction
Michele Landsberg

40   CHAPTER 1
Women's Liberation: A Toss of Silk

70   CHAPTER 2
Hot Buttons, Charged Topics

108   CHAPTER 3
Dual Oppression: Harassment and Rape

144   CHAPTER 4
Wounds Against Society: Violence Against Women

176   CHAPTER 5
In Defence of Children

214   CHAPTER 6
Women Without Borders

250   CHAPTER 7
Charting Equality: Feminist Activism and the Charter of Rights

288   CHAPTER 8
Feminism Forward

329   *Acknowledgements*

330   *Author's Reading List*

333   *Photo Credits*

FEMINIST HISTORY SOCIETY

The Feminist History Society is committed to creating a lasting record of the women's movement in Canada and Québec for the period between 1960 and the year of the Society's founding, 2010. Our objective is to celebrate fifty years of activity and accomplishment by creating a written legacy, for ourselves, our families and friends, our communities, students, and scholars. The beautiful books we publish, with membership support, will be as spirited and diverse as the movement itself, meant to stand together, and to encourage and challenge those who follow.

Invoking the image of a wave on water – of a visible, moving, growing rise of energy – many have described the feminist campaigns for suffrage and temperance during the nineteenth and early twentieth centuries as the "first wave of feminism." Thus the upsurge of feminist activism that began in the 1960s has often been characterized as the "second wave." The concept of "waves" with respect to the history of the women's movement is debated. Feminism has a history that predates the 1960s and will continue long after 2010. The energy that women brought to their quest for equality in these decades, however, is beyond dispute, and it is that energy that we seek to capture in this series.

In 1960, the Voice of Women was founded. The decade of the 1960s also saw the founding of the Fédération des femmes du Québec, the appointment of the Royal Commission on the Status of Women, and the creation of "women's liberation" groups across the country. By 2010, as some of the founding mothers of our generation of feminism have begun to die, it serves as a wake-up call regarding the pressing need to chronicle our history. Our movement is not at an end. But new waves are upon us, and now is the time to take stock of what we did and how we did it.

Over the next decade, our goal is to publish two or three books a year chronicling different aspects of the movement from sea to sea to sea. Members of the non-profit Feminist History Society receive an annual book at no extra charge, and may also purchase other books published by the Society. The topics will be as diverse as our wide-ranging campaigns for equality through transformative social, economic, civil, political, and cultural change. We will make every effort to be inclusive of gender, race, class, geography, culture, dis/ability, language, sexual identity, and age.

We maintain an open call for submissions. There will be many different authors, as individuals and organizations who participated in the movement are encouraged to contribute. There will be a variety of formats, including autobiographies, biographies, single- and multi-themed volumes, edited collections, pictorial histories, plays, and novels.

Beth Atcheson, Constance Backhouse, Lorraine Greaves, Diana Majury, and Beth Symes form the working collective for the Society. Shari Graydon has shared her expertise and time to help move the Society forward. Mary Breen, Miranda Edwards, and Jane Will have helped with the Society's administration. Martin Dufresne is providing expert translation services. Dawn Buie has created the Society's web site, making it simple to join and contact us. Zab of Zab Design & Typography has created the distinctive visual identity for the Society, as well as the book design for the series. We offer our heartfelt thanks to all of the talented and committed feminists who are providing encouragement, advice, and support.

We urge you to join, and to participate as an author, in the Feminist History Society.

www.FeministHistories.ca
info@feministhistories.ca

LA SOCIÉTÉ D'HISTOIRE FÉMINISTE

La Société d'histoire féministe s'est donné pour mandat de créer un portrait durable du mouvement des femmes au Canada et au Québec entre les années 1960 et 2010, l'année de fondation de la Société. Nous voulons ainsi célébrer cinquante ans d'activité et de réussites en créant un legs imprimé pour nous-mêmes, nos familles et nos proches, nos communautés et nos élèves, ainsi que pour faciliter la recherche. Les superbes livres que nous publions, grâce au soutien de nos membres, seront aussi vivants et diversifiés que le mouvement lui-même, et nous espérons que leur combinaison encouragera et provoquera celles qui nous suivront dans cette voie.

Invoquant l'image d'une vague avançant sur l'eau – symbole d'une montée graduelle d'énergie visible et mobile – beaucoup ont décrit les campagnes féministes organisées pour revendiquer le droit de vote et la tempérance, au dix-neuvième et du début du vingtième siècle, comme la « première vague du féminisme ». Ainsi, la poussée d'activisme féministe qui a débuté dans les années 1960 a souvent été caractérisée comme une « deuxième vague ». Toutefois, cette notion de « vagues » ne fait pas consensus comme modèle de l'histoire du mouvement des femmes. Il est certain que le féminisme date d'avant les années 1960 et se poursuivra bien au-delà de 2010. Mais on ne peut mettre en doute l'incroyable dynamisme des femmes dans leur quête d'égalité au cours des cinq dernières décennies; c'est cette énergie que nous voulons illustrer avec notre collection.

L'année 1960 a été celle de la fondation du groupe La Voix des femmes. Cette décennie a aussi vu la fondation de la Fédération des femmes du Québec, la mise sur pied de la Commission royale d'enquête sur la condition de la femme au Canada et l'apparition de groupes de « libération des femmes » partout au pays. Cinquante ans plus tard, le décès de quelques-unes des pionnières de ce mouvement sonne le rappel d'un besoin pressant, celui de rédiger la chronique de notre histoire. Ce n'est aucunement la fin du mouvement. Mais de nouvelles mouvances nous sollicitent, et il est temps de faire le point sur ce que nous avons accompli et comment nous y sommes arrivées.

Au cours des prochains dix ans, notre objectif est de publier deux ou trois livres par an, qui relateront différents aspects du mouvement féministe dans toutes les régions du pays. Les membres de notre société sans but lucratif reçoivent gratuitement un livre par an et peuvent aussi acheter les autres livres publiés par la Société. Nos thèmes seront aussi diversifiés que nos grandes campagnes pour l'égalité et leurs réformes sociales, économiques, civiles, politiques et culturelles. Nous nous efforcerons d'être inclusives à tous les titres : genre, origine ethnique, classe, géographie, culture, (in)capacité, langue, identité sexuelle et âge.

Nous maintenons une invitation générale à nous soumettre des manuscrits, en y encourageant toutes les personnes et organisations ayant participé au mouvement. Cette diversité de plumes pourra exploiter une foule de genres, qu'il s'agisse de biographies, d'auto-biographies, d'ouvrages à un ou plusieurs thèmes, d'anthologies, de récits en images, de pièces ou de romans.

Beth Atcheson, Constance Backhouse, Lorraine Greaves, Diana Majury et Beth Symes forment la collective de travail de la Société. Shari Graydon contribue à notre avancement en nous faisant bénéficier de son expertise et de son temps. Mary Breen, Miranda Edwards et Jane Will nous ont aidées à mettre en place la procédure administrative. Martin Dufresne s'acquitte de services experts en traduction. Dawn Buie a mis en ligne le site Web de la Société, qui facilite les adhésions et nos contacts avec le public. Zab, de Zab Design & Typography, a créé notre identité visuelle distinctive et une maquette de livres pour notre collection. Et nous adressons nos remerciements les plus sincères aux féministes talentueuses et engagées qui nous assurent sans relâche encouragements, conseils et soutien.

Quant à vous, nous vous incitons ardemment à vous joindre à la Société d'histoire féministe et à y participer à titre d'auteure.

www.FeministHistories.ca
info@feministhistories.ca

ABOUT MICHELE LANDSBERG

Constance Backhouse and *Lorraine Greaves*

MICHELE LANDSBERG, one of our earliest feminist newspaper columnists, is widely recognized as a clarion voice of women's rights in Canada. Writing with wit, passion, and incisive analysis for twenty-five years in more than three thousand columns and feature articles, she used her platform to advocate fearlessly on behalf of women and children, peace and pluralism, human rights, and social justice. It is no exaggeration to state that her popular columns helped to galvanize the remarkable wave of the Canadian women's movement that emerged with such force in the 1970s. The film documentary that profiles Michele Landsberg's career summed it up well: she "touched millions of hearts."

Michele Landsberg was born in Toronto in 1939. Her father, John Abraham Landsberg, the son of Russian immigrants, was born in Toronto in 1894 and made his living as a travelling salesman selling "ladies' frocks." It was a career he found frustrating, and Michele remembers him as a man who could "curse and swear" at times but "quote Shakespeare" effusively at other times. Michele's mother, Naomi Leah Glassman (Landsberg), born in Russia in 1901, had come to Canada via England at the age of ten. She raised three children – Michele and two older brothers – before taking up work as a real estate agent when Michele was twelve.

Michele's schooling took place at Allenby Public School in mid-Toronto, where she was subjected to some nasty incidents of anti-Semitism. She and the few other Jewish students would get "beaten up in the school yard" and chased with taunts of "Jews killed

Jesus." It was an early insight into intolerance and discrimination, and Michele found refuge in books. "Books were my escape and salvation," she recalled. "In books I found magic and adventure and possibility."

From an early age, she also rebelled against the feminine norms that her mother tried to instil in her. She wanted no part of "the idiocy of girls' roles," as she put it. "I was a feminist so long before there was a movement," she laughed. "There just wasn't a word for it." So in her teenage years, she became "a blue jean rebel" who "swaggered and smoked Export As." And her rebellious streak proved disruptive at Earl Haig Collegiate, the high school she attended in Willowdale, where she generally had a "terrible experience from beginning to end." She looked longingly at her brother, who was sent to UTS (University of Toronto Schools), a public school for students of exceptionally high academic ability. It was cost-free but only took boys. There was no equivalent for girls, and so Michele navigated her way through a high school that seemed to her bereft of intellectual challenge.

She was rescued by a remarkable Latin teacher, Vera Vanderlip, who recognized Michele's thirst for learning and offered up her early mornings for three years running to give the promising pupil special tutoring in Greek. "She was a wonderful teacher," recalled Michele. "It was thrilling. By the end of it, I was in line for a Prince of Wales scholarship in Greek, but instead I left to go to Israel." It was a decision that would give Michele her first experience in an international setting.

In 1957, Michele went to Jerusalem to study with the Institute for Youth Leaders from Abroad for six months, and then she put in another six months of "hard toil" on a kibbutz. Her growing recognition of social injustice became an invigorating passion to transform the world around her. She returned that fall to enrol at the University of Toronto, becoming the first woman in her family to go to university. Friends of the time describe Michele as exotic and enchanting, her singularity marked by her romantic beatnik image, as she walked across campus to class, clad in a signature trench coat and beret. She aspired to write poetry and novels.

Yearning to become another John Keats, she was crushed to find the Department of English Language and Literature to be

By her early twenties, Michele had a point of view and was ready to challenge the world.

"profoundly chauvinist," populated by professors who believed that all writers had to be male – and preferably English. Although Michele graduated in 1962, she recalls that her confidence was badly shaken. Despite her extraordinary authorial voice, she confides that she is "still anxious about writing, even after all these years."

In Michele's final year at university, the country was enmeshed in political debate over the introduction of nuclear missiles to Canada. It was a policy that outraged her and caused her to join the NDP to canvas against the Conservatives and Liberals in the federal elections of 1962 and 1963. It was during the second of those campaigns that she met Stephen Lewis, who was the NDP campaign manager in the riding. The first time she heard him speak, she was mesmerized. For his part, Stephen recalls Michele as radiant, intense, and irresistible. Their first date was for a movie, and Michele laughs that Stephen suggested they "go to see a movie in York South…. It was typical Stephen," she explains. "He thought of the whole city as a bunch of ridings."

Stephen proposed to Michele that first evening, and although she described herself as initially resistant, she was also captivated. The two were married in her mother's garden six weeks later. "Stephen made me laugh constantly, and he was the only man I had ever met who was really an egalitarian in his heart. In 1963, there were no such men – I had never met them. There were nice men, men I persuaded to be pro-feminist, but no man was really like that." Today, reflecting back on her forty-nine years of marriage to Stephen, Michele added: "He was as idealistic as I was. It was a meshing of goals, and it has sustained us."

Michele landed a plum job right after graduation – a tribute to her writing talent – as a news reporter at Toronto's *Globe and Mail*. There, the twenty-three-year-old feminist found herself immersed in a "completely male world." The culture was unrelievedly sexist, filled with sexual harassment that was taken for granted as something that came with the job. It was also deeply resistant to left-wing politics. Michele kept her birth name after her marriage to Stephen because the editors did not want it known that one of their reporters was married to a socialist politician. (In 1963, Stephen Lewis had been elected to the Ontario Legislature and would eventually lead the provincial NDP, although he would laugh that Michele was never willing to "do the political wife thing.") Michele was delighted with the newspaper's ultimatum, since she was more than happy to retain the Landsberg surname. She worked at *The Globe* as a feature writer until the birth of her first child in 1965.

Stephen Lewis was already involved in politics when he and Michele met in 1963. By the time he was campaigning as leader of the Ontario NDP in the early 1970s, Michele was working for *Chatelaine* and raising Avi, Ilana, and Jenny.

At home for six years while raising three children, Michele juggled night feedings and toddler tantrums with freelancing for the CBC and various Canadian and U.S. magazines. Stephen, meanwhile, was often sitting until midnight in the legislature, and once he became leader of the NDP, he was on the road travelling all the time. In 1971, she returned to work for pay full-time at *Chatelaine* magazine, where she flourished for seven years under the inspired leadership of the legendary Doris Anderson. In 1974, she received a gold medal in journalism from the University of Western Ontario for an article she had written on women and trade unions. By 1978 Stephen had resigned from politics, and in that same year, Michele moved to the *Toronto Star*, Canada's largest daily newspaper, to become its "woman columnist." During the 1980s, as a resident in New York City with Stephen, who had been appointed Canada's Ambassador to the United Nations, Michele also wrote columns for *The Globe and Mail*. She recalls that no newspaper ever gave her a mandate to "write a feminist column," but that was what she wanted to do, and she did it.

Full-time journalism, inherently a pressure-filled job, was even more so when combined with little children. Michele recalls "working so hard, doing all my own research, three kids under twelve, cooking, running to parent meetings at school." The work was gruelling. Says Michele:

> "I'd get to the office in the morning, read the volume of mail, read the papers to see what I wanted to write about, go out and interview people, take notes, go home, and work all evening until three in the morning as often as not, writing and rewriting (pre-computer). I remember that I was working about ninety hours a week. It was never a problem to think up ideas. There were thousands jumping out of the paper. The hardest part was finding time to research. I had a mania for research, which was drummed into me when I studied English at U. of T. When I had contentious columns, I had dozens of filing cabinets filled with stuff. I had to be prepared to defend my views."

Michele was under such pressure that she didn't even notice that her readership was growing by leaps and bounds and that her reach and influence were becoming manifestly evident to those with power and those without.

As a trailblazing feminist columnist, Michele drew the public's attention to wrongs, injustices, and anomalies that had been publicly invisible before she brought them so vividly to life. She was among the first journalists in Canada to raise and illuminate the issues of sexual harassment, the plight of child incest victims, the existence of systemic racism in employment and education, mass rapes in war-torn countries such as Rwanda and Bosnia, the harms of female genital mutilation, and the profound imbalances in Canada's divorce and custody laws.

And her writing found an eagerly responsive audience. John Honderich, publisher of the *Star*, pronounced her the "top read staff columnist" at the paper. Her readers loved or hated her, and they sent her volumes of letters, stacks of mail that she had to open, read, and digest. Some of her columns provoked debate, backlash, and visceral personal attack. Others were described by women on the front lines as "the voice for those without a voice" and "a beacon of hope." Her male colleagues at the paper sometimes became outraged over Michele's work–so incensed that at times they slammed their fists down on her desk. But no one questioned the massive clout of her writing.

Fleck women put fire back into feminism

MAY 1 6 1978

Bored by women's liberation? Feel your raised consciousness sagging just a bit?

Meet the Fleck women — the 150 who last March went on strike from their factory jobs making automotive wiring at Fleck Manufacturing Co. in Centralia, Ont. They'll put new fire in your feminism in a single morning; together, they're worth a year's subscription to MS. Magazine and any number of Herstory (women's history)

riot sticks. Jeez, it was movies!"

"I couldn't believe all gear was coming straigl chimes in 33-year-old F cey. "We had to pretend braver than we were. Y most of us are mothers, a been bringing up our k spect the police. And here walking a picket line shoved around, getting : and angry that we were stuff you wouldn't believe Intimidation? They've c

Because of her commitment to women and children, Michele Landsberg became an activist in inspiring, supporting, and fighting for childcare programs, education reform, and women's agencies of all kinds, from rape crisis centres to specialized hospitals and health services to shelters and anti-violence agencies. Gradually, she became a behind-the-scenes advisor and lobbyist for the poorest and most voiceless in society: women and children on welfare, refugees, autistic children, divorced mothers struggling to make ends meet, battered women, women and men unjustly persecuted for their race or sexual orientation. Observers note that there is scarcely a women's or children's agency in Canada that has not appealed to Michele for behind-the-scenes strategic advice or journalistic support at one time or another.

Diverse women from all groups came to see Michele Landsberg as their champion. Because of her unswerving "gender lens" and her creative ability to popularize feminist concepts, she encouraged thousands of women to understand their lives more politically. Teachers and nurses, working in predominantly female professions, honoured her many times for her staunch advocacy on their behalf. Eventually, the "silenced" women – the anonymous rape victims, the unnamed incest survivors, the guardians of child witnesses in sexual abuse cases, the women depicted negatively by the mass media – all turned to her to "tell the story." Even the fifteen rape survivors of the notorious sexual sadist and murderer Paul Bernardo came out of the shadows to ask Michele Landsberg to sit with them (many times) and hear their tortured stories so the world would know what he had done.

It is fair to say that Landsberg's literary panache and painstaking research combined to make her columns a powerful force for social and legal change. Time and again, her columns were usefully cited in the legislature during debates about proposed laws that would have an impact on women and children. She was consulted by Canadian ministers of justice as changes to sexual assault, custody, and support laws were underway. She used her connections to cabinet ministers to bring front-line women activists from the anti-violence movement to meet for the first time with those in power. Her passionate, stubborn advocacy on the part of battered and oppressed women from the Caribbean, the Middle East, and Africa, who were threatened with deportation, not only saved these individuals from peril, but actually helped to inspire a new and more generous Canadian immigration policy, one that accepted flight from gendered violence as grounds for legal refugee status.

Landsberg's voice was particularly strong during the great constitutional battles in Canada's recent history. During the epic struggle to have women's rights enshrined in the Charter of Rights and Freedoms, Landsberg's many columns and feature articles on the Charter clarified the labyrinthine subject for readers, electrified the public's support for women's equality rights, and inspired the front-line activists engaged in the daunting, but eventually successful, grassroots campaign to enshrine women's equality rights in the Constitution. One of her feature articles on the subject was awarded the profession's highest honour, a National Newspaper Award.

Landsberg never shied away from the most difficult of topics, always seeking to add depth and complexity to her readers' grasp of controversies, whether she was advocating for peace in the Middle East or debunking the so-called False Memory Syndrome. Her more controversial columns eventually circled the globe on the Internet and inspired thousands to activist causes.

In 1994, Michele Landsberg was diagnosed with breast cancer.

She was overwhelmed with "agonizing fear" and steeled herself to move through nine months of radiation and chemotherapy. "I'm not a brave person when it comes to these things," she explained. "Everybody is always saying if you have an optimistic attitude, you will survive. That is such bullshit. I believed

When Michele was awarded the President's Medal for Journalism from the University of Western Ontario in 1972, she informed the university that she would be bringing her husband, then leader of the Ontario NDP, to the ceremonies. To the couple's amusement, Stephen's place card was labeled "Mr. Landsberg."

it was a death sentence; I was not optimistic. But my wonderful oncologist told me I was wrong. A year vanished out of my life. But I got my life back – more than my life back." After the treatment terminated, Michele returned to her column at the *Toronto Star* and decided to take up the cause. She gave major coverage to the first World Conference on Breast Cancer (the first to include grassroots activists on an equal footing with scientists), wrote about the environmental link to cancer, and encouraged thousands of women by sharing her personal experience.

In 2005, Michele became the chair of the board of Women's College Hospital as it regained its independence from a merger with Sunnybrook Hospital. This surprising turn of events was a uniquely fitting triumph after a decades-long battle she had fought through her columns to keep alive the cherished woman-centred institution. For four busy years, she was occupied full-time as chair of the board at Women's College, even though it was a volunteer position. Michele continues to provide vigorous leadership to the hospital as it embarks on its new life as Ontario's first academic ambulatory hospital and the only one with a special focus on women's health.

All three of Michele Landsberg's books have been bestsellers. The landmark *Women and Children First* (Macmillan 1982, Penguin 1985) spent years on post-secondary curricula across Canada. A commentator and regular children's book critic on the CBC for more than two decades, Michele turned her astute opinions into a fascinating critique of children's literature, titled *Michele Landsberg's Guide to Children's Books* (Penguin 1986). Subsequently published in revised editions in the United States and United Kingdom (Prentice Hall and Simon & Schuster), it was recommended as a Book of the Year by *The London Times*. Chronicling her years in New York City, when her husband, Stephen Lewis, served as Canadian Ambassador to the United Nations, Michele wrote *This is New York, Honey! A Tribute to Manhattan in Love and Rage* (McClelland & Stewart 1989). It became a #1 best-seller on *The Globe and Mail* list in 1989.

In addition, Michele has been published in a variety of Canadian and U.S. publications such as *Ms.* magazine, the *New York Times Book Review*, *The Washington Post Book World*, *The New York Post*, *Entertainment Weekly*, *Parenting* magazine, *Herizons*, and *Canadian Woman Studies*.

In her many other endeavours, Landsberg has been a keynote speaker for LEAF (the Women's Legal Education and Action Fund), among many other large women's organizations; a member of the board of Sisterhood is Global; an active fundraiser for MATCH International (a Canadian-based organization guided by a feminist vision of sustainable development); a board member of PEN International (a worldwide association of writers designed to promote literature and defend freedom of expression); a member of numerous boards of women's agencies and shelters; a delegate (preceding the U.N. conference on the environment) to the Women's World Congress for a Healthy Planet; a member of the board of Nightwood Theatre (Canada's national women's theatre); and a member of the Judicial Appointments Committee in Ontario, from 1988 to 1990, charged with creating a more inclusive, democratic process for appointing judges. For the last twenty-three years, Michele has been an active participant in the renowned New York feminist seder group, which counts among its members such well-known feminists as Gloria Steinem, Esther Broner, Letty Pogrebin, and, until her death, the great human rights champion and environmentalist Bella Abzug.

In recognition of her extraordinary life and career, Michele has been honoured with a number of significant awards. She was twice a winner of the National Newspaper Award. She was named a Woman of Distinction by the Toronto Y WCA in 1983. In 1986, she was awarded the Robertine Barry Prize by the Canadian Research Institute for the Advancement of Women. In 1990, the Canadian Association of Journalists gave her the Women in Media award. In 1991, the feminist organization MediaWatch presented her with the Dodi Robb Award, describing her as a "life-long catalyst for change, mentor, inspiration and advocate." In 1996, she received the Florence Bird Award from Rights and Democracy (International Centre for Human Rights and Democratic

Daughters Jenny, 13, and Ilana, 16, admire the Woman of Distinction award given to Michele by the Toronto YWCA in 1983.

Development). The Elizabeth Fry Society of Toronto named her its Rebel for a Cause in 1997. In 2002, she was awarded the Governor-General's Award in Commemoration of the Persons' Case.

In 2006, she was named an Officer of the Order of Canada. In 2005, the Canadian Women's Foundation created the Michele Landsberg Award, a $1,000 prize for a student active in feminist advocacy and/or journalism. And she has received seven honorary doctorates from Canadian universities: Mount Allison University (1988), Acadia University (1989), Brock University (1990), McMaster University (2005), York University (2006), Ryerson University, jointly with Stephen Lewis (2007), and the University of Toronto (2009).

Pro-choice supporters Norma Scarborough (left) and Michele (right) were honoured at a 1996 dinner for 600 guests, including Dr. Henry Morgentaler. Norma Scarborough was lauded for her eight years of service as president of the Canadian Abortion Rights Action League (CARAL), Michele for her many columns in support of the abortion cause. Anti-choice advocates picketed outside the Toronto restaurant in the January cold.

Michele continues to live in Toronto with Stephen Lewis. Over the years, Stephen's career also blossomed into international prominence with his work as the United Nations' Special Envoy for HIV/AIDS in Africa and for his extraordinary, ongoing humanitarian activism. Together they have raised three children, Ilana Naomi Landsberg-Lewis (a lawyer), Jenny Leah Lewis (a casting director), and Avi David Lewis (a journalist and film-maker). For Michele, who describes herself as a "besotted grandmother," there are now three grandsons: Zev, Yoav, and Zimri.

As an exuberant gardener, mother, grandmother, and forever a feminist, Michele's verdict on life is inspiring: "Basically, I'm an optimist, even if I get heartbroken at times. I love life...and I'm not always in a rage. I want to fix things, and I want to know what happens next!" Gloria Steinem, one of the most prominent leaders of the women's movement in the United States, offers a last ringing endorsement: "[Michele] understood [feminism] better than I did. If I could put her every day on CNN, I would do it."

ENDNOTE

Information for this biographical introduction has been drawn from discussions with Michele Landsberg and from the documentary film *Michele Landsberg: Iron in Her Soul* (Davey Production, 1998), produced and directed by Donna Davey in association with Vision TV.

INTRODUCTION

MARTY GOODMAN, hard-driving editor of the *Toronto Star*, leaned back in his office chair, fingers laced behind his head, and tried to explain the nature of the job for which I was somewhat reluctantly interviewing. the *Star*'s "woman columnist" was a job I wasn't sure I wanted.

"You see the CN Tower out there?" he asked, gesturing widely. "If I look out and see a man climbing up to the top of the tower, that's a news story. See?" I nodded. "But if I look out and see a woman climbing up the tower, now that's a woman's story."

"I see, Marty," I said, keeping a straight face. Suddenly, I wanted the job. Marty, king of his realm and so sure of his wisdom, sat in for all the men I knew who simply assumed their right of leadership. But, reader, he hired me. Now I was handed the slingshot to aim straight at the forehead of male hegemony.

It was 1978, and the women's movement had been exploding like popcorn for at least a dozen years, and yet, when my column first appeared in the *Toronto Star*, halfway through May of that year, it was apparently the first time that a feminist analysis of the news had made it into daily circulation in a major Canadian newspaper. To judge by the amazed, vociferous, and adulatory reaction from the *Star*'s readers, this analysis was brand-new and burning hot to many of them.

For most of the next quarter century, give or take a few leaves of absence to write books or the three years I wrote columns for *The Globe and Mail* from my privileged perch in New York (as the wife of Canada's United Nations Ambassador Stephen Lewis), I was the feminist columnist in the *Star* beginning in the "Women's" section and eventually ending up on page two of the news section, and, in inverse ratio to my advancing age, going from five columns a week to four to three to the final sum of two, on weekends.

At age six, Michele says she was "the perfect little lady my mother wanted."

I had begun life as a docile little girl, with bows in my hair and smocked dresses for "best," in a lower-middle-class family in midtown Toronto. We were fish out of water – Jews in a mostly Christian neighbourhood, living perilously on the edge on my father's erratic earnings among the more upwardly mobile at our Reform synagogue, and advancing to the middle class only when my mother went out to work in the 1950s (scandal!) as a real estate agent. At age twelve, I wrote a lengthy, indignant essay (on the backs of my father's order forms from his work as a travelling salesman of ladies' frocks) on the use of "he" as a universal pronoun that supposedly "included" the female. "It excludes me from the English language and literature!" I wailed.

It was *difference* that made me what I became. I was a child feminist because of the gender preference, privileges, and entitlements heaped on males in our mid-century culture, made sharply visible to me in the special status awarded my beloved brother, older than I by only a year and a half. The frightening main-stream anti-Semitism of Toronto in the 1940s and '50s singled us out and held us at arm's length; the anti-intellectualism of my schoolmates, who did not share my passion for reading, highlighted my isolation. I swam against the current in every possible way, defiantly wearing pigtails and my brother's fly-front blue jeans to my suburban high school in the crinolined and simpering 1950s. The other girls actively hated me for being so strange. The principal, a blustering and agrammatical dunce, threw me out of school for several days for insolently striking a wooden match on my fly, right in front of him, and brassily lighting an Export A cigarette.

Simone de Beauvoir explained it all to me. I had to sneak *The Second Sex* from the adult library (I was still chained by a children's library card), and it burst on my consciousness – the most thrilling, though frequently impenetrable, book I had ever read. It was the first time I had met, in person or in print, anyone who shared my extreme agitation about the prison bars that encaged female lives. The rules for females in the '50s ranged from wearing conformist clothes, which included girdles and long-line bras, to exhibiting insane decorum, modesty, and chastity while doing our all-out best to "get" a boy, without whom we were led to believe we were nothing. My guidance counsellors tried to dissuade me from going to university instead of "normal school" to become a teacher.

In university, where I had hoped at last to find others who could see the injustices, I was quickly smacked down by the prevailing sexism – the lordly, indulgent male smugness that could afford to be kind in dismissing, from Olympian

Writer Myrna Kostash (left) converses with *Chatelaine*'s Doris Anderson at sculptor Maryon Kantaroff's 1970s all-women party.

heights, the wee squeakings of the female. I once remarked casually to a first-year classmate on the total absence of female-written texts in our literature courses. He made some comment about women's proven inability to write great novels. "Women are just as intelligent as men…" I began, and I'll never forget the flash of astonishment across his face and his outburst of spontaneous laughter at my ridiculous comment.

Despite all this, I was part of the lucky generation – the small cohort born just as World War II was beginning, and before the enormous wave of the baby boom. Only six percent of my generation went on to post-secondary education. True, cultural stereotypes were rigidly fixed, but at least there were few enough of us that we didn't have to struggle for jobs. Straight out of university, my BA in hand, and baffled about what my future should be, I landed a reporter's job at *The Globe and Mail* through sheer luck. My boyfriend, a bluff, good-hearted police reporter for *The Globe*, lured me into writing a news story to which he was assigned but for which he felt ill-prepared. Young poets were defying Toronto's "Sunday blue laws" (nearly every activity except breathing and praying was legally banned on the Christian Sabbath) in order to read their poetry aloud in Allan Gardens. On the strength of the story I wrote, *The Globe* employed me.

I loved my job (imagine earning ninety dollars a week for writing!) and felt I was in an adult world at the centre of Important News. After I married, I would sometimes finish work late, go downstairs to the huge King Street windows of *The Globe and Mail*, and watch the enormous printing presses spit out copies of that evening's paper – all the more exciting when a bylined story of my own was on the front page. Then I'd drive up to Queen's Park to watch my husband, Stephen Lewis, then an NDP MPP, if he were engaged in parliamentary debate. (Day and night sittings were the norm.) At twenty-three, with black stockings and long black hair, I was not the usual MPP's wife. Once an indignant Tory leapt up to protest, "Mr. Speaker, there's a beatnik in the visitors' gallery!" Stephen had the delectable pleasure of rising on a point of order: "Mr. Speaker, that's no beatnik; that's my wife."

But by 1965, when the women's movement was surging, I was at home with my first baby, and the outside world quietly vanished…

including *The Globe and Mail*, where I had spent three years as a feature writer and reporter. Now my whole universe was five inches in front of my nose, and it would be

The Royal Commission on the Status of Women held hearings in Winnipeg, Manitoba, in 1968. Chair Florence Bird is third from the left.

years before I again had the time to raise my eyes. You could say that I was born too soon, or that my timing, from a feminist point of view, was lousy. News of the movement's amazing life came to me dimly, at third- or fourth-hand, and most often in sarcastic snippets from the malestream press. I remember standing in my kitchen in 1970, holding the latest baby in my arms, and glancing at a story in the newspaper about Betty Friedan's incredible impact on the burgeoning feminist movement, following publication of *The Feminine Mystique*.

"Hmph," I thought grumpily. "Fine. Where were you, Betty Friedan, when I needed you?"

When I headed back to outside work the following year, after six years of babies and freelance writing, it was to *Chatelaine*, where I wrote feature articles and a column on "parenting." With three small children at home and a husband in politics, I spent the next seven years juggling job and motherhood. The work at *Chatelaine* was all focused on feminist issues, but the unique and historically determined truth of Doris Anderson's magnificent leadership was that she never used any of the movement jargon.

With all the ferment going on outside the walls of Maclean Hunter – the publishing house on University Avenue that produced its flagship newsmagazine *Maclean's*, *Chatelaine*, and a host of small industry journals – I went right on thinking that the women's movement was happening somewhere else. And it was. While we at *Chatelaine*, with its huge national readership of a million urban, rural, and small-town women, were pushing the ideas of the movement without ever labelling them as "feminist" (we wrote about racism in Canada, violence against women, divorce, abortion, women's poverty, women's shelters, incest, the Royal Commission on the Status of Women, the need for more women in electoral politics, and recipes and fashion on a budget), a far more radical contingent in Toronto was coming to life. By and large, we were oblivious of each other.

When I began writing at the *Star*, I was in the odd position of being a relatively untutored feminist. Women's studies didn't exist in my university days – almost no women writers, in fact, were even on the literature curriculum, and we had no female professors. In the later '60s, I had been busy nursing babies, cooking dinner, and fighting for progressive school reform, while younger women were raising their consciousness and marching for reproductive choice. I was committedly on the side of women and dedicated to winkling out women's hidden realities from the male-dominated news of the day. But because I was learning nuance and complexity as I went along, the columns unfold as a sort of running chronicle of the way we were, the way we thought, the way we were figuring things out.

As I sift through some three thousand of my columns and feature articles, some as early as my features in *The Globe* in 1963, I often have to blush (or even cringe) at attitudes I've long since shed. It's a brisk tutorial in self-knowledge, however – we often fancy that we've always been as enlightened as we supposedly are now. In my case, at least, it wasn't true. I was constantly learning from the women whose stories I retold, women I interviewed in shelters, on street corners, in university offices, or at rallies. The outrageously biased reporting of even the friendliest male reporters taught me how deeply ingrained were the sexist ideas in which we are all raised. And I learned that no one, especially not me, got a free pass out of the dominant culture. Every time I fiercely resisted tackling a new feminist subject, I forced myself to examine why – and then struggled to dismantle those mental barriers. For example, I was so loath to interview the first author of an incest memoir to come through Toronto that I later had to admit I had been unconsciously stigmatizing the victim, as though the repulsive acts still clung to her. When I finally met her, I found her delightful and illuminating.

My work on the column was a continuing education and challenge. It was exhilarating, exhausting, often painful, and frequently joyous. The readers responded with enormous openness. In the first years, I laboriously cut open hundreds of envelopes a week; later, in the e-mail era, three hundred to five hundred messages a day was the norm after a provocative column. Often there were startling stories to be mined from my readers' correspondence.

It was the best job in the world, and the *Star* was an outstanding employer. Fortunately, I was ready to "write the revolution:" I'd been born at the right moment in history and had stumbled into the perfect assignment at a time when the very themes dearest to my heart were making headline news. The rewards have been ample. I know that the feminist anecdotes, true-life accounts, analyses, and revelations in the columns had a direct and sometimes life-changing impact on many, many women – I know because they still seek me out to tell me so.

I've chosen for this book the columns that seem to chart the path of the movement most tellingly, and those that I think might resonate for readers today. I have kept an eye open for columns where my hasty judgements or unconscious prejudices are clangingly obvious today; some of these are included to show how attitudes slowly bend and change shape over time.

What an amazing few decades it was! At the height of the feminist movement in the late '60s and '70s, we were like a snowball rolling down a steep hill, gathering momentum, flinging new ideas into the air at reckless speed. Sexual harassment, glass ceiling, marital rape, no means no, the "click," safe touch, children's rights,

Braving the bitter winter weather in 1997, Michele interviews striking workers of an old-age home, who were fighting to keep their benefits.

Ms., bra burning, consciousness raising, primary caregiver, the personal is political, pay equity – none of these concepts had existed before the women's movement, and all of a sudden the new phrases were on every civilized person's tongue. Academics were snapping up themes and elaborating them, publishers rushed to publish books on new feminist subjects (whole new imprints and publishing houses were created), and young people were galvanized into action.

The media, naturally, were agog. Newness and upheaval are the media's bread and butter, and though they were slow off the mark (you know something is getting old when the media begin to report it), they did eventually figure out that something was happening out there, something more than a target for mockery and scorn. Of course, simultaneously with the birth of the movement came the solemn, wish-fulfillment pronouncements of the movement's death. The feminist movement has existed, to one degree or another, in every era of human history, and it has always been deemed dead on arrival by the forces that wish it were. The conviction that "feminism is dead" was so widely mouthed – and believed – that when I began my *Toronto Star* column in 1978, one of the first columns I wrote invited women to "raise their sagging consciousness."

So what happened to that snowball? It got bigger and bigger as it rolled, it picked up all sorts of little debris (factions, arguments, in-fighting), and heavier and heavier, it rolled to a stop. Gradually, that stalled snowball melted into little rivulets, streams, and brooks, trickling into and infiltrating every aspect of society. Feminist achievements became so much part of the mainstream that the movement seemed to dissipate.

Those who weren't on our side to begin with were quick to pronounce us dead and to theorize gloatingly about our slowing momentum: It was our struggles with racism that did us in, they crowed, or the "pornography wars," or the fact that young women despised the very name of our movement. These are all symptoms and side effects, not causes. The most significant factor in our declining impact was the slowly entrenching backlash and the increasing power of the conservative movement. ("Backlash" and "conservative movement" may be read as a redundancy.) The more laws we got through legislatures and the courts, the more equality we demanded and won, the more our female presence began to fill medical schools and legal offices – the more those with established power resisted us. The first prime minister to cut back our Trudeau-era funding was Brian Mulroney. Successive prime ministers, Liberal and Tory, slashed more and more from the federal money that kept our national organizations going. It's too big a country, with far too little philanthropy aimed at women, to sustain national organizations without government support. Entire networks of social advocacy, research, and activist organisations were closed down, one by one, as the country veered right and deficits – rather than equality or the public good – became the dominant concern.

The wider political context is important. In the '80s and '90s – the decades of greed, extreme consumerism ("Because you deserve it!"), and rampant individualism on the American neo-liberal model – the collectivism and idealism of the Second Wave of feminism began to look fustian. Young women especially, raised to believe they were already equal ("You can be anything!"), leapt through the newly opened doors to education and careers – and many were seduced away from a social consciousness by the demands and rewards of individual pleasure-seeking and consumerist distractions. The media became skilled at finding privileged, upper-class women who abandoned their careers to stay home with children, or defiant young women who would obligingly insult feminism or proclaim their devotion to "pussy power" to satisfy an anti-feminist news peg.

Nevertheless, I never doubted for a moment that feminism was as alive as ever and would rise to meet the next massive political pushback with fury and determination. In the meantime, of course, now that we were no longer coming up with new concepts and new ways to deconstruct our world, the media moved on to the next little series of upheavals in the status quo: the fathers' rights movement, the so-called False Memory Syndrome, then the whole Cosmo Girl throwback – oops, I mean *Sex in the City*. Because we were no longer new, the media lost interest. News is about the new, after all. Without that dazzling media spotlight, people lost track of what we were up to. And many of the most idealistic youth quite rightly took feminism for granted and moved on to more immediate battles: globalization, climate change, the oil wars.

Preparing this book, I began to keep track of feminist-focused activism wherever I could find it, especially among the young. My findings were amazing. Canada is buzzing with youthful feminist activism, now that a decade of conservative values has eroded our gains. Dozens upon dozens of feminist blogs spark debate on the Internet, engaging thousands. The Abortion Rights Coalition of Canada speaks out forcefully, researches the state of services, organizes press conferences, and lobbies with sharp effectiveness to prevent anti-abortion bills from sneaking through Parliament. Younger activists stage readings of abortion monologues and, through Canadians for Choice, help isolated young women with the money and travel assistance they need to get abortions; in Prince Edward Island, the only province with no abortion services, women have begun to organize to fight for access.

When a clumsy police officer in Toronto warned students that they should avoid "dressing like sluts" to prevent being raped, the protest mushroomed into an outrageously successful Slut Walk on April 3, 2011, in downtown Toronto, with two thousand wildly dressed women, young and old, protesting their right to wear anything without being blamed for rapists' crimes. Within weeks, similar Slutwalk protests had burst into action around the world, from the Northwest Territories to New Zealand.

In Québec, the FemRebelles came together in a feminist grassroots collective and linked up with the FemRev in Winnipeg, where several hundred diverse young women gathered to "share struggles." In Ontario, the Miss G Project began five years ago when a small group of undergraduates – inspired by newly discovered feminism sparked by their university women's studies courses – determined that women's history should be taught in secondary schools. By 2011, their membership numbered in the thousands across Canada, and the Ontario Ministry of Education agreed to offer a women's studies curriculum, which Miss G helped to create. Meanwhile, they reach out to offer education sessions to wildly enthusiastic teens in high schools.

In Vancouver, the dynamic WAM (Women and Media) conference met for the first time in 2011, exploring and challenging the role, portrayal, and career possibilities of women in the media. And in Ottawa, Canada's largest-ever international gathering of women (two thousand attendees) occurred in an academic and grassroots conference called "Women's Worlds" in the summer of 2011. In all these activist endeavours, the words "young" and "diverse" and "feminisms" bubble up to describe – the Fourth Wave? (The Third Wave, which announced its birth in New York in the 1990s, never caught on very persuasively in Canada.)

Most of us in the Second Wave weren't quite ready, as our wave subsided, to be cast as the "older generation." It was only yesterday, after all, that we ourselves were wearing cheeky slogans and taking back the night. We reacted with indignation when young women began to rebel by declaring themselves "not feminist." We should have played it cool because youthful scorn can always be expected. We should have trusted our achievement: We had equipped those young women with the language and the understanding that they were equal and entitled to justice and a fair share. Sooner or later, when the world showed them its uglier side, they would feel enough indignation to rise up in protest again.

Feminism is a protest movement, the deepest possible attack on the masculinist status quo. And protest movements don't last. They rise, they flood the public conversation, and they recede, leaving behind a new tidemark. Perhaps you have to be old enough to have grown up in the repulsively smug and oppressive 1950s to know how deeply and lastingly our society has changed, no matter the surface victories of the backlash. Nothing is now unquestioned by feminism. In my youth, nothing at all was questioned by anyone.

As Gloria Steinem said when the term "sexual harassment" was first used, "We thought it was just life."

The recipients of the 2002 Governor General's Awards in Commemoration of the Persons Case celebrate in Ottawa in front of the statue of the Famous Five on Parliament Hill. From left to right: Michele, Margaret-Ann Armour, Megan Reid, Elisapie Ootova, Françoise David, and Nancy Riche.

How will this newest rising of women change the future? I can't wait to see.

AUTHOR'S NOTE *All the headlines on the columns in this book were originally written by various copy editors and never by me. They don't necessarily represent my view of the column's message.*

Chapter One

WOMEN'S LIBERATION: A TOSS OF SILK

THE ARC OF the Women's Liberation Movement, or "Women's Lib" as it was dismissively dubbed in the 1960s and '70s, is bewilderingly difficult to follow – more like a toss of silk, billowing and sagging and then soaring across the sky, than the clean swoop of a rainbow.

In Canada, feminist work had been doggedly pursued from the late 1950s and right through the '60s by the generation ahead of me: middle- and upper-class white women of means and confidence whose mostly lady-like demeanour masked their iron determination. As a young *Globe and Mail* reporter in the early '60s, I was sometimes sent to cover meetings of the Association of Women Electors [AWE]. I saw them as starchy ladies in gloves and hats, preoccupied with the minutiae of municipal affairs – but that was my youthful stupidity. A keener, more experienced observer might have detected the first murmurings of a coming revolution in political engagement.

Indeed, an early president of AWE, June Rowlands, was to become the first female mayor of Toronto in 1991. Among other forerunners were the Voice of Women, an anti-nuclear and pro-peace women's organization founded in 1960 and led by such shining lights as Ursula Franklin and Kay Macpherson. Much less visible, but bursting with new energy, were fledgling groups of francophone women, aboriginal women, union women, black women, lesbians, and political radicals.

In the late '60s and early '70s, a vibrant, adrenaline-charged lesbian movement was bursting out in Toronto, with many short-lived but vivid nightclubs, coffee-houses, magazines, newsletters, rock bands, and all the internecine fury, exultation, and factionalism that any movement could spawn. Many of the lesbian activists identified with feminism. Only later did I learn of the mainstream straight movement's panic-stricken rejection of lesbianism ("the lavender menace!"). Straight women's homophobia – more than anything, I believe, a fearful and defensive reaction to accusations that feminists were just "a bunch of man-hating lesbians" – was, nevertheless, a hurtful and destructive reflex that cost the women's movement dearly in wasted energies and squandered womanpower. In any case, this stream of feminism was pulsing away beneath the radar of most Canadians. Any media attention was reserved for women like Doris McCubbin Anderson, who began editing *Chatelaine* magazine in the late '50s, and Laura Sabia, who began pushing for a Royal Commission on the Status of Women in the early '60s.

Young women were a forceful element in the New Left that emerged in the United States from the civil rights struggle and the protest movement against the Vietnam War. It didn't take them too long to register the vaulting egotism and sexual entitlement of the movement's male leaders, and from the protest-within-protest surge came the rebirth of feminism, mostly dormant since the days we won the vote.

Betty Friedan's 1963 book *The Feminine Mystique* had suddenly released the pent-up forces of women's self-discovery. It was an explosion of joyful creativity and expression: Consciousness-raising groups, intense and thrilling, sprang into existence, as did women's avant-garde theatre, collective daycare ventures, fledgling women's book publishers, adventures in sexuality of all kinds, Take Back the Night marches to protest the idea that women should cower indoors at night

THIS WOMAN'S PLACE IS IN THE HOUSE ...
THE HOUSE OF COMMONS

Kay Macpherson

INDEPENDENT – ST. PAUL'S

Kay Macpherson is working for :

Equal rights and opportunities for women; a better life for pensioners and a fair chance for all our children; greater pollution control and conservation of resources; ending the threat and hardships of unemployment; greater independence for Canada; international disarmament, co-operation and peace.

LET WOMEN SHARE THE RESPONSIBILITY

263 men : 1 woman M. P.

VOTE FOR A BETTER BALANCE

WILL YOU HELP ?

KAY MACPHERSON'S COMMITTEE
1066 YONGE -North of Rosedale
485 4268· 486 6226   Station

Kay Macpherson, one of the Voice of Women founders, ran as an Independent in the 1972 federal election gaining 5.5 percent of the votes in a Toronto riding.

to "prevent" rape, grassroots rape crisis centres, the very first battered women's shelters, cervical self-examination and "menstrual extraction," and do-it-yourself abortion groups. (Yes, really – in California.) The art world was electrified by the new feminist voices and visions. Women across North America threw themselves into the transformative excitement of the liberation movement.

And in Canada, there were, among others, the Fleck women.

FLECK WOMEN PUT FIRE BACK INTO FEMINISM
May 1978

Bored by women's liberation? Feel your raised consciousness sagging just a bit?

Meet the Fleck women – the 150 who last March went on strike from their factory jobs making automotive wiring at Fleck Manufacturing Co., in Centralia, Ont. They'll put a fire in your feminism in a single morning; together, they're worth a year's subscription to *Ms.* magazine and any number of Herstory (women's history) courses.

They're spunky, ribald, salt-of-the-earth, riding high on a wave of sisterhood as unaffected as their bright green eye shadow and double negatives. Fifteen of them have been in Toronto, briefly, to testify before the Ontario Labour Relations Board concerning charges their union, the United Auto Workers, has brought against Fleck management and police – charges of intimidation and illegal anti-union activity.

Waiting to testify before the pin-striped board members, they fill the sedate lobby with the slap-slap of cards (euchre and crazy eights) and good-natured banter.

"Guess we're a bunch of country bumpkins," they laugh, poking fun at themselves for not knowing how to operate the 10-cents-a-spray perfume machine in their downtown hotel.

Back in March, the Fleck women struck for decent wages and the right to have union security – a right conceded even by Ontario Labour Minister Bette Stephenson. Many of the strikers are sole-support mothers who were bringing home about $100 a week, far less than the plant's maintenance men were earning.

They thought it would be a quick, straightforward little strike, though many were badly scared when the OPP came into the plant before the strike to lecture on picket-line behaviour. Many of them got the impression that strikes were illegal, that they might go to jail for five years. They struck anyway.

Union? Strike? They never even thought of such things before they decided to get organized last fall. Once the idea of joining a union was proposed, it ran like wildfire through the plant; in the first week, 82 percent of the women signed up.

"The management ripped down my notice about the organizing meeting," laughs Sheila Charlton, 35, "so I wrote the notice on my T-shirt with black marker and wore it to work. All the girls were running over to see it."

The 150 Fleck "girls" who struck in 1978 for the right to have a union and decent wages were a down-to-earth but determined lot who faced harassment in the workplace and riot police on the picket lines.

Girls. All the women call each other "girls." Even inside the hearing room, where their sass, ingenuity and gritty determination keep cracking up the lawyers, everyone calls them "girls."

They don't have any sophisticated movement jargon, obviously.

"That first morning of the strike, every one of us was scared to death," says Mary Lou Richard, 30. "I climbed in the car and my legs were shaking. And when they brought out the riot police against our picket line...hundreds of cops, a helicopter...they had these shiny black helmets and big riot sticks. Jeez, it was like the movies."

"I couldn't believe all that black gear was coming straight at me," chimes in 33-year-old Fran Piercey. "We had to pretend to be a lot braver than we were. You know, most of us are mothers, and we've been bringing up our kids to respect the police. And here we were, walking a picket line, getting shoved around, getting so scared and angry that we were shouting stuff you wouldn't believe."

Intimidation? They've overcome their initial disbelief and fear. "One guy, who didn't go out on strike, he's a big 300-pounder. We were told he'd be coming after us with a baseball bat," says Sheila Charlton. A great whoop of laughter goes up from the crowd of women who are by now listening in to the interview. "There are more of us than him!" shouts one.

Sexual harassment by male supervisors on the job: To hear their stories, these women have put up with more leers, jeers, mauling, grabbing and sexual insult than any 100 office workers are ever likely to encounter. They handle it with their favourite weapon: bawdy, biting humour that slaps down the offender with belittling wit. (Too bad their best one-liners are unprintable.)…

The ultimate proof of their liberation, despite the "girls," despite the way they stayed up all night on picket duty and then automatically took on the task of making sandwiches for hundreds of male picketers who had joined them, was the way they misinterpreted one of my questions.

"Would all this have happened if you weren't all women?" I asked, referring to the intransigence and bullying tactics used against them. "Jeez, no," exclaims Sheila Charlton. "The men would never have had the guts to do what we've done."

One by one, as the Fleck women are called to testify, they sail proudly, if nervously, into the hearing room. "Stick to the truth!" is their rallying call to each other.

As each one comes out, she's greeted with cheers and hugs. Sisterhood and sticking to the truth as they've lived it: two tough and triumphant achievements for the Fleck women.

• • • • • • • • •

DURING MY YEARS at the *Toronto Star*, between 1978 and 2003, I marched often on picket lines (it always seemed to be snowing or raining) with women at Radio Shack, Bell, and Irwin Toy, where the immigrant workers assured me that the Irwin brothers were so mean because they were Jews. (They weren't, as it happens; they were non-Jews of German origin.) Sisterhood is complicated.

On another front, women's liberation began to shift into the legal arena and the era of securing our rights.

EXCLUDING GIRL FROM LEAGUE EXPOSES ABSURD LAW
August 1978

We still hold the law to be so sacred that those who make it, write it, and interpret it are very seldom criticized.

That's why you don't hear a public outcry and gnashing of teeth even when the law seems absurd. Take, for example, the strange business last week about Gail Cummings, the Huntsville 12-year-old who wanted to play hockey. Gail was good, so good that she quickly outclassed the local girls' teams and was snapped up by the boys' all-star team, with whom she played four games, as goalie, in 1976, when she was 10.

That was fine with Gail and the other kids and the coach. But it was dreadfully scary to the Ontario Minor Hockey Association [OMHA]. Why, those big sports fellows were all atremble and aquiver at the thought that a girl could play their game better than a lot of boys. In the distance, they heard the rumbling and the roar as the foundations of western civilization began to crumble.

And when they booted Gail out of the league, and when Gail's parents asked the Ontario Human Rights Commission if it were quite kosher to bar a kid from sports because of her sex, and when the Human Rights Commission said it was not kosher, and Gail must be allowed to play...well then, is it any wonder that these he-men ran crying to the Ontario Supreme Court to protect them from that little girl?

The Court pondered. The whole case hinged on whether the OMHA was in violation of the Ontario Human Rights Code, which forbids discrimination on the basis of sex, colour, race, creed, nationality, or origin in respect to "accommodation, services, or facilities available in any place to which the public is customarily admitted."...

Chief Justice Gregory Evans, in his written judgment, concluded that the law is directed only at discrimination in facilities which are "open to the public." The OMHA, he said, is not really open to the public, but is a service "extended to and to the advantage of boys." That the league plays in publicly owned arenas "is not a dominant factor in the case."

Chief Justice Evans felt that "a reasonable view" of the league's activities is that it does not discriminate against girls because "it is a facility capable of being used by boys only." Surely, said the Chief Justice, "a volunteer organization of this kind has the right to limit the scope of its activities." Besides, he argued, if the league had to accept girls, it "may well destroy an organization which has contributed so much to the development of boys."

• • • • • • • • •

ONE SIMMERING DEBATE through the 1960s was whether housewives should be paid for their labour. The idea seems outmoded today, when most women are employed outside the home. It's strange to remember how many stay-at-home mothers accepted the divisive propaganda that feminists despised housewives, even while we were out there withstanding ridicule for making the argument for housewives' pay.

Even progressives were mostly opposed to this idea as, well, impertinent. We feminists thought it would demonstrate the dignity and worth of our work in the home; left-wing men thought it would bankrupt the economy and maybe, just maybe, demean the value of their labour. It was a never-fail provocation for me to slip into conversations with my father-in-law, David Lewis, a noble socialist but of a more chauvinist era.

HEY, HOUSEWIFE, YOU'RE WORTH $6,000 A YEAR
June 1978

Look up from that dishpan and smile, Canadian housewife. Today, the federal Canadian Advisory Council on the Status of Women announced that our work is worth at least $26 million a year to the economy, or $6,000 for every household in the country.

It's the first time ever that thorough research has been done into the content and value of Canadian housework, and it's an eye opener. The Council's 90-page report, called "Five Million Women," says that those 5 million are producing services equal to 27 percent of the gross national product.

Something else emerges from the report. If "fear of flying" [a reference to sexual inhibition, borrowed from a 1973 Erica Jong book title] and "midlife crisis" were the trendy phrases of the mid-'70s, then we'd better quickly add "housewife ambivalence" to our vocabulary for the end of the decade. Not only are housewives ambivalent about their role, but the Council itself can't make up its mind about the pros and cons of housework and how it should be rewarded.

Though the Council pays tribute to the overwhelming dollar value of all this cooking, cleaning, and childcare, it also cautions against the "psychological dependency" of unpaid housewifery, and warns young women against "shutting themselves into dead ends."

For all that, the Council could not come up with any workable suggestions for paying housewives or even letting them in on the Canada Pension Plan (CPP). Universal pay for housewives would be staggeringly expensive; voluntary contributions to the CPP would exclude exactly the women who need pensions most, the ones who couldn't afford to contribute. So after all their charts, graphs, and analysis, the Council comes out plumping squarely for "a change in attitudes," that universal and meaningless panacea that is the last resort of every government commission I can remember.

The most interesting thing about the report is not its conclusions, though, but its glimpses into the housewives' state of mind. A majority of housewives, it says, are dissatisfied with housework. In an English study, cited in the Council's report, 72 percent of the housewives found their work monotonous, lonely, and fragmented.

I know, I know. A couple of years ago, I took a three-month leave of absence to steep myself in the remembered joys of "being at home with the kids." Nothing, I thought, could be quite as frenetic, as emotionally draining, as the constant rush between home and work.

I was right. Being at home is incredibly soothing to the frazzled nerves...in some ways. Each day dawned with a rosy prospect of unstructured hours softly spreading before me. What I'd forgotten was that little Catch 22 of housewifery: You shall have all the time in the world, at last, but it shall be divided into segments of no more than seven minutes each. You will never settle down with the morning paper without remembering at the last minute that it's shopping day. You will remember the school bake sale (too late) while in the grocery store, comparing the merits of five different kinds of lettuce.

I'd forgotten what it was like not having a bank account of my own. I'd forgotten how housework swells to fill every available crack of time, so that I was soon trying to make time to be with the children, instead of luxuriating in hours of playtime.

The average Canadian housewife spends 50 hours a week

doing housework, says the Council's report. In tiny European villages where water is drawn from wells, a woman's hours of work are the same. And housewives are actually working more hours per week now, surrounded by their gleaming machinery, than they did 50 years ago.

I could have told the Council that myself. How many hours did I spend cleaning that glurk out of washing machine agitators, or potting and repotting plants? How many frazzled hours were spent poking bent hangers up the clogged tubes of vacuum cleaners, or phoning servicemen who didn't show up?

It was all worth it, though. The chance to sit in the sunshine on the back porch steps to chat with a child who'd just arrived from school; the chance to dream up special recipes for someone home with a cold; the time to whomp up a giant batch of gooey playdough for a gang of neighbourhood kids.

Ambivalence? Don't ask. It's just part of being a woman in one of history's more chaotic, transitional times. The pity is that women feel they have to square off and attack each other's choices instead of wryly admitting to each other that there are at least 15 sides to this home-or-job dilemma.

• • • • • • • • •

WHEN FEMINIST SUPERSTAR Gloria Steinem came to town in August 1978, I was ecstatic to get a chance to interview her. Gloria not only spoke our feminist truths with wit and infinitely quotable clarity, she also was a living refutation of the often-voiced idea that feminists were only soured "old maids" who were too ugly to "get a man," a presumably devastating sexual insult hurled indiscriminately at any woman who spoke up, whether she was ugly, single, or not. Gloria, though, was so obviously beautiful, calm, and assured, with enough female confidence to masquerade as a Playboy bunny in order to get a news story, that this accusation instantly died on the lips of any would-be slanderer. She had the added glamour of being a founding writer for *New York Magazine* and is still, fifty years later, billed as "the most famous feminist in the world."

EQUAL PAY IS STEINEM'S FINAL GOAL

August 1978

A decade after she first flashed on the scene as a feminist spokes-woman, Gloria Steinem can still dazzle us. Lucid, funny, at ease but totally in control, the president of *Ms.* Magazine Corporation seems to embody the growing-up and the staying power of the movement.

In town to speak to the American Psychological Association convention, she held a press conference yesterday at the Sheraton Centre and leavened her remarks with rapid-fire one-liners:

"The most sophisticated argument against the feminist movement is that men's egos are too fragile. But," she grins devilishly, "we have more faith in men than that."

"Militant? We're not militant. The Pentagon is militant; we don't even have a helicopter."

"A majority of the U.S. population agrees with all the major issues of feminism...freedom of choice about abortion, equal pay, daycare, equal opportunity. But that's just in the opinion polls. I'm not saying what they think when we move in next door. A black nuclear physicist is always just a nigger in the south, you know, and a competent woman is a bitch anywhere."

The one-liners were just the spice, of course. Steinem's message is serious, her logic knife-sharp, and her intelligence luminous. She looks out from behind her famous round granny glasses and, far in the distance, she sees a bloodless revolution.

"When all women get equal pay, at last, that will be a transformation of society, not just a simple reform. Equal pay, as our opponents know all too well, means a massive redistribution of wealth. Because right now the whole economy rests on the cheap labour of millions of women. The average U.S. secretary is two years better educated than the average boss."

For those of us who feared the feminist movement was faltering, Steinem brings a wry but bracing optimism....

"...[T]he shift in attitudes on the part of the public has been enormous, and that's been an accomplishment of the movement. And we have networks now, alternate structures that are nourishing and supportive to women. We have more minority role models. And the movement is more cohesive now than it's ever been."

"This is a revolution, and we're in it for our lifetime."

• • • • • • • • •

IT WAS A REVOLUTION waged with words instead of swords, and if we pushed back the obstacles in our path by the sheer force of numbers, determination, and the obvious justice of our cause, there was one barrier that remained and is in place to this day: the obduracy of capitalist economics, which sees early childhood as insignificant, high-quality childcare as a luxury, not an economic and societal necessity, and the raising up of the human race as a woman's private problem.

WORKING MOMS AND THEIR KIDS DON'T GET FAIR DEAL
May 1978

The United Nations says, in a recent report, that working wives are exhausted. Be it Canada, Finland, or Peru, it's the same old economic squeeze: once you have the home and kids, you have to go out to work to help pay for them.

But since working mothers are no less devoted than the stay-at-home kind, they end up doing two full-time jobs. France reports that "It's quite a physical strain" and West Germany notes that "dual-role women" are suffering more health problems.

Well, yes. We know all about that here in Toronto where roughly half of all mothers are out in the labour force.

It's what I call the Elevator Syndrome. Five o'clock in an office building and the men are strolling to the elevator with a certain rosy expansiveness. Sometimes they almost miss the next down car because they're busy chuckling over the day's anecdotes, swinging their briefcase with that cheerful expectation of a good hot dinner waiting at home.

The working mums look different. They come pelting down the corridors as though headed for the last boat out of a flood zone. You can practically hear their blood pressures swooshing upward each time the elevator lumbers to another maddening halt.

Their mental calculators are clicking: "Let's see, 25 minutes to make it through rush hour...did I remember to defrost the hamburger? Damn, forgot to buy Jane's gym shoes at lunchtime. I'll write a note to that nag of a teacher...."

There'll be another three hours of work at least before the working mum can call it quits. The cooking pots clang, the kitchen rings with the voices of children competing for a few minutes' attention, the adrenalin pumps, the mind races ahead to the next seven fussy details of running a house. (Yes, confirms the U.N., working mothers go to bed later and rise earlier than their husbands.)...

Despite the fact that half of Canada's mothers are working to pay the bills (mostly at boring, low-paid jobs), often exhausting themselves in the effort to do a decent job of parenting, too, society persists in treating them like pampered minxes who are selfishly indulging a taste for diamonds.

How many after-school programs do you know about? In-plant daycare? *Any* daycare centres? Doctors or dentists who keep evening hours? Hot lunches for primary school kids? Flexible working hours for women? Neighbourhood drop-in centres where kids can play safely till their mothers get home? What about child-care exemptions on income tax...still a piddling drop in the bucket compared to the real cost of paying for competent care?

Those experts at the U.N. think they have an answer: international standards, education, and mass media campaigns. Thanks, fellas, but it's going to take a more basic turnaround than that before working mums and their children get a fair deal.

• • • • • • • • •

WHILE THE FEMINIST MOVEMENT was making some inroads in the greater society, inside the movement stress fractures began to appear. At the end of the 1960s, Marxist feminists had clashed bitterly with "apolitical" feminists. By the mid-1970s, differing sexualities were testing the tensile strength of the movement's bonds.

While I was working at *Chatelaine* magazine, I had not a single contact with feminist activists outside the magazine. Sometime in those early '70s years, I heard the exciting news that A Woman's Place, a drop-in gathering place complete with feminist research materials, had opened in midtown Toronto, on Dupont Street.

There were no "centres" for women at that time, no building we could claim as our own, no single meeting place where you could go in search of like-minded feminists. I was thrilled by the news. On my lunch hour, I rushed up to this beckoning haven and stopped short just inside the door. I remember a tempting rank of bookshelves at one side – a collection of books and documents that was to grow into the Toronto Women's Bookstore. At the back of the room was a desk where two young women halted in mid-conversation, looked up, and glared at me. I was surprised to see that both were wearing the legendary "army boots" that were supposed to characterize "women's libbers," but which in fact were almost unknown in Toronto.

Haltingly, I introduced myself as a sister feminist working for *Chatelaine*, anxious to consult their shelves of research. Their hostility seemed to deepen. Dismissively, they waved toward the shelves and told me I could "look at stuff" if I really wanted to. Then they turned to each other and began passionately to kiss. That kiss, clearly meant to shock me, barely registered on my consciousness. I was already too rattled by their evident scorn and distaste. What could it mean? Here at last were the feminist activists with whom I'd longed to connect, and they clearly wanted nothing to do with me.

We've all travelled so far since the early '70s that it would be pleasant not to revisit the misunderstandings of earlier decades, but it's important to remember the struggle lesbians had, even with other feminists. I feel a little defensive now about my ignorance in those days, but at least I can plead that there was practically nothing about lesbians in the public eye or in feminist conversation to help me understand the depth of their sense of exclusion, their fierce resentment, their defiance of bourgeois types like me and the mainstream society I represented to them. My pathetic lack of awareness when I first visited A Woman's Place paralleled, come to think of it, the serenely unconscious sexism of men.

Later, I realized that homophobia was a deep and destructive strain in the women's movement. Some women may have been threatened by lesbian sexuality, but I think most were merely falling prey to hoary divide-and-conquer tactics. Men opposed to feminism loved to dismiss us all as "frustrated lesbians" (whatever

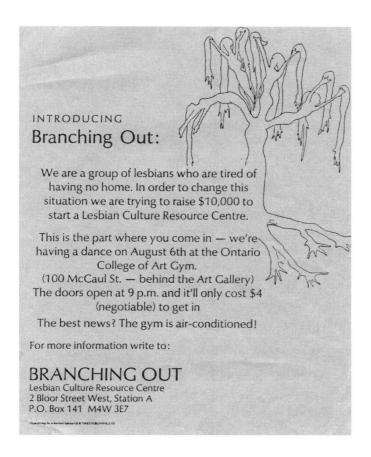

INTRODUCING

Branching Out:

We are a group of lesbians who are tired of having no home. In order to change this situation we are trying to raise $10,000 to start a Lesbian Culture Resource Centre.

This is the part where you come in — we're having a dance on August 6th at the Ontario College of Art Gym.
(100 McCaul St. — behind the Art Gallery)
The doors open at 9 p.m. and it'll only cost $4 (negotiable) to get in

The best news? The gym is air-conditioned!

For more information write to:

BRANCHING OUT
Lesbian Culture Resource Centre
2 Bloor Street West, Station A
P.O. Box 141 M4W 3E7

that meant), and many heterosexual feminists were threatened by this delegitimizing of their beloved movement. Naturally, lesbians were enraged by the kind of feminist who wanted

By the end of the '70s, lesbian groups such as Branching Out had become more active and public, as evidenced by the group's 1984 pamphlet.

them to set up the chairs for the meeting but never to chair the organization for fear of what outsiders would say.

The gay and lesbian liberation movement changed all that, first by forcing homophobia into the open and then by showing the world its ugly destructiveness. Feminists had to evolve, along with the rest of society.

By the turn of the decade, I allowed myself a moment of tempered optimism as I surveyed the progress of the movement. Amusingly, in retrospect, the "peg" for my column was a poll done by a tobacco company, heavily invested as it was in "liberation."

THE DIE IS WELL CAST FOR EQUALITY
March 1980

The women's movement may not have won us equal pay or decent pensions...yet. But a new U.S. poll proves that the movement has started a massive shift in public perceptions, as quietly inexorable as a beginning avalanche.

The poll, of 3,007 women and 1,004 men, was the latest in 10 years of surveys done by an American tobacco company to gauge the progress of women's liberation.

A decade ago, say the pollsters, only a minority of U.S. women (40 percent) approved of the struggle for equal rights. The most resistant to change were the older, less-educated women.

Today, a significant majority (64 percent) of U.S. women favour social change, though the base of support has shifted: now the older, less-educated women are more convinced, while proportionately fewer young, privileged women support social change.

Even more astounding is that 64 percent of U.S. men, too, support a change in women's status. Three-quarters of the women felt that abortion should be decided by a woman and her doctor; they supported the Equal Rights Amendment by a ratio of two to one, and 62 percent approved of divorce as a way out of an unhappy marriage.

Though the survey revealed many of the hesitations and anxieties of post-liberation women (nearly two-thirds feared that the change in male-female roles might cause stress and adjustment problems among children), it also revealed the key to understanding the last decade: women are now a permanent, full-time, major part of the work force.

All change, present and eventual, hinges on that crucial new fact.

Just last week, before this poll came along to shore up my argument, I was half-heartedly debating the triumphs of the women's movement with a friend.

"We've all been led down the garden path," snorted my chum, not entirely facetiously. "Here's the National Action Committee on the Status of Women having its annual meeting about women and equal pay, for God's sake. What progress have we made?"

"C'mon, you know that women have incredible opportunities now compared to 10 years ago," I said...and faltered, because it

didn't take my friend's beadily skeptical glance to remind me that though a few privileged women have made it to the top, the vast majority find that sexism bars the way to advancement.

An illustration by Heather Walters from a Canadian Council on Social Development booklet, "Women In Need."

"Well," I forged on, "at least attitudes have changed enormously. We'll never go back to the *Father Knows Best* '50s."

"Oh, yeah?" said the cynic, ostentatiously flipping the paper open to the column in which I wrote about teenage stereotyping. Score a point for pessimism: teenagers wrote me overwhelmingly to confirm that peer pressures still force them into silly sex stereotyping à la Fonz [the cocky alpha-male teenager in *Happy Days*, a popular TV sitcom about the '50s].

Why do things seem so hopeless and so promising at the same time? How can we reconcile the clashing statistics: more people than ever before believe in women's equality while at the same time women's wages are slipping backward in relation to men's?

There are women prime ministers now, sure. Meanwhile, the powers-that-be are closing down the rape crisis centres and slamming the lid on daycare.

The see-saw is glumly depressing for feminists and sympathizers. Clarity is so much more invigorating: either we would celebrate or grit our teeth and fight harder. But the battle seems to lose focus when the good news is daily spiked with the bad.

The trick, I think, is to take a longer perspective. It's going to be a grim decade economically, and a minority chorus of reactionaries (including Liberal cabinet ministers, if they hold true to form) will continue to scapegoat working women and to press for cutbacks in women's services. They'll succeed, undoubtedly, in embittering the lives of many individual women.

But look beyond the immediate economic setbacks and you see a pattern that is truly astonishing. Eighteen years ago, when I graduated from university, the head of the English department could smugly inform me that there would never be a female professor in his department as long as he lived. He echoed the prevailing tenor of society: chauvinists ruled supreme, openly discriminating against women everywhere from the courts to the kitchen.

That was before Irene Murdoch and the surge of family law reform across the country. It was before the Pill, when women finally got control of their fertility, and, above all, it was before the landslide of women working outside the home.

All that is irreversible. North American women will never again be chattels before the law, or enslaved by unwanted pregnancies, or forced to stay at home. Whatever the temporary reversals along the way, the larger pattern is set.

● ● ● ● ● ● ● ● ●

THE LANDMARK *Our Bodies, Ourselves* was published in Boston in 1973, sending shock waves of recognition through the women's movement. Radicals in California had already been experimenting with self-administered abortions, and I was writing an impudent article in *Chatelaine* magazine about the need to be defiantly questioning of medical and hospital rules.

So it was stunning to realize, in 1980, that, despite all of our sexual enlightenment and bodily self-assertion, we had been numbly unaware, in Canada, of just how wilfully we women had been exposed to deliberate harm by the authorities we naively trusted (in those days before deregulation) to protect us in the marketplace.

When I wrote the following two pieces about toxic shock and

about the Dalkon Shield, the women's health movement (and consumer awareness) was still very young. The same astonishing abuses could easily arise again, but I don't think they would escape feminist notice, analysis, and confrontation. The difference this time: our feminist consciousness.

WOMEN'S BODIES HAVE NO PRIORITY
October 1980

What was your reaction to the recent news stories about toxic shock syndrome?

Did you, like me, tch-tch nervously over the reports that 350 U.S. women had suffered, and 29 had died, from an illness caused by tampon use? Did you, like me, think with some distaste, "Oh, well, those women couldn't have changed their tampons often enough?"

Actually, news reports offered two other, equally plausible, explanations – a new strain of bacteria or dangerous new materials in the Rely tampons – but how quick we all were to blame other women for their misfortune.

It wasn't until much later, when I had done some investigation, that I suddenly recognized that our reactions and the toxic shock syndrome are both part of an old, old pattern.

First I called some tampon manufacturers. Richard Illis, president of Playtex Ltd., talked willingly about the "san-pro industry" (san-pro means sanitary products). Then I asked him about the ingredients in the deodorant tampon. "Oh, no, we don't reveal that information at all," he said with finality. I asked him what government standards or regulations his product had to meet. "None whatever."

We women are supposed to buy and use, in the costly millions, a product which we insert in our bodies, but we are not to ask what it is we are using.

I called some doctors. Gynaecologist Dr. Dawne Jubb, of Women's College Hospital, said tampons were only part of the story. "Vaginal sprays, deodorants and douches serve no real purpose and are a common source of irritation, rash, infection, and actual chemical burn," she said. A general practitioner laughed in cynical

Holding their International Women's Day Committee banner in 1981 are (from left) Nancy Adamson, Susan Genge, Sandy Fox, and Pat Hughes.

resignation. "Go ahead. Ask the government what labelling requirements they demand?"

So I started to call government offices. Dr. Ajit DasGupta, head of the medical devices bureau of the Health Protection Branch, spoke to me impatiently about tampons.

"No, we don't test them. Tampons have not caused us any concern until now. We respond to priorities, and they have not been a priority."

I was interested to learn that none of the hundreds of intimate products used by women is a priority. But the one intimate product used by men, the condom, is "a very high priority indeed," said Dr. DasGupta, "especially as it is a protection from disease."

Condoms are tested "rigorously" by our federal government. Strict standards are set, Dr. DasGupta said, for the safety and efficacy of materials and for dimensions, strength, and pinholes.

The nearest female equivalent I could think of was contraceptive diaphragms. Are they tested? "No," Dr. DasGupta said, and went on, somewhat imperiously: "We can hardly test all 250,000 medical devices on the market, from dentures to diaphragms."

I see. The pattern is getting clearer. Though condoms are used for a few minutes and discarded, and diaphragms are used for years, and may remain inside a woman's body for hours at a time, condoms are a priority and diaphragms are not.

Toxic shock syndrome, I began to realize, was not just another commercial exploitation and unfortunate accident. It is part of an old pattern of government indifference to women's health. Our own secretive shame about our bodily functions, our own guilty eagerness to blame ourselves and each other, are an essential part of this pattern.

Remember the morning-sickness drug thalidomide, and its heartbreaking parade of deformed victims? And then there was DES, taken by millions of women to prevent miscarriage and paid for in suffering (vaginal cancer, deaths, stillbirths, sterility) even unto the third generation.

Remember the birth control pill revelations, and the banning, too late, of certain lethal types? Then the Dalkon Shield intra-uterine device, which lacerated its users, killing some, and damaged infant brains before it was yanked off the market?

Toxic shock syndrome is just one more betrayal of women's well-being that we can add to the list. And perhaps we were right, in some measure, to blame women. The tampon companies can honestly say that they never received questions or challenges about tampon ingredients. The only letters they get are from women who are ashamed to see sanitary napkins advertised on television.

How weak we are, how brainwashed, to waste our energies on prudery while our health is under assault.

• • • • • • • • •

MEANWHILE, the gruesome Dalkon Shield case was winding its way through the U.S. courts, ripping away the veils of secrecy that had protected these hateful exploiters of women's bodies. When the founder of the A.H. Robins company, maker of the infamous Dalkon Shield, finally declared Chapter II bankruptcy (a uniquely

American dodge) and sold his company for millions, I reviewed its sad history of criminal neglect...and our society's indifference to women's health.

USING LOOPHOLE, DALKON SHIELD MAKER PROFITS FROM LAWSUITS

February 1988

...Many may have forgotten the Dalkon saga. In 1971, the A.H. Robins company of Richmond, Va. – a company selling patent remedies such as ChapStick, Robitussin and Sergeant's flea collars – decided to move into the booming contraceptive market. They latched on to the IUD as a medical device that did not yet need approval from the Food and Drug Administration.

They bought the Dalkon design from a gynaecologist and rushed on to the world market with a gigantic promotion campaign claiming that they had the "safest, superior, modern" IUD. To prove that wearers of the Dalkon Shield had a spectacularly low 0.5 percent pregnancy rate, they cited false statistics.

The Dalkon Shield is a vicious-looking little crab-like plastic device with a string attached. It cost 25 cents each to manufacture. Almost from the beginning, the Robins company knew, and suppressed the fact, that the string was faulty. It acted as a wick that led bacteria up into the woman's uterus. (A ChapStick quality control supervisor saw the flaw right there in the factory, and suggested a modification that would have prevented untold suffering. It would have cost an extra five cents. He was fired.)

Thanks to aggressive marketing, 4.5 million devices were sold around the world. As late as last year, some were still lying on clinic shelves in remote countries, being inserted in trustful women, and causing pain and death.

Reading the superbly researched book *At Any Cost – Corporate Greed, Women and the Dalkon Shield*, by Morton Mintz of *The Washington Post*, you have to be both outraged and heartsick at the company's cold-blooded pursuit of profit. For example, when it learned that the device became more lethally infective as time went on – "a deadly depth charge in women's wombs, ready to explode at any time," in the words of Judge Lord – Robins removed a label warning that the device should be changed after two years, and redoubled its advertising.

In the United States alone, 36 women are said to have died from acute pelvic inflammatory disease caused by the shield. Thousands suffered such massive infection that they had to have emergency hysterectomies. It's estimated that thousands of Third World women died without their massive infections ever being traced to the Dalkon Shield.

The shield's failure rate was high – at least 5 percent of users became pregnant – and many doctors believed Robins's false insistence that the shield was harmless to foetuses. Hence, a frightening onslaught of dangerous septic abortions, ectopic pregnancies, at least 11,000 foetal deaths, and hundreds of children born handicapped, deformed, or brain-damaged.

Throughout the mounting horror, and through hundreds of lawsuits during the 1970s and early 1980s, Robins maintained an injured innocence. In lawsuit after lawsuit, Robins was guilty of lying, cover-up, stonewalling, destruction of evidence, and harassment of plaintiffs.

Then, facing 5,000 individual lawsuits, Robins hit on the perfect solution. In August 1985, it declared Chapter 11 bankruptcy. The success of this dodge is a delicious lesson to other culpable U.S. businesses. The minute Robins filed, all lawsuits were frozen. Even plaintiffs who had won handsome awards were unable to collect.

Meanwhile, Robins got richer. Its stocks rose. Vermont lawyer Bob Manchester, who represents several thousand claimants, explained to me in an interview that the current climate of takeover and merger mania made Robins a juicy target. It's a profitable company with a large, trained sales force. And any new owner would be able to write off plaintiffs' claims as a bad debt. The women's suffering, in other words, turned out to be a plump bonus, a tax break, for some corporation....

• • • • • • • • •

BY NOW, most of us had begun to realize that some aspects of chauvinist behaviour would go on smouldering underground as stubbornly as a subterranean coal seam fire, off-gassing toxic fumes into the atmosphere and bursting unpredictably into open flames. The passionate attachment to sexist language is one of those seams. It always, without fail, signals the presence of deeply sexist and male-dominant attitudes.

MEDIA ATTACK STRAW WOMAN IN RIDICULING NONSEXIST LANGUAGE
June 1986

Whoa, hey, wait a minute. Nobody minds when journalists pick on a straw man now and then (I may even have done it once or twice myself); it's a handy way to make a point, and besides, there's usually a chorus of dissent standing by to pick up the straw man, dust him off and pay him due respect. But picking on a straw woman? It's just too easy.

For the past couple of years the media have been getting what amounts to a free goal kick at their favourite target: egalitarian language change. If there have been any loud, clear dissenting voices in the press, I haven't heard them.

Recently, I noticed that *The Globe and Mail* was editorially harrumphing at a non-sexist style manual being proposed for the Scarborough Board of Education. In magisterial tones, *The Globe* allowed as how it didn't really mind cleaning lady being changed to cleaner, or office girl to secretary, but that the committee got carried away altogether – "shot from the hip" – when it proposed access cover instead of manhole cover.

Hmmm, I thought. True, that's ridiculous. Why access cover when sewer cover would be clearer, more practical and even better English (because simpler) than manhole cover? I sent away for a copy of the manual, and guess what? That's just what the committee recommended. Access cover was second choice, a sort of afterthought – though you wouldn't have known that from *The Globe*'s indignant account.

A picayune point, but revelatory.

Thwacking away at non-sexist language has become the gentleman's sport of the eighties. When the National Museum of

Man tottered into the limelight last year, and women objected to its sexist name, the press grew choleric in response. Colonel Blimp rose from the grave and took umbrage in letters and columns coast to coast.

But Museum of Man is a preposterous name. All the laboured witticisms of those letters to the editors cannot obscure the very simple truth that "man," to our modern ear, means "male." Repeated studies of youngsters from kindergarten to college come up with the same result: when students are asked to describe man in space, or primitive man, or urban man, or man in society, they talk about males – and usually about warlike, aggressive males. Less biased words and phrases, like society, or space, or primitive peoples, on the other hand, evoke images of women and men in a variety of peaceful and cultural pursuits.

Every time we insist on using "man" to denote all human beings, we are thumping into children's minds a distorted version of the world, one that defines humans as male, males as dominant, real, and universal, and females as a kind of variant or subspecies.

It may be a nuisance to say "he and she," but the use of the universal "he" reverberates with a not-so-subtle glorification of the male and a dismissal of the female. No, you say? It's neutral? A mere convenience? Fine. Then let's use a universal "she" instead, just in the name of fairness after all these centuries. No again? That would be ridiculous, implying that everyone in the world is female? Thank you. My point exactly.

In fact, our entire beloved English language is land mined with explosive little relics from centuries of patriarchy. Why does it sound so right to say "he and she," "male and female," "husband and wife," "Mr. and Mrs." and "man and woman"? Is it just an accident that the female always comes second? Nonsense. As Dr. Freud once said, there are no accidents.

And it's no accident, either, that non-sexist language change is the butt of so much media crossfire. We care about language passionately, viscerally, because we know it shapes us, our culture, our history, and our future. Words are powerful. Those who have power never cede it willingly.

Opponents of language change may pose as staunch defenders of tradition or even as beings of superior sensitivity who, like that ninny of a princess in the fairy tale, are bruised and battered by a pea under a stack of mattresses. But they often betray their true motives – their lurking ambivalence about gender equality – either by attacking straw women ("access cover" indeed) or by ludicrous overstatement. Consider the *North Bay Nugget*, which seized on the Scarborough style manual and went absolutely berserk. In an editorial revealingly called "Sexless Scarborough," the *Nugget* raved on about English as a "lusty brute of a language...virile, fertile...(whose) roots are in the blood and slaughter of the Battle of Hastings..." a language which is about to be "emasculated and neutered" by a pack of "linguistic eunuchs and sexless scribes."

Doesn't all this bluster about sex seem a little contradictory, not to mention fixated? After all, if English is already neutral and universal, as opponents of change insist, how can it be neutered and emasculated?

It won't wash, fellows. The strangled shrieks of outrage get sillier and sillier. Letters to the editor on this issue are particularly unilluminating. Either these wits are sophomoric ("I guess we'll have to change 'Manitoba' to 'Personitoba'") or else they just don't know much about English: "Tee-hee, what about 'manual'?" Well, what about it? Simple etymology will tell you that "manual" is derived from the Latin word for hand.

Tinkering with words may not always produce an elegant alternative, but at least it is a rational, optimistic response to built-in prejudice in English and in society. There is nothing malign in the effort. None of the changes excludes or denigrates men. Reformers, too, love and value the language – love it enough to want it to be more realistic, less biased, less hurtful. They want to include the other half of humankind in our modes of thought and speech....

• • • • • • • • •

I BEGAN MY ADULT LIFE as a graduate in English Language and Literature, almost accidentally landing a job at *The Globe and Mail* straight out of university, with a rebellious feminist soul and virtually no language, ideology, or known allies to buttress my passionate but incoherent devotion to women's equality. A year later, in 1963, I married impetuously, but as it turned out lastingly, the first man I'd ever met with genuine egalitarian impulses.

By the time I wrote about my wedding, I was applying my feminist instincts – still relatively untutored, because there was no such thing as "women's studies" in my day – to the daily news in my columns. Those columns, daily for several years, and then three times a week, chart the public consensus of the time, my growing critique of that consensus, and my personal development.

ROMANCE JUST CREEPS UP ON YOU
March 1979

My mother's wedding picture hung on the wall for years, a soft-focus shimmer of dark-eyed loveliness, white lace, and baby's breath.

By the time my turn came along, the formal wedding struck me, an early bird rebel of the '60s, as a little outdated. Nobody had yet invented the word "liberated," but there I was, briskly planning a no-nonsense wedding that would embody the new free spirit of womanhood.

Besides, if the truth must out, I wasn't at all sure I could manage a graceful slide down the aisle without tripping on the train, sneezing, or springing a few loose bobby pins at unsuspecting relatives.

I settled on a traditional ceremony at home, with just the family. Warmth and intimacy, I ruled, but no soppy romanticism, please. In keeping with this austere philosophy, the groom and I completely forgot about the need for a wedding ring until two days before the event. I took a few minutes off from my job as a reporter to dash into Eaton's, where I shocked a salesperson into a state of almost terminal disapproval by demanding the "cheapest wedding ring you've got...quickly, please."

That was in 1963. Heaven knows what steamy imaginings passed before her eyes. By the way she handed my $16 ring across the counter at arm's length, it was pretty clear she thought I was even then sprinting to an abortionist's back room or a sleazy motel rendezvous.

Despite my plans, everything became both more romantic and nerve-racking from that point on. When people heard that I was about to marry someone I'd met only six weeks earlier, their eyes would light up with a kind of dazzled incredulity. Try as I might to be sensible, I couldn't help but feel like a wild romantic adventurer.

As a minor concession to propriety, I agreed to have my hair "done" the morning of the ceremony, while my mother put the last floral touches to our already gleaming home. As I fidgeted under the dryer, wondering how I'd managed to get myself into two situations (hairdresser and marriage) in which I didn't believe, all in one day, a delivery boy showered a fragrant armful of red roses into my lap.

Blue-rinsed heads and towers of pink plastic curlers all swivelled my way. "From my fiancé," I mumbled bashfully, abandoning all allegiance to a bohemian vocabulary. "We're getting married today."

It was like magic. Eyes misted, sighs were sighed, smiles were smiled, and I was sent on my way (curled and sprayed and weighed down by roses) in a scented cloud of good wishes.

With a $16-ring and an upswept "do," 23-year-old Michele wed Stephen Lewis in her mother's backyard. Despite the fact that she didn't believe in marriage, Michele admits she was swept up in the romance of it all.

The wedding was fine, too. It was May, the sun shone, and instead of the perilous march down the aisle, there was the rabbi eating a corned beef sandwich in the hall, goggled at solemnly by my two tiny nephews in their best blue cardigans.

Like any wedding party, fancy or plain, we were smitten with an awestruck sense of the occasion. A strange solemnity stiffened our faces as we crowded into my parents' little den for the ceremony. In a panicky moment ("What the hell am I doing?"), I found reassurance from the steady gaze of my aunts and grandparents, all happily married, looking down from their photographs on the wall.

We got through the ritual bits all right. Then the rabbi, desperate for some words of relevance, decided to orate on the wedding ring as a symbol of our vows. "This ring, so lovingly and thoughtfully chosen by the two of you," he said, holding my Eaton's special. I felt a giggle spreading upward and I knew it was all going to be all right.

Afterward, there was a splendid wedding feast laid out in the living room, the only room large enough to hold us all at one long table. I remember impromptu singing, the fragrance of flowers, affectionate jokes, and a blur of festivity that wrapped us in a surge of familial love, high hopes…and yes, romance.

MORE THAN BABY CARRIAGES
child
repeal anti Abortion laws
sign here
make every mother a willing mother every child a wanted child

Chapter Two
HOT BUTTONS, CHARGED TOPICS

THE HOTTEST DEBATES in society in the 1980s and 1990s raged over the female body – who controlled it? Whose right was it to dictate its behaviour, its functioning, its uses, its adornments? The use of just one word could send the debate careering down a wayward path, the way "choice" became the sword with which we battled for reproductive rights. Instead of framing the discussion as one of women's rights and equality (without the right to control one's bodily fate, how could there be equality?), we let our American sisters, with their unique blend of individualism and consumerism, frame it as a person's private choice. That's not entirely wrong, certainly, but isn't reproductive freedom an essential component of public health and society's wellbeing as well as a personal right?

It's hard to imagine equal heat being kindled under issues surrounding men's bodies. Perhaps only their "right" to enjoy all kinds of pornography under the rubric of free speech is as ferociously contended – although, as I point out in this chapter, no journalist in our culture enjoys as much unfettered free speech as any pornographer does.

Progress has been made on all the "hot" issues that were featured in these columns – gun control, gay marriage, porn and censorship, race and racism – yet the struggles continue, the passion and fury can erupt at any time, and many of feminism's most cherished victories are continually menaced. The media constantly polarize the debates by pitting groups of women against each other, like stay-home moms versus daycare users, or pro- and anti-choice campaigners, or "pro-sex" women against those dried-up "prudes" who want to spoil all the fun. The tactic isn't new: First Wave suffragists were also derided and parodied as anti-sex killjoys and harridans. The trick to evading these binary traps is to think more widely. Whose economic, sexual, class, or political interests are being served by the female mouthpieces and role models provided by the media? The answers can be complex, but at least they're more thought-productive than the simple-minded oppositions (home or career? breast or bottle?) so dear to the media.

The first "hot button" issue, the one that drove women into feminist activism, was that of reproductive choice. It was the oldest, established, permanent, floating outrage against women in Canada – the ever-present knowledge that whoever you were, no matter your circumstances, if you were female and Canadian, your womb belonged to the clergy. It was the Catholic Church and its fundamentalist Protestant counterparts that wielded the power to intimidate legislators and control women on the subject of procreation. And it was this illegitimate male power that so enraged women that it became one of the motive forces for the explosion of women's resistance.

Abortion had been illegal in Canada since 1869, the same year that the Pope decreed all abortion, from the moment of conception, a mortal sin. One hundred years later Prime Minister Trudeau finally decriminalized contraception in 1969. But the power to decide on abortions was put in the hands of all-male physician committees in hospitals, a paralyzingly slow and difficult, not to say humiliating, process. Illegal abortions, consequently, were still rampant, terrifying, and often deadly.

In 1983, a flamboyant, anti-choice crusader from the Prairies named Joe Borowski – an extremist already convicted of contempt of court and assault – was in court in Saskatchewan to protest the abortion clauses in the Criminal Code, on the grounds that they denied the foetus's right to exist. Joe, the self-appointed spokesman for all fertilized ova in Canada, had been granted the right to proceed to trial. The court ruled that CARAL (Canadian Abortion Rights Action League) and CCLA (Canadian Civil Liberties Association) were not permitted to participate in the trial.

"It was an appalling atmosphere," said Norma Scarborough, a grandmother of six and a CARAL activist who was in the courtroom the first day. "I had no idea how depressing

At the 1987 International Women's Day March in Toronto, the Canadian Abortion Rights League supporters were front and centre.

it would be. I left in tears after listening to all these men – judge, lawyers, witnesses – jousting and game-playing about the most personal things in a woman's life, while we women sat by helplessly."

BOROWSKI CASE NEEDS CLOSER SCRUTINY
May 1983

...[Joe] Borowski's fanaticism is amply on display in the current court case in Regina, where Borowski is contending that abortion, for any reason – rape, incest, it doesn't matter – should be banned. Women's and civil rights groups were denied standing in the case.

That means that it's a curiously one-sided argument being heard in Regina. Mark MacGuigan, the minister of justice directly responsible for defending the therapeutic abortion law, has gone on record stating that he is implacably opposed to abortion. Not surprisingly, the federal government's defence effort seems to many onlookers to be singularly weak and tepid. It's really something to stand by and listen, without being represented in court, while a bunch of men (most of them religiously opposed to a woman's rights to birth control or abortion) argue about women's bodies.

I know that men find this point hard to understand. They are so used to having the right to rule that it doesn't strike them as the least bit grotesque that it should be men, all men and only men, who are making and challenging the laws on abortion.

And there isn't any real parallel that could make them see how silly, how preposterous the situation is. But imagine this: Suppose this country had always been ruled exclusively by women – women priests, MPs, judges, sports heroes, company presidents. Suppose the all-female Parliament decided that male masturbation was a very great evil, and that all the wasted and lost sperm were real little potential human lives. Suppose it became a federal crime for a man to masturbate. If any man or boy wanted to waste his sperm, he would have to apply to an all-female hospital committee for a special license. It would debate his emotional and physical health in detail before ruling whether he had the right to take such a regrettable step, which might lead to bitter remorse in years to come. Then imagine a challenge in the courts: An extremist woman from the Eternal Multiplication Church argued that even those few men with medical licenses to masturbate were murderers and should be stopped.

Into the court would traipse the great women of the world. The female judge would brood over the evidence; female lawyers would banter and joke about male sexual traits. A man would take the stand to sob about his past amorality and reckless waste of tiny lives. Every twitch of male habits, every gland, sac, and vascular cell, would be scrutinized. A famous woman specialist would be called to testify about the incredible beauty, the muscular vigour of the little sperm – alive, and already imprinted with its human destiny –

swimming with a grace equalled only by an Olympic champion.

Ludicrous, isn't it? There's something madly unbalanced about the entire procreative fate of one gender being placed in the hands of the other. There's a faint whiff of something worse than ludicrous coming from that courtroom, too – the men talk about cows, about women as mere containers for the precious fertilized egg, about how easy it would be for a man to carry a foetus. It's as though they resent or are jealous of our procreative power.

The weekend papers carried too many disturbing snippets of abortion news for any woman to feel sanguine. There was a picture of three men picketing the Morgentaler [abortion] clinic in Winnipeg, their signs trumpeting their opposition to "death camp clinics." The anti-abortion movement's fondness for the death camp metaphor is one of the ugliest and most sinister things about it.

Then the *Star* quoted Dr. Heather Morris, a gynaecologist at Women's College Hospital [Toronto], as one of several experts asked to comment on the ideas of Jerome Lejeune. He's the one who testified in Regina about 8-week-old foetuses cavorting in the womb. Morris was quoted as saying it would be "presumptuous" to criticize Lejeune, who has "pretty remarkable credentials." The paper did not mention that Morris is a past president of Alliance for Life, the national co-ordinating committee for all anti-abortion groups. Keep your eyes open for this kind of thing happening over the next month or so of the abortion trial. Since women are not represented in the case – as far as I'm concerned, Joe Borowski and Mark MacGuigan are all but dancing cheek-to-cheek – we out here in the public will have to carry out the task of real analysis and debate, what our cowardly Parliament should have been doing all along.

· · · · · · · · ·

THAT SUMMER, emotions, heated to a pitch, boiled over when the Toronto Women's Bookstore, just below the Morgentaler Clinic, went up in flames. The bookstore was later rebuilt and still stands, despite many more financial and ideological crises. The Morgentaler Clinic later moved to a safer and more anonymous location than its perch above the bookstore. As for Borowski, by the time his court case wound its way to the Supreme Court of Canada in 1989, it was deemed irrelevant and dismissed, because the abortion law had been happily overturned the year before.

ANTI-CHOICE FANATICS TRIGGER CHAIN REACTION
August 1983

Scorched books and daggers of broken glass littered the ground outside the Toronto Women's Bookstore last Friday, after an arsonist set fire to the building. Boards were hastily nailed up over the shattered windows. Inside was the pitch-black darkness, filthy puddles, charred rubble and the overpowering stink of smoke that you can never forget.

Attempting to destroy Dr. Henry Morgentaler's second-floor abortion clinic, arsonists set fire to the pregnancy and childbirth section of the Toronto Women's Bookstore, which occupied the space below the clinic. In a chilling twist of fate, Michele stares out the shattered front window from a poster promoting her book, *Women and Children First*.

I'm supposed to be on a leave of absence this summer, but I called my editor to ask if I could jump back into the paper, this once, to say what I feel must be said.

The Toronto Women's Bookstore was one of my favourites: bright, sparkling in its sweetly renovated old brick house on Harbord St., run for the past nine years as a non-profit venture by two book-loving women, Patti Kirk and Marie Prins.

Both women are married and both have very young children and it is just one of the ugly ironies of this business that the arsonists – trying to destroy Henry Morgentaler's abortion clinic, which just happens to occupy the second floor – set the fire in the pregnancy and childbirth section of the bookstore. That section is – was – the most comprehensive in Toronto, and happily pregnant women rushed there to buy books available nowhere else.

When the unbalanced members of our society start burning bookstores, alarms clang in my conscience and bells of memory start tolling. I wonder how such cruel destruction and waste can happen...

A Canadian Medical Association poll released last week showed that more than half of all doctors agree with Morgentaler that abortion ought to be a woman's private decision. An even greater majority agrees with the idea of freestanding abortion clinics. How many of them go on disregarding the law in their private practices, or treating it as a joke – yet refuse to make a public stand for change? We have a cowardly, antiquated law, and Morgentaler, admittedly abrasive and single-minded, is at least trying to reform it, at the risk of his income, his liberty, and – it turns out – his life.

Who is to blame for the violence? I blame anti-choice fanatics, who have freely used wild language like "mass murder" and "Holocaust" to describe legal abortions in Canada. Their crusading hysteria has triggered a chain reaction of excess. They do this in the name of love of life. But they should know that hatred is contagious; berserk language and extreme emotion can catch many alienated souls in their net, and pull them toward irrational acts of violence.

I blame anti-choice campaigners like Dr. Robert Mendelsohn, a man I once admired, who flew to Winnipeg recently to join the anti-Morgentaler protest, and who was quoted in the Winnipeg press as suggesting that the way to stop abortion was to buy a Saturday Night Special, walk into a hospital, and shoot the first two abortion doctors you meet. Murderous talk – even if he later claimed it was all a joke. [In the winter of 2011, Canadians may hear a

This flyer was produced by Women for Political Action to support the Toronto Women's Bookstore.

This is the defaced and vandalized plaque for the Morgentaler Clinic, Toronto. Morgentaler continued to challenge Criminal Code restrictions on abortion, which would not be struck down fully by the Supreme Court of Canada until 1988.

precursor of current events in this U.S. conversational style].

I blame Roy McMurtry, Attorney-General of Ontario, who allowed the police to stage their ridiculous cowboy raid against the Morgentaler Clinic. Police raids are an extreme measure, usually reserved for those cases in which evidence might be destroyed or fugitives escape.

The Morgentaler case was the exact opposite. The doctors made their activities public from the beginning and did not try to conceal them from the law. Why then did the police have to blockade Harbord St. [where the razed building is located], bring a fleet of ambulance buses, storm into a room where a woman was recovering from an abortion, and seize files and equipment? The raid was pure grandstanding – just one more exaggerated action calculated to inflame an already raging debate. The Attorney-General should have demonstrated more level-headed judgement.

I blame Crown Attorney David Cooper, who was so aggressive at Morgentaler's bail hearing that even the judge was irritated. Cooper wanted Morgentaler and his colleagues to be kept in jail over the summer until the trial. Implication: Morgentaler is a common and dangerous criminal. Result: more public vilification of a man who is defying an unjust law – and providing a safe medical service for women.

And I blame all of us, who have sat around and been content to let a brave handful of activists fight this one for us while we watered our lawns and drifted through another spring and summer. We who believe in freedom of choice are a huge majority – 72 percent according to a Gallup poll – and we could easily, long since, have forced a more rational law into existence. But we didn't bother. Uneasily, we told ourselves that abortion is a dreadful business, and that though we must all be allowed to make our private decision, we would rather not get involved publicly.

But public events have a way of reaching out and grabbing private people by the scruff of the neck. The bookstore was an accidental neighbour of the abortion clinic. Yet all of us who have been enriched by that little treasure-house of books will now, because of public apathy and anti-choice acrimony, be made to suffer a loss....

• • • • • • • • •

I WAS LIVING in New York in 1988 (where my husband was Canada's Ambassador to the United Nations) when I got the incredible news that the Supreme Court of Canada had struck down the century-long bitter injustice of the abortion law. I felt in that moment intensely patriotic as a Canadian.

JUBILATION: IT'S ALMOST DIZZYING
January 1988

At a stroke, the Supreme Court of Canada has wiped out one of our country's meanest injustices. The abortion law, a shabby and cringing deal made among men who rule, and made at the expense of women, has been named for what it is: painful, arbitrary, and unfair.

Ever since the Murdoch case [in 1975, the Supreme Court of Canada denied prairie ranch wife Irene Murdoch any financial share in her divorced husband's ranch after she did hard manual labour there for 25 years], I've always thought that the Supreme Court of Canada could be counted on to rule blandly, blindly, in favour of the status quo, and against the rights of women. I had begun to think that the Charter of Rights was a cruel hoax, a victory turned to ashes as men rushed to court to undo whatever frail protections women had wrung from parliaments. And I had certainly thought that the powers-that-be would go on forever, hounding and baying after Henry Morgentaler, because they were too cowardly to face down the anti-choice extremists.

Those who have not been personally touched by the women's movement may find it hard to credit the depth of emotion we feel today. It's important to understand that the abortion fight has not been about abortion, but something which runs far deeper: the right of women to be autonomous.

I've never had, nor needed (thank heaven) an abortion. But ever since I've been a thinking adult, the power of a fanatic minority to control my body's most intimate functioning has been a biting gall. No woman's life is truly her own unless she has control over her reproduction – which is precisely why so many men, high and low, have invested such bitter ferocity in denying us that self-determination.

More than any other single factor, the abortion laws have alienated me from and made me cynical about government. They were a constant reminder that the individual fate of women all over Canada – especially the poor, the distant and the powerless – was a matter of total indifference to the men in Ottawa. Brutally and cravenly, they ignored the will of the majority of Canadian voters for decades. The agonies, the medical endangerment, the desperate straits and the humiliations caused by the law – it all meant nothing to them…But nobody blamed them, nobody called them to account for their dereliction. The man who took the punishment was, instead, the one man who had the courage to lead the battle against them.

Henry Morgentaler is an important hero of mine. He may come across as irascible or abrasive, words that reporters have used about him, but whenever I've spoken to him, he's been gentle, rational and idealistic. In private conversation he would brush off the personal hurts; his anger was saved for the stupidity and inequality of the laws...He's been dragged to court over and over again, thrown in jail (just imagine what jail is like to a Holocaust survivor), harassed and threatened beyond most mortals' endurance. A doctor who could have become smugly affluent in quiet private practice, he repeatedly risked everything to confront an unjust law....

We were affected, too, by the richly funded public relations successes of the anti-choice religionists. They managed to make it seem that anyone who believed in reproductive choice didn't care about life, about babies. They never had to take the rap for the miseries and deaths they themselves caused; instead, we women – women who created and nurtured life and yet argued for our rights to decide when and how – were bullied into defensiveness and silence. But not the women of CARAL. The women who slaved away, understaffed and overworked, at the Canadian Abortion Rights Action League, did have the courage to face the callousness of parliamentarians and the hatefulness of the extremists. They are today's heroes, too; it was they who backed Morgentaler, raised money for his legal defence, and laboured to give women the bravery to speak out.

When the truth is finally told, it will emerge that there's hardly a family in Canada where someone, at some time, didn't desperately seek and sometimes get an abortion. Because of a bad law imposed by the few on the many, that extremity had to be faced, most often, in fear, shame, isolation, and danger.

The long lie is over; long live the Supreme Court of Canada.

• • • • • • • • •

THE LAW WAS HAPPILY overturned, yes, and overnight abortion became a medical procedure like any other. But like dumped sewage seeping back into the harbour, the anti-choice status quo in health services never goes away by itself. Canadian public opinion remains firmly and steadily pro-choice, especially among the educated (63 percent). But reality does not meet the serene expectation of most Canadians that the debate is over and abortion services are readily available.

A spunky young group called Canadians for Choice has stepped into the void left by CARAL, and it reports that only 15.9 percent of Canadian hospitals provide abortion. Dedicated doctors like Morgentaler are a declining and aging minority, doctors are legally able to refuse to do abortions, and the admirable Medical Students for Choice reports that in both Canada and the United States, more class time is devoted to Viagra than to abortion. In Canada, medical schools spend an average of less than one hour teaching about abortion in their four-year curriculum.

Abortion was only one of the hot topics that caused roiling controversy during the crest of the Second Wave. Everything that touched on sex – and on male sexual entitlements and privileges – dominated debates and pitted feminists against one another. Journalistic lore has it that the rocky shoals of pornography and free speech were the destructive Scylla and Charybdis of the women's movement.

It makes for a juicy story and a much-desired denouement (i.e., the death of feminism), but it didn't feel like that from the inside. It felt as though only some women, usually high-profile media types – not necessarily feminists – were co-opted into the defence of male phallic privileges. For decades, while under the sole direction of lawyer Alan Borovoy, the Canadian Civil Liberties Association pitted itself ardently against the slightest infringements of male sexual entitlements – battling anti-harassment and rape shield laws, for example – while largely ignoring all forms of inequality and discrimination against women.

The courts, too, colluded in protecting male appetites, even when their decisions left women to sink or swim. The disgusting language used by the judge in the infamous lap dancing case reveals a lot about the mentality of some of the men who are empowered to rule over the lives and livelihoods of women.

HOW DID JUDGE EVER RULE LAP DANCING NOT OBSCENE?
June 1995

Let's face it: most exotic dancers aren't qualified to work as brain surgeons or pastry chefs. They strip for a living, many of them because they bolted from rotten families in their early teens, never finished school, are reluctant to prostitute themselves and have few marketable assets aside from their willingness to flaunt their flesh.
So when a judge makes their jobs dangerous or obsolete, with a single ill-considered stroke of the pen, they can't usually "just get another job." They have kids to raise, bills to pay, and not many available options.

In the winter of '94, Judge E. G. Hachborn of the Ontario Court ruled that lap dancing was not obscene. Police officers had testified for the Crown about the way lap dancing was being conducted in local strip joints. The judge said that it was within community standards of tolerance for dancers to sit nude on a customer's lap and grind their buttocks against his groin, to masturbate the customers, to let the men variously "touch, fondle, kiss, lick, and suck" the women's buttocks, genitals, and breasts, and to permit cunnilingus.

In a flash, the bar owners began to build booths along the walls of their murky establishments; within a year, some of these open booths were closed off by curtains or doors with locks, leaving the women even more vulnerable as naked prey.

Table dancing, brought to Toronto in the early '80s by a henchperson of [Brian] Mulroney's Tory party (see Stevie Cameron's book *On the Take* for details) had already eroded the fragile, sequinned fantasy world of the exotic dancer. "I loved the glamour," said exotic dancer Katharine Goldberg in an almost naively wistful conversation recently. "Up there, in my costume, with men applauding, I felt like a star."

Table dancing gradually changed the business from elaborate stage performances, for which top dancers could earn $1,000 a week, to the sleazier, one-on-one $5 impromptu performances beside the customer's chair.

Still, it wasn't until the advent of lap dancing that the great divide was breached. Now touching, fondling, grabbing and what

Katharine calls "fingering" became part of the game. But it was still considered illegal and was, therefore, conducted furtively.

Until Judge Hachborn's decision. Then, suddenly, in the unvarying way of consumer capitalism, what had become possible instantly became commercially obligatory. Many of the dancers hated it, but prostitutes came flocking to exploit the new liberties. Instead of being paid by the bar owners, strippers had to work freelance, even paying "administrative fees" to the tavern for the privilege of sitting nude on men's laps and allowing themselves to be groped....

Whether or not you sympathize with exotic dancers and their scruples against being manhandled, ask yourself: By what "community standards" did Judge Hachborn rule this open, unconcealed practice of prostitution "not obscene"?

Curiously, Judge Hachborn's ruling would likely have gone the other way had he taken into account the landmark 1992 Butler decision of the Supreme Court, which outlaws sexual expression that harms and degrades women.

Why didn't Judge Hachborn rely on Butler? Good question. The Butler decision is the only court ruling in the world known to define obscenity from the woman's vantage point, taking harm, degradation, and dehumanization into account, rather than conventional male-defined morality. It's a uniquely progressive and enlightened set of guidelines for interpreting Canada's obscenity law. So far, Canadian courts have honoured it more in the breach than in the observance.

The lap dancing tempest-in-a-D-cup shows that it's time judges did their homework, read Butler, and began applying the law in the interest of women as well as the interests of pornographers, pimps, and strip-joint proprietors.

• • • • • • • • •

THE CITY OF TORONTO mopped up Hachborn's mess by passing no-touch bylaws two years later. Meanwhile, in the midst of the bitter porn debates, there were moments of amusement.

PHONE SEX WORKERS PUSHED TO TAKE CALLS
FROM CHILDREN
September 1995

The scene is mordantly funny: Within a stone's throw of the Royal York Hotel, in an old office building, 60 women are sitting in a huge room filled with tiny, three-sided booths. Some are knitting, crocheting, drawing, or paying bills. Many are pregnant. They are all colours, all shapes, all ages. But each has a phone tucked into her shoulder, and as she peers through her bifocals to crochet, or paints her nails, she is moaning, gasping and groaning in fake sexual ecstasy.

They're phone sex operators: safe-sex verbal performance artists. Two of them have come to see me at the *Star* to complain about the mounting pressure they're under from their boss to provide phone sex to under-age callers. Children.

"You go on automatic pilot," said Joanie, a middle-class, mid-30s former professional person who was sidelined from her career after an illness. Victoria, a pretty blonde teenager with a painful history of abuse (she's confronting her abuser in court this month) is tougher and more worldly-wise than Joanie.

Both say that the job is a "last stop" for them. "Where else can you earn $9 an hour, plus 25 cents a minute for every call over 10 minutes?" asks Joanie. "I've cleared $320 a week, and for a job that requires no skills, that's pretty good. Many of the girls are single mums; they need every cent to get by."

That's why it's so hard to resist the pressure from the boss – a blustering, Florida-based businessman who treats the operation like "an offshore company." He once tried to deny the women statutory holidays because he'd never heard of them.

Management, it seems, is obsessed with something it calls "whole time" – the average length of each woman's calls over an eight-hour shift. If, after three calls, a woman isn't averaging 8½ minutes per call or more, she's "earlied out" – sent home with only three hours' pay. For a single mother, that could threaten the rent money.

Management is especially incensed about what it calls D.I.H. calls, blaming the "girls" for not prolonging the conversation with fantasy talk. D.I.H. stands for "dick-in–hand;" these are the experienced, savings-conscious callers who dial only when ready for action, ordering the women to skip the talk and "just moan." They're usually off the phone in less than three minutes.

Between the tide of competition and the practised ejaculatory skills of repeat users, revenues are falling and the pressure is on to exploit every customer to the full.

"Switchboard used to screen out the kids with a couple of questions, using a chart that matches birth dates and high school graduation years. Now, with all the competition and falling revenues – the market is just swamped – they ask, 'Are you over 18? Fine, I'll put you through.'"

Most of the women comply. Joanie and Victoria, each for her own reasons, resist. But even they agree that, sometimes, the calls are pathetic and hilarious at the same time. Some of the exchanges they've had with U.S. callers who are obviously children:

"What state do you live in, sugar?"

"I don't know, I just moved here."

"Wow, you're a heart surgeon? How old are you?"

"Twenty-two."

"Oh, you're an electrical engineer? Gee, that's great. How old are you? Thirty-five? And you say your daughter is 25?"

Both Joanie and Victoria are matter-of-fact about the gamut of secret sexual weirdness they deal with daily. A lot of it sickens them, and they admit that their private lives are tainted by a distasteful after-echo. But the calls from children are the worst; they estimate that in the late afternoon shift, 25 percent of the callers are underage.

"I'd say my pay cheques are $100 lower a week since I started hanging up on child callers," said Joanie.

Canadian parents who discover that their adolescent has secretly rung up $3,000 in phone sex bills (don't laugh – it happens) can take two steps: argue with Bell to have the bill wiped out or reduced; or pay $10 to have a call block installed on their phone.

Joanie and Victoria, however, work for a firm taking 99 percent of its calls from the U.S., using what's called a redirect system. Callers phone, leave their number on an answering machine, and (through the magic of computers) get an instant call back, billed either to their phone or their credit card.

Well, hard times make for tough grinds. Still, it's odd to think of Canadian women grubbing away in the phone-moan trade, many of them feeling compelled to pander to the lonely, curious, or sexually over-stimulated children of the United States.

• • • • • • • • •

THE HARD BATTLE fought by feminist lawyers and activists to establish a legal standard by which to judge pornography had culminated in the Butler decision of 1992 – the decision so spectacularly ignored by Judge Hachborn in the lap dance case. But there was never any unanimity about porn issues in the women's movement, nor did we ever pretend there was. Indeed, our progress had its own little shadow: every advance brought its own contradictions and complications.

"The objective of the legislation...is aimed at avoiding harm, which Parliament has reasonably concluded will be caused directly or indirectly, to individuals, groups such as women and children, and consequently to society as a whole, by the distribution of these materials. It thus seeks to enhance respect for all members of society, and non-violence and equality in their relations with each other."

Justice Sopinka, writing the majority decision of the Supreme Court of Canada in R v. Butler, concludes that the definition of obscenity in the Criminal Code is constitutional.

Now that women's studies was ensconced at universities and women could actually secure a career and advancement through academic work on feminist theories, we had theories to fit snugly to every predilection.

By the mid-80s, the energy of feminism streamed in dozens of directions, and pornography was one of them. Identity politics had, like Reagan-era "me-ism" [narcissistic gratification as an ideology], lent a glossy shine to the assertion of one's right to any kinky pleasure that came along. Jay Scott, *The Globe and Mail*'s talented film reviewer of the time, didn't hesitate to label filmmaker Bonnie Klein's anti-porn documentary *This is Not a Love Story* "an example of bourgeois, feminist fascism," though the film did not even advocate censorship. There were plenty of women – lesbian activists, mainstream liberals, and academics alike – who would advocate for this position.

Because the media were, and are, so heavily invested in the

"freedom" end of the argument, it sometimes seemed impossible for feminist anti-porn views to get any kind of fair hearing. The demonizing of porn critics such as Andrea Dworkin and Catharine MacKinnon was so extreme that their media depiction was almost grotesquely cartoonish. I remember a well-regarded left-wing male columnist screaming at me drunkenly at a wedding party one night that I couldn't call myself any kind of real columnist (unlike his own noble self) because I hadn't attacked MacKinnon in print. He knew nothing about her writings other than her anti-porn "municipal ordinance" activism, and he misunderstood even that.

"FREE SPEECH" GIVES FREE REIN TO SUPPORTERS OF PORNOGRAPHY
June 1987

Censorship is so explosive and so labyrinthine an issue that it would take several columns just to touch on the main points. It's dismaying, therefore, to realize that, once again, in the public debate on the pornography bill, one phrase will dominate every discussion, and one key element will be virtually absent.

The phrase which shapes the debate, a phrase made sacred and absolute by pornographers, pro-pornographers and civil libertarians, not to mention writers, artists, and mediacrats, is "free speech."

The missing element is discussion of the deep, pervasive harm that pornography is inflicting on all of us.

The civil libertarians and pornographers will have the most free speech in the debate, and the victims of pornography will have the least. As always, the free-speechers will try to silence the anti-pornographers by ad feminam insult ("housewife," "prude," "anti-sex," and "fundamentalist" will be the most common and shaming terms of personal abuse) and the media, which naturally have an enormous financial and ideological stake in unfettered liberty, will give far more free speech to the free-speechers than to their opponents.

For those of us who cherish civil liberties, the last decade has offered an extraordinary spectacle: that of the American and Canadian Civil Liberties Unions, besotted by noble theory, rushing to ridiculous extremes to defend Nazis, rapists, and pornographers while resolutely ignoring the grievous injuries these people inflict on the civil rights of others. It's a classic case of well-motivated but irrational excess.

Free speech is, indeed, a precious ideal, though one much honoured in the breach. Society has long since recognized that speech must be regulated in many ways, most of them invisible and now taken utterly for granted. Journalists are daily prevented, by libel and contempt of court laws, from reporting what could be relevant information. Government servants are bound by oaths of lifelong secrecy; the most ardent proponents of liberty for themselves will eagerly sue others to keep them quiet.

It strikes me that the people who have a corner on the free-speech market in our society are pornographers, who enjoy an $8-billion a year industry in the United States, and who can count on an automatic, impassioned defence by media and free-speech idealists.

Even the gruesome torture and debasement of women is now respectable, so long as it is done elegantly. When a Manitoba judge acquitted *Penthouse* magazine of obscenity charges, he cited the testimony of a respected civil libertarian spokeswoman, who praised the artistic merits of the "strange and beautiful" photographs in question. The photographs (later ruled obscene by two Ontario courts) showed Japanese women hanged by their necks from trees, or naked, bound, trussed, with ropes tightly lashed around their breasts and through their genitals, and wearing death masks.

Much fine and high-minded scorn is reserved for those feminists, like me, who are concerned about the harm that such despicable – and widespread – images do. Civil libertarians demand rational, objective proof of harm. But no proof, it seems, will ever be good enough for them. When Linda (Lovelace) Marchiano described in detail how her pimp beat, brutalized, and terrorized her into performing in *Deep Throat* and pretending she loved it, her horrifying testimony was received in silence by the free-speechers. I know of no instance in which it moved them to reconsider. When women in rape crisis centres or battered women's shelters tell how their men forced them to emulate *Deep Throat*, or insisted on other violent, painful, humiliating, or dangerous practices in imitation of popular porn, their voices, too, are simply shrugged off by the libertarians. Not heard....

The civil libertarian blindness and deafness on these issues is disturbing. We know, after all, that our sexuality is profoundly conditioned by society. Fashions in women, like fashions in clothes, change, at the dictate of men, every few years. Generations of Chinese men learned to be aroused by tiny, bound, suppurating feet. (They've unlearned it now.) Now our own generations of little boys – almost all of them, in fact – get their sex education from *Playboy* and *Penthouse*, learning that bondage is sexy, that women are consumer items, and that violence is a turn-on.

PORNOGRAPHY DEBATE DISTORTS REALITY
January 2000

Pornography is the most combustible fuel in modern culture.

You have a little simmering tension between different groups in society? Throw on a bit of pornography – aah, a satisfying fire. You want more heat? Toss in some whips, chains, and academics who write about the "transgressional" glories of sado-masochism. Yikes, the bonfire is roaring out of control!

Unfortunately, the raging fury of this debate distorts reality, just like the shimmering, off-centre effect of a heat haze. Even more unfortunately, the bonfire threatens to blaze up again in March, when the Little Sisters bookstore case, which challenges the constitutionality of our customs regime, goes to the Supreme Court.

First, some background: For generations, Canada had an obscenity law that almost automatically discriminated against depictions of gay and lesbian sex. Gay and lesbian bookstores insisted that they were being unfairly targeted by Canada Customs, who imposed far harsher restrictions on gay porn than on other material.

The real conflagration started, however, in 1992, when LEAF, a feminist legal organization, intervened in a pornography case at the Supreme Court. LEAF's argument was affirmed in the Court's ruling. This was the famous Butler case (named after the convicted porn video store owner).

The Butler decision redefined pornography in Canada: No longer were "morality" and "obscenity" to be the measure – in a diverse population, whose morality gets to rule? – but now the defining factor would be harm to women and children because of violence or degradation. Porn's pervasive imagery of submissive women enjoying violent rape or torture, said the court, is an impediment to women's equality.

On the other hand, Butler was clear that depictions of consensual adult sex are not degrading or obscene in any way. And artistic or educational merit would always be taken into account.

At the time, I wrote enthusiastically about this new, harms-based definition of pornography, sure that it would be a liberating force for everyone.

Sex radicals emphatically disagreed. Some gays and lesbians and civil libertarians were enraged by Butler. They were, apparently, even angrier than they had been in all the preceding years of the far more restrictive obscenity law.

Why? My hunch is that it had to do with Butler's being hailed as a feminist victory. The very word feminist – once a red flag to the establishment – is clearly not "cool" to rebellious young libertarians, or aging wannabe groovy radicals. Civil libertarians, in particular, have been stridently opposed to women's equality rights that might impinge on male sexual liberties.

That's the only way I can explain the dishonest propaganda war that the sex radicals have waged against the Butler decision. For example, the president of the American Civil Liberties Union accused Butler of causing "an explosion of censorship," and giving Canadians "a taste of state repression."

"This view of Butler is, unfortunately, an article of faith among my gay and lesbian students," said Karen Busby, a University of Manitoba law professor.

It's an article of faith among the mischievous and uninformed as well. Now that pornography is coming back before the Supreme Court, Toronto's alternative press is already running a fever. A rant in the gay weekly *Xtra*, in which Toronto law professor Brenda Cossman railed against feminists and reviled the "infamous Butler decision," was headlined "The loonies are back."

In *NOW* magazine, reporter Colman Jones falsely accused

LEAF of having "pressured Canada's legal authorities to make our obscenity laws the most restrictive in the western world." Butler, said Jones, "resulted in a slew of subsequent convictions," chiefly against queer porn.

Hopelessly wrong.

"There have been only two cases in Canada that used Butler," emphasized Busby. One was a prosecution; the other a lost appeal against a customs decision.

Only two cases in seven years – hardly a slew or an explosion of censorship. In fact, the opposite is true. Butler has added to sexual freedom. Here it is, for the record: Revenue Canada spokesman Michel Cleroux told me in an interview last week that, "Because of the Butler decision, we revised our customs guidelines in 1994. Before that, anything depicting anal penetration was considered obscene. But Butler says consensual adult sex is okay, so we removed anal penetration from the obscenity guidelines."

"Butler has worked to liberate sexual expression," agreed Bruce Ryder, Osgoode Hall professor of constitutional law, in an interview.

Ryder pointed out, however, that Revenue Canada was also pushed by the court challenge from Little Sisters bookstore. [Little Sisters, a Vancouver gay and lesbian bookstore, challenged customs rulings repeatedly.] Cleroux agreed that was a factor.

So the complicated truth is that both Butler and gay activism have widened our freedom of expression.

Sadly for the radical chic rebels who would love to see LEAF implode with internal strife, LEAF will actually take another – and united – step forward when the Little Sisters case goes to court this winter.

The LEAF factum strongly upholds the harms-based Butler definition of pornography. It also argues that the customs regime has not gone far enough in applying Butler.

Gay porn, it says, should be judged by a more subtle and complex customs standard because gays and lesbians are a minority group, subject to oppression, and with different sexual standards and needs.

In order to create this better mechanism for judging pornography, LEAF will ask the Court to strike down the current customs regime.

Traditionally, when the Court does strike down a law, Parliament speedily creates a new and better one. That's what it did in 1985, creating a new customs rule for porn within three weeks of the previous law being axed.

With each go-round, Butler is being more finely tuned to increase freedom of sexual expression while seeking to prevent harmful degradation.

It's typically Canadian: a balancing act, a careful, walk-the-tightrope advance toward a fair and inclusive compromise.

● ● ● ● ● ● ● ● ●

IT'S ALL MOOT NOW. It's laughable to look back and see how much heat and sound and fury we all expended on rules that were going to fade from prominence, for entirely unexpected reasons. Butler did set a benchmark, the first time in history that obscenity was defined from a female perspective. In the Butler decision, the Court ruled that harm to women from depictions of violent degradation could be simply assumed. Three years later, in two further decisions (Kourie 2005 and Lebaye 2005), the Supreme Court ruled that real evidence of harm, of a very high standard, would have to be shown in order to convict anyone of obscenity. The government would have to hire scientists and prepare briefs to have any hope of a conviction against a pornographer, unless the case was sensationally egregious.

So much for the ridiculously hyperbolic claims of the pro-porn crowd; so much for the ludicrous ecstasy of feminists who thought we had actually corralled the slavering beast.

A little matter of evidentiary standards has pulled the fangs of the law – except for child pornography, which continues to be prosecuted aggressively, rightly with no resistance.

As contentious as porn was the issue of racism. Decades after Americans had confronted issues of slavery and sought to expunge the remaining stains of racism from their culture and workplaces, most Canadians were still oblivious of our own history of slavery, racism, and discrimination. Confronting ourselves came hard to Canadians, so accustomed to the easy, self-regarding balm of not having been slave owners and Ku Klux Klan types like the Americans. Or so we were brought up, falsely, to believe.

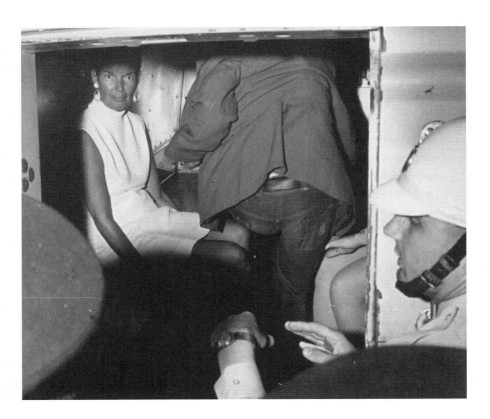

June Callwood, seen here in the back of a police van after being arrested during a 1968 protest against police conduct, was a founder of Nellie's.

Behind the scenes, the feminist movement had been wrestling with its own white supremacy and black fury for a decade or more. Huge progress had been made – the National Action Committee on the Status of Women had taken many significant steps toward racial equity – but the general public seemed unaware of the issue. Until, that is, the furor over June Callwood broke out in early 1992.

June, as I wrote at the time, was a "hugely admired celebrity, a woman of rare social commitment, and one who has powerful media friends." From the 1960s on, June had been in the thick of social protest movements, using her powerful network of allies to secure advancement for the marginalized. She founded Digger House as a refuge for rebellious street hippies and yippies in the late '60s, started Jessie's, a multifunction resource for teenage mothers, dreamed up Nellie's, the first hostel for homeless women, launched Casey House for AIDS patients when AIDS still made you a pariah.

While she worked as a journalist, her good works seemed limitless, and her elegance – she carried herself with the confidence and panache of the beauty she had been and still was – swept her through the doors of the mighty where she pleaded the case of the lowliest. It came as an enormous shock to the public, therefore, when every liberal columnist in Toronto, from Pierre Berton down, began to trumpet his outrage that persons unnamed at Nellie's hostel – the very institution she had founded – were calling June a racist.

"If Callwood is a racist, then so are we all," thundered the headline on Pierre Berton's *Toronto Star* column, unconsciously confessing to the core of the problem.

In all the indignant furor, in the spate of choleric columns and editorials, there was not one word quoted from the Women of Colour Caucus – the group of Nellie's workers who had allegedly challenged June. Months went by, and the controversy simmered on, but always from only one viewpoint, the white viewpoint. The white viewpoint, in brief, is the total refusal to understand that all our beliefs, institutions, structures of thought and practice are drenched in mostly unconscious racist assumptions. Whether June and her allies on the board of Nellie's consciously intended to suppress the women of colour was irrelevant. The way Nellie's was structured and managed, like every other institution, kept the black women in their place. The black women knew it in every fibre of their being. The white women mostly did not.

"Racial thought police," roared June's allies in one newspaper. "Fascism," they snarled at one another.

I knew that when the jackal-pack of the press howled in perfect unison, something was wrong. I desperately wanted to hear from the Women of Colour Caucus, but its members remained stubbornly silent, refusing all overtures. They were terrified by the way the acid commentaries had splashed back in their faces, and silence seemed their only defence. It took weeks, step by step and careful call by call, till I could arrange a secret meeting with the Women of Colour Caucus, plus behind-the-scenes interviews with other staff and board members.

It emerged that no one had really called June a racist. What had happened was a welling up of resentment from the staff who were women of colour, as they saw white staff promoted and trained on computers while they continued to do the drudge work. When they complained, they met with furious denial and outrage. When one of them rose to confront June personally at a board meeting, she was furiously scolded by June that she should be grateful to June for the rest of her life.

It was the usual stand-off. June, a high-profile target, was super-sensitive to any slur on her considerable progressive credentials. When I called her to hear "her side" of the story, she dug a deep hole for herself with unguarded and enraged remarks. Then and now, I refuse to push her into that hole by repeating what she said. (We were casual friends, and I had long championed many of her causes.) And it didn't do me any good: to this day, twenty years later, many of June's influential friends still harbour a coldness toward me for having tried to give voice to what the Women of Colour Caucus felt about their situation.

A year after I tried to explain the systemic racism complaint at Nellie's, I found a more helpful way of dragging the subject into the open. I think I had more requests for reprints of the following column than for almost any other of the thousands I've written. People were thrilled to have "systemic racism" explained, in academic Dr. Peggy McIntosh's genius formula, in the most kitchen-sink items of everyday experience, without individual guilt or finger-pointing.

• • • • • • • • •

UNPACKING A LIFETIME OF WHITE PRIVILEGE
February 1993

It's more than halfway through Black History Month; have you checked your racial awareness recently?

My own awareness received a sharp and exhilarating little jolt when I read an article by Dr. Peggy McIntosh in a journal published by the National Association of Women and the Law.

When you're struggling with a difficult new concept, sometimes a lively metaphor brings everything murky into vivid focus. That's what McIntosh, the associate director of the Centre for Research on Women at Wellesley College, has done for the concept of systemic racism.

Her idea came to her as she tried to convince her male academic colleagues to introduce more material about women into their courses.

"I have often noticed men's unwillingness to grant that they are over-privileged in the curriculum, even though they may grant that women are disadvantaged," McIntosh wryly notes in her article.

Her male colleagues, she says, seemed mostly "oblivious to the connections between over- and under-representation. Denials which amount to taboos surround the subject of advantages which men gain from women's disadvantages."

McIntosh was struck by the realization that white privilege, in just the same way, gives whites an automatic, unearned advantage while making them oblivious to its existence.

And now we come to that inspired metaphor: "White privilege is like an invisible, weightless knapsack of special provisions, assurances, tools, maps, guides, codebooks, passports, visas, clothes, compass, emergency gear, and blank cheques."

McIntosh launched into an exercise of "unpacking" her knapsack, naming and writing down all the previously unnoticed ways in which she, in her daily life, enjoys "over-advantage" by contrast with her African-American women colleagues in the same building and line of work.

Here are just a few of the 46 privileges she lists: she can move into housing she has chosen and be pretty sure her neighbours will be neutral or pleasant to her; she can go shopping alone, assured that she won't be followed or harassed; she can turn on the TV or open the newspaper and see people of her race widely and positively represented; she can speak in public to a powerful male group without putting her race on trial; when she is told about "our national heritage" or about "civilization," she is shown that people of her colour made it what it is.

She does not have to educate her children to be aware of systemic racism for their own daily physical protection; she can swear, dress poorly or not answer letters, without having people attribute these choices to the bad morals, poverty, or illiteracy of her race; she can do well in a challenging situation without being called a credit to her race; she can criticize the government without being seen as a cultural outsider; she can worry about racism without being seen as self-interested or self-seeking; she can easily find academic courses and institutions which give attention only to people of her race; she can remain oblivious to the language and customs of persons of colour, who constitute the world's majority, without feeling any penalty for such oblivion. She can go home from meetings of organizations she belongs to feeling tied-in rather than isolated, out-of-place, outnumbered, unheard, or feared. She can buy "flesh-coloured" bandages that more or less match her skin.

McIntosh's list is a provocative, sometimes scathingly funny recognition of daily experiences which, she writes, she once "took for granted as neutral, normal, and universally available to everybody," just as she once took the male-focused curriculum as neutral.

The problem, McIntosh writes, is that "I was taught to see racism only in individual acts of meanness, not in invisible systems conferring dominance on my racial group."

That's why McIntosh's metaphor of a knapsack, stuffed with comfy clothes and blank cheques, is so valuable. If we follow her example and take a close, honest look at our unearned assets, we may, like her, have to give up the self-flattering "myth of meritocracy" and recognize how many doors swing silently open for us because of our skin colour. We may suddenly understand how much fear, anxiety, and painful marginalization we've escaped just by being born white in a white-dominant society. And if we're honest, we'll see that unearned advantage, like hereditary wealth, can also be soul-damaging and character-deforming. Because we think we're exempt from racism (after all, we didn't choose our white privilege) we may lay claim to a moral purity to which we're not entitled.

"If we could just see our own over-advantage, and not merely others' disadvantage, it would change the way we act," McIntosh said in a phone interview.

• • • • • • • • •

SHOCKINGLY, when a Canadian judge examined racism in the judicial system toward the end of the twentieth century, there were still men on the bench as ignorant in their bigotry as any red-neck cracker.

IN BLACK AND WHITE: RACISM REPORT CAN'T BE IGNORED

January 1996

The most powerful lesson Judge David Cole learned in his three years of work as Co-Chair of the Commission on Systemic Racism in the Ontario Criminal Justice System from 1992 to 1996 was, he told me, "the absolute centrality of race in the lives of people of colour, and its complete invisibility to the rest of us."

Yes, systemic racism is a difficult concept to explain to those who haven't suffered its maddening constraints and hindrances. But the Commission has done a wonderful job in finally showing us just how it works – and what its appalling consequences are. The racism is not in the intent of anyone's actions, but in the differing impact on people of different races.

For example: of black people charged with a crime and later found not guilty, 21 percent are denied bail. For whites, the comparable figure is only 14 percent. When it comes to drug offences, 60 percent of accused whites but only 30 percent of blacks are released by the police – even though the whites were more likely to have a criminal record. Of those charged with assault, 37 percent of whites but only 24 percent of blacks are released on bail....

I find it frightening that a number of judges quoted anonymously in the report told the Commission that the idea there is racism in the system is "patently false"...ascribed to "self-serving interest groups...the socialist government...the left-liberal establishment..."

I almost expected them to start blaming "outside agitators" in time-honoured Mississippi style.

These Colonel Blimps with their political prejudices hanging out are judges, people with the power to rule over others' lives in the most serious ways. Given the report's absolutely irrefutable evidence – gathered by Statistics Canada and independently analyzed by two expert criminologists – one has to question the capacity of these judges to sit on the bench.

• • • • • • • • •

GUN CONTROL is another of those hot buttons; press it and the rhetorical bullets start to fly.

Virginia Woolf once wrote that as a woman, she had no nation. Although Canada enjoyed a dramatically declining number of gun murders over the years since the gun control law was passed in 1995, now that Canada is in the governmental embrace of the gun-lovers, we learn all over again the painful truth that no party is a reliable ally of women.

In 2010, the minority government of Stephen Harper vowed "never to rest" until the long gun registry was abolished. It's still a mystery to me why anti-control advocates can whip themselves up into such a hysterical state of victimhood over a simple gun license. No one, after all, is threatening to take away their toys. At this point, after the initial cost of the registry, it costs peanuts to keep track of who has what weapons, and many lives have been saved by being able to do so. Nevertheless, a western-front woman pushed the bill in the House of Commons and, astoundingly, a handful of rural New Democrats, supposedly under pressure from their constituents, vowed to support it. Only an intense lobbying campaign, mostly by women, swayed some of the key New Democrats to change their minds and defeat the bill.

It was a sobering lesson. When it comes to women's rights, concerns, and interests, no ally is trustworthy, and no victory is carved in stone.

WHO CAN PUT A PRICE TAG ON SAVED LIVES?
December 2002

Gun control is a gender issue.

That's what Chief Justice Catherine Fraser of the Alberta Court of Appeal said back in '98. Studies from Harvard University show that the more firearms there are in any area, the more women are killed.

It's a gender issue because 80 percent of Canadian women favour gun control, and no wonder. The gun control movement in this country was initiated and led by women – the mothers and the sisters of those who were murdered in the Montréal Massacre, as well as some survivors. The Coalition for Gun Control, led by Ryerson [University] professor Wendy Cukier, now represents more than 350 anti-violence, police, women's, community, and public health organizations.

Women are using the gun control laws to save their own lives. The new law requires that when anyone applies for a gun licence, the spouse (or recent ex-spouse) must be notified. Since '98, more than 26,000 spouses and others have used the toll-free line to alert authorities that the applicant may pose a threat. More than 7,000 gun licences have been refused or revoked since that law came into force.

So how many women were saved from death? We don't know. Firearm deaths have declined steadily since the introduction of the law, but it's notoriously difficult to prove a negative – that is, to say precisely why several hundred people were not killed.

We do know, however, that guns double the likelihood of death in any assault. And since the first gun control laws began to be introduced in the 1970s, the rate of spousal killings by firearms has declined 80 percent.

If you just love numbers – and the Tory and Alliance opposition in Ottawa are feasting on them these days – here's another juicy figure for you. The annual cost of gun deaths and injuries in Canada, not to mention the pain, the loss, and the grief, is estimated by public health officials at $6.6 billion.

That puts things into perspective, doesn't it? Not, of course, for the bellowing and bleating gun lobby in Parliament. Ever since early December, when the Auditor General scolded the federal government for huge dollar over-runs in implementing gun control, and for misleading Parliament about the real costs, the gun-lovers have revelled in righteous denunciations.

True, the cost of the gun control legislation over 10 years will be $800 million. The Alliance has joyfully accused the government of "wasting" $1 billion, and, unfortunately, the leadership wars between Allan Rock and Paul Martin have led some Liberals to leap into the blame game as well.

They should be thoroughly ashamed of themselves. Paying for public health and safety is a responsible way for governments to act. In New Brunswick, the feds are spending $400 million to widen a stretch of highway where 43 people died in just four years. And in Ontario (think Walkerton, think public schools, think hospitals) we know very well how to count the cost of reckless government cutbacks.

Perhaps the most sick-making aspect to the current uproar about gun control is not the jelly-like consistency of Liberal backbones, but the stench of hypocrisy wafting from the opposition benches. The very people going purple in the jowls about that $1 billion are the same people whose sabotage techniques swelled the cost.

Tory premiers like Ralph Klein and Mike Harris ignored public support of gun control and crusaded against it all the way to the Supreme Court, causing endless, expensive delays. Two NDP prairie governments refused to enforce the law. Gun lobbyists in Alberta, sounding close to their paranoid U.S. militia counterparts, boasted to the media about deliberately snarling the gun registration system with sophomoric guerrilla tactics in order to make it unworkably expensive.

Gun control, of course, is also an intelligence issue. The more educated you are, the more you support it, according to Gallup. Opposition to registering guns, you might say, can be counted in inverse ratio to reasoning power.

The federal government, faced with the vicious backlash by a minority of Canada's 2.3 million gun owners (out of 31 million Canadians), waived or lowered registration fees as an enticement to the hostile. Chalk that up as another cost imposed by the gun lobby on the rest of us.

Toughen up, you feeble federal Liberals. You owe it to the vast majority of sensible Canadians to fund and enforce the gun control legislation. As for Anne McLellan, who was the shilly-shallying justice minister when the costs were allowed to escalate, maybe it's time she was sent to the backbenches.

• • • • • • • • •

WHILE GUN CONTROL is still exploited as a wedge issue by the governing Harper Conservatives, some hot buttons, such as gay marriage, have cooled in Canada. In 2011, visiting some friends in New York and discussing gay politics, I mentioned an activist in Toronto who was, I said, "married to an architect." A few minutes later, my friend said hesitantly, "Er…is her partner a man or a woman?" I was equally taken aback. "A woman, of course!" I replied. "You see," said my friend sheepishly, "when you use the word 'married,' we Americans are a bit thrown off.…"

Gay marriage was legalized in Canada in 2005 (eight of ten provinces had made it legal several years earlier), and it quickly became so accepted that it seemed hardly worth mentioning in casual conversation. This is one social advance so firmly established that it's confounding to look back just a few years and to remember the tedious, tendentious arguments of those who opposed it so bitterly and for so long – and for so little reason.

GAY MARRIAGE CRITIC STUCK ARGUING IN CIRCLES
July 2003

The debate about same-sex marriages is as exasperating as a car alarm that wakes you at 3 a.m. It beeps and bleeps on and on, a meaningless noise that makes your nerve endings scream. Bury your head under your pillow as you will, you can't seem to shut it out.

At least in this 750 words' worth of bleeps, you'll know exactly what biases I bring to the keyboard. There's absolutely nothing sacred about marriage, in my view, except the equality, respect, tenderness, comradeship, and love that two people create together. This form of marriage is very recent, and it can be practised by the non-churched, the common-law, and people of the same sex. Why not? Gays and lesbians have just as much possibility of being loving and faithful partners and extraordinarily good parents as do heterosexuals.

The history texts tell us that the formal institution of marriage was created not by any God, but by men's desire to amass, protect, and perpetuate property. From the beginning, women were traded about and sold off like cattle, and men got to seize, own, and bequeath the real estate. Not only the wives but also the offspring were men's marital property for most of human history.

Whatever stability or protections marriage offered to women and children, there are also entire libraries that document the unspeakable cruelties made possible by this "sacred" institution.

Only in the last century did we begin to struggle free from such gross injustices. Piece by piece, we improved the law. Finger by finger, we pried the icy grip of established religions from around our throats.

Now that marriage has evolved beyond the grasp of religionists (it was such a convenient way of keeping the women under control and procreating!), it has become a matter of free choice and, in the best of cases, equal partnership. A far better framework for rearing children, in my view, than the patriarchal nonsense of earlier generations.

I've tried and tried to think how it is possible for the existence of same-sex marriage to harm, insult, or take away anything from heterosexual marriage.

I undertook this mental exercise to better understand "the other side" of the argument, and it was in this spirit that I forced myself to listen to ethicist Margaret Somerville on a CBC radio broadcast recently.

Somerville is a professor of medicine and law at the McGill Centre of Medicine, Ethics, and Law. In print and on the air, she is both ubiquitous and honoured. She is always presented as a lofty moral authority of strict scientific objectivity. (What fools we mortals be to think that science is objective.) She herself insisted in a phone interview that she is strictly secular and attached to no political point of view.

Strangely, however, Somerville's views often coincide with the most conservative and male supremacist attitudes of right-wing politicians and various churches. She opposes euthanasia, reproductive technologies, and stem cell research, and was appalled by the striking down of Canada's abortion law because, she said then, so many women would rush to have pre-vacation "designer abortions" to preserve their svelte figures in swimsuits. Last week, she told me during our interview that she is definitely not pro-choice, because the absence of a criminal law allows a woman "to abort the day before her due date."

Now, she has become prominent in the crusade against same-sex marriage. On the radio, she hypothesized that the next step, which she thought was "simply awful," would be the creating of an embryo from two ova or two sperm. (The ethicist seems to be haunted by strange premonitions of sci-fi doom.)

"There has to be a basic rule," she said. "Marriage is inherently procreative. It must be about the child; it's about the child's rights." She argued that the number of childless marriages, or marriages that are downright harmful to their children, don't count in the argument. "The institution symbolizes procreation, no matter what couples do."

When Somerville kept repeating that heterosexual reproductive marriage has to be a basic rule of society – without ever saying just why it must be so – I challenged her to provide a reason, rather than going around in circles. "I'm getting very nervous about your simple-minded interpretations," she retorted. "All religions have always believed in heterosexual marriage, for millennia and millennia." Precisely.

To me (and, thankfully, to the courts), equality, dignity, and freedom from discrimination – not the dictates of religion – are basic rules of our pluralist society. I'm still waiting to hear a sensible argument on the other side.

• • • • • • • • •

THAT CONVERSATION with the ethicist was not the first time I had contemplated the obtuseness of the gay-averse. Back in the early '80s, I found it necessary to argue for the rights of gay male teachers to be in the classroom – as though gays had a monopoly on pedophilia – and even at the turn of the millennium, there was fun to be had in considering the views of the heterosexist majority.

HETEROSEXUAL FAMILY LIFE A SOURCE OF SMUG PRIDE
June 2001

When I first heard about it, the idea was so preposterous that I dismissed it as just another Internet hoax. Then my latest copy of *Briarpatch* ("Saskatchewan's independent alternative newsmagazine") arrived in the mail. Good old *Briarpatch*'s enterprising editors had actually reprinted the entire, official announcement:

The office of the mayor of the city of Regina proclaims Monday, June 18, as Heterosexual Family Pride Day.

The long list of "whereas's" makes the mayor's orientation abundantly clear. Whereas the intact heterosexual family unit is ordained by God as clearly revealed in the Holy Bible, and whereas "large bodies" of research show that the intact hetero families [i.h.f.] provide excellent nurturing for children, and whereas the i.h.f. provide necessary stability for the good of society, and whereas the i.h.f. provide "sexual satisfaction for the men and women who are committed to them," and whereas monogamous husbands and wives have no reason to worry about AIDS or broken hearts (oh yeah?), Mayor Pat Fiacco asks citizens to recognize Heterosexual Family Pride Day.

My first reaction was a burst of hearty laughter; my second was a slight queasiness at the thought of the small-eyed, snake-belly-white kind of homophobe who would come up with such a farrago of nonsense.

Smug majorities are given to this kind of thing. They lash back at any disadvantaged group that pesters them with demands, needles them into the painful exercise of thought or disturbs their placid enjoyment of their monolithic rightness, whiteness, and entitlement.

The first stage of reaction is denial. Wife-battering? Child sexual abuse? Systemic racism in Canada? I could cite you chapter and verse of the respectable commentators who swore up and down that none of these harms existed.

The second stage of majoritarian panic is, pardon the expression, appropriation.

The same misogynists who insisted that there was no such thing as wife-battering soon began to change their tune: from a bellow to a whine.

"Me too!" they began to whimper. "Men are battered too." Despite the obvious idiocy of this claim – women who are deemed "battered" are subject to a complex mesh of submissive conditioning, threats, intimidation, physical violence, crushed self-respect, terror, and financial dependency, usually because of responsibility for the children – the wails of the copycat victim are heard world-wide.

In Cairo, where women can choose female-only subway cars to avoid gropers, a male lawyer is threatening to sue unless the city provides men-only cars. In Austria, where women earn one third of the male rate of pay, Herbert Haupt of the far-right Freedom Party is not only the minister of women's affairs – he's also a backlash bozo who thinks there should be a men's department. And in British Columbia, a shelter for men who have suffered "verbal or physical abuse" (cry me a river) had to close down for lack of public support. The *National Post* was aghast at their plight.

Heterosexual Family Pride Day, however, is the ultimate in embarrassing acts of appropriation. Can you imagine the mind of someone who thinks he has to strut the "pride" of heterosexual men? The smarmy language doesn't hide the all-too-obvious motives: to assert the supremacy of conservative family values, to denigrate the claims of the gay rights movement, and to try to enshrine one Christian or "missionary" brand of sexuality as the only legal style of union.

Seems these evangelicals feel all shook up unless the state enforces their form of belief. Their idea of social stability, however, is just what threatens us all. It creates the kind of parents who teach their children to hate and taunt their schoolmates who are children of lesbians or gay men. It gives licence to the kind of thugs who would beat a Matthew Shepard to death because he was gay. It breeds the toxic intolerance that drives gay youths to a 30 percent higher suicide rate than other teens.

Heterosexual "intact families" – a tiny minority – already bask at the top of the social-approval ladder. Surely that's enough legitimation for anyone. Besides, I just read in *The New York Times* that the divorce rate in the evangelical Christian heartland of the United States is 50 percent above the national average.

The patriarchal system isn't working any more, fellas! It's plumb broke. Proclaim all you want, you're driving last century's model. Maybe, instead of copy-catting gay pride days, you ought to learn something from feminists, lesbians, and gays about real love and commitment in the arms of equality.

On second thought, nah. Equality is one thing you can't fake.

Chapter Three
DUAL OPPRESSION: HARASSMENT AND RAPE

LONG BEFORE THE WORD "feminism" was in common usage and before "sisterhood" could even be imagined, the grim spectre of rape hovered over every young female life. The possibility of rape was ever present as a curb on a girl's freedom and a plausible excuse for denying her the same liberties as her brothers enjoyed. The fear of it pulsed through us whenever we were out alone at night. The thought of rape, the ultimate helplessness and vulnerability of it, was devastating, even in the abstract.

And yet, until the feminist movement began to name harassment as abuse in the 1970s, most of us numbly accepted that we would be viewed, judged, dismissed, approved, hired, or rejected on the basis of our sexual attributes. Boys and men were entitled to "rate" us noisily, with so-called wolf whistles or jeers, and there was nothing we could do about it except try to avoid drawing attention to ourselves – while at the same time striving to be as attractive as possible to the opposite sex. Sexual harassment, in other words, was our unavoidable fate; rape was the "fate worse than death." Both types of assault were understood through the lens of patriarchy: Harassment kept us pinned down, excluded, and disarmed; it suited the purposes of male dominance, so it went unnamed and unrecognized. Rape, on the other hand, destroyed the property rights of male "owners" (boyfriends, husbands) and was therefore, quite apart from its impact on women, a hanging crime.

I'll never forget my shock, in 1979, when a book called *The Secret Oppression: Sexual Harassment of Working Women,* by

Published in 1978, *The Secret Oppression* opened the closet door and told women what to do to fight debasement and harassment on the job. It included case studies and offered actions plans for unions and management.

Constance Backhouse and Leah Cohen, thumped onto my desk in the *Toronto Star* newsroom. Naming is so powerful. At first, I was jolted and repelled by the idea of "sexual harassment;" my instinct was to brush it off as more "victim" stuff. Of course, I was by now aware that this brush-off was often a defence against a painful truth, so I let my mind rove back over the decades of my female experience. I remembered the camp director who, when I was a sixteen-year-old counsellor, tried to persuade me how prudish and repressed I was not to let him see me naked. I recalled the university professor who insisted I write a missed test in the privacy of his office, where he ran his fingers through my hair and whispered that there was a way I could be sure of getting an A. I remembered these incidents and many more, and how I had brazened through and survived them, no matter how demoralizing they were inwardly.

With an almost physical jolt, I suddenly apprehended all those incidents not merely as mortifying – not somehow my fault, and not at all as a sought after and desired tribute to my irresistible female allure – but as an infringement on my person, on my freedom, and on my rights. Thanks to this feminist work of analysis, I was able to understand my own experience without the fog of masculinist culture. And thanks to my incorporating the authors' analytic tools into my understanding of the world, I was able to comprehend abuse when others might just see "flirting."

Later, in 1990, this analysis came to mind again when a recurring news story caught my eye. An older and "eccentric" engineering professor had been banned from the Hart House swimming pool at the University of Toronto for having "leered" at a student in the pool, and the media were up in arms about the "ludicrously" strict sentence he received. No one could resist the story: Columnists, news reporters, writers of letters to the editor, and writers of editorials themselves, all used the same tone, over and over, to rehash the case. All heaped ridicule on the mere thought of branding a leer as "sexual harassment." Progressive men and reactionary women all agreed.

Such unanimity, I had begun to intuit, was a signal. If the entire jackal-pack of journalists was yipping and howling the same tune, it must be that male sexual entitlement was under fire. Nothing is more sacred in our society than a man's right to impose his sexual inclinations on a woman, any woman. (And women are supposed to be grateful. How many times have feminists been chided by male and female critics to "appreciate the compliment" when verbally harassed on the street?)

Sure enough, when I studied the stories, every last one was written strictly from a male point of view. Would all men have to wear sunglasses? How could a man be punished for a mere "stare"? The commentaries were universally sophomoric, and not one of them – even when the writer was striving for a serious tone – attempted to consider the story from the woman's point of view or to remark on the impact on a woman of being persistently ogled. Hummel (the professor who had been charged), in one of his many creepy remarks to the media, vowed that he liked to look at and photograph women, that he liked to open doors for women, "especially the curvy ones," and that he would never insult a woman.

I longed to hear the woman's story. Unlike Professor Hummel, however, the student in question, Bev Torfason, obeyed the confidentiality of the hearing and the appeal – a confidentiality requested by Hummel and immediately broken by him in his frequent missives to the press. Several months went by with the entire story being interpreted through Hummel's ogling eyes. Then my phone rang at the *Star*. "Hello," said a timid voice. "This is Bev Torfason..."

NO JUSTICE FOR VICTIM OF LEERING PROFESSOR
January 1990

Beverly Torfason is a shy young woman with long blonde hair, round glasses and an angelic kind of prettiness. She is an engineer, quiet, articulate, and very private. All during the past year, she's been the butt of merciless media ridicule.

Beverly Torfason is the woman who blew the whistle on Professor Richard Hummel, the former frogman of Hart House.

Professor Hummel's persistent ogling of Beverly Torfason and other swim-suited young women was, according to witnesses who testified at the sex harassment hearing at the University of Toronto, "way beyond normal."

Hummel was found by the hearing to be guilty of sexual harassment and, even after appealing his punishment, was barred from the Hart House athletic wing for five years. Now Hummel is going to the district court for a judicial review; his lawyer will attack the procedures of the original hearing on legalistic grounds.

If the media hold true to form, Torfason's complaint is going to be ridiculed again. And Hummel, a 60-year-old engineering professor twice found guilty of peculiar and repulsive behaviour that violated the rights of others, will be treated as a jolly old rogue.

The unfairness of the public perception was due, perhaps, to the fact that Hummel broke the agreed-on rules of confidentiality. Eagerly, he circulated long, incoherent, misspelled letters arguing his case and making bizarre innuendos about Torfason. He publicly named her and her place of work. He posed for newspaper photographs in his office, showing off his photographs of female swimmers (with a girlie calendar on the wall behind him), and made sure that the press heard his side of the story.

Torfason maintained the rule of confidentiality and refused to talk to the press until both hearing and appeal were completed. "I was determined to fight dirt with dignity," she told me, tears of outrage welling in her eyes.

Still, even given that Torfason refrained from lobbying, why were so many commentators – in editorials, on radio, in magazines – so quick to champion Hummel's right to leer and so eager to sneer at Torfason's right to privacy and freedom from harassment?

Torfason takes evening courses at the university and swims at Hart House, the main on-campus recreation centre, three times a week. In the spring and summer of 1988, she gradually became aware that Professor Hummel was consistently swimming in the lane beside her, staring at her with his head out of the water.

"It was weeks before I could grasp that this man was definitely following me and staring at me," she told me. "At first I thought I must be over-reacting. But he was always there. I became so uncomfortable that I changed my swim times, first to the weekends, then to lunch-time. But it wasn't long before he showed up then, too."

The ogling went on for months, witnesses testified. At one point, Hummel donned swim goggles and followed Torfason closely – a couple of feet away – for four lengths. Three lifeguards testified that Hummel's persistent staring, at Torfason and at other women, was obvious, prolonged, and troublesome. One student said he stared at her breasts; she was so unnerved she discussed Hummel's ogling with her parents, and then rearranged her swim times.

During the summer and fall, the lifeguards, the athletic director of Hart House, and Torfason herself all confronted Hummel; according to Torfason, he didn't stop.

A lifeguard testified that Hummel stared so hard at women walking on the deck that he actually bumped into pillars. Laughable? Not to the young women who felt so vulnerable and exposed to his obnoxious gaze that they actually hid behind those pillars to avoid him.

Is this just a giggle? When a 60-year-old haunts you in a swimming pool until you can't be at ease in your own skin, is this a knee-slapping joke? A hearing panel and an appeal panel didn't think so. They were quite clear that Hummel was a sexual harasser.

Meaningful glances may be delightful when they're mutual; an unwelcome leer from a passing stranger is no big deal. But since when does a young woman's desire to exercise mean that she must agree to be the sex object of any aging and prurient gawker who has figured out her swimming schedule?

Beverly Torfason had the courage to fight for her right not to be harassed. Several women who had suffered from Hummel's unwanted attentions were more fearful; they were willing to testify only if they could remain anonymous, and therefore the panel refused to hear them.

Maybe they knew something that Torfason didn't: when it comes to questioning male sexual privileges, or asking that a woman's experience be given serious and equal consideration, most of the mainstream media are, alas, wilfully, complacently, blind and deaf.

• • • • • • • • •

TODAY, IT WOULD BE obvious (at least to most women) that Hummel was doing more than harassing Torfason. His many months of watching her in the pool, peering at her breasts, following her on the pool deck, and even into the change room, amounted to stalking. By the '90s, even the sluggish federal Conservative government felt it had to recognize in law this common precursor to assault.

A fairly tepid anti-stalking law was brought forward. "When the Tories come wooing the women's vote, their gifts are highly suspect," I warned in a column in May 1993.

What the Tories give, the Tories may take away. In Ontario, after the Mike Harris Conservatives were elected in 1995, laws designed to promote justice for women were rapidly struck down. In 2001, I was again writing about sexual harassment and what it might eventually lead to.

SEXUAL HARASSMENT IS A CRIME – LET'S TREAT IT LIKE ONE
June 2001

Theresa Vince might be alive today, delighting in a loving family life, if Ontario had had strong safeguards to protect women from sexual harassment on the job. But she was shot to death by her supervisor at Sears just days before she was to take early retirement at age 56. Vince had complained to Sears about the years of torment she had endured, but nothing was done.

She was not the first. Three other Ontario women had previously been murdered in the workplace after a history of harassment.

Sexual harassment is not a wink-wink, jokey little peccadillo; women are not "over-reacting" to harmless flirtation and, most important, despite the wide and erroneous impression that sexual harassment rules have "gone too far," there is virtually no law to stop women being sexually hounded and humiliated out of their jobs.

In 1995, the year before her obsessed stalker murdered Theresa Vince, the Mike Harris right-wing government was elected. One of its early deeds was to repeal the employment equity law, which had compelled employers to take active measures against workplace harassment. Ever since, the government has steadily whittled away at other remedies, protections, and avenues of redress.

"I believe sexual harassment in the workplace is only there because the people at the top condone it and maybe practise it themselves," said the still-grieving Jim Vince, at a recent Queen's Park press conference. (Sandi Thompson comes to mind: She was fired after revealing that she had been sexually harassed by her boss, Al McLean, then Tory Speaker of the Legislature. She had to go to court before the Tories stopped defending their buddy and offered her a settlement.)

Jim Vince was at Queen's Park because his local MPP, Liberal Pat Hoy, has brought forward an anti-harassment bill in Theresa's memory, with the steady encouragement of the Chatham-Kent Sexual Assault Centre, the local women's shelter, and the Chatham-Kent Labour Council.

Hoy's bill to amend the Occupational Health and Safety Act was drafted by lawyer Geri Sanson, a noted human rights expert. He also consulted with the Chatham activists and the Vince family. This is a genuine, community-based effort to turn a grotesque crime into a springboard for better laws.

The bill puts the responsibility where it rightly belongs: in workplace legislation, not just in the more amorphous realm of human rights....

Hoy's bill would require an immediate investigation of a complaint and give the investigator the power to order a halt to the behaviour. A complainant would have the right to refuse work, without penalty, until the situation is resolved, and the employer would be compelled to take steps to remedy the offence.

The Harris government prides itself on a get-tough, law and order regime. But here's a crime that can result in unemployment, economic loss, depression, illness, and even death – and there are no workable structures in place to protect the victims or hold the assailants accountable.

Studies show that between 40 and 70 percent of women, and 5 percent of men, suffer from sexual insult and aggression at work, usually from supervisors. Experts say that "talking it over" with the harasser commonly escalates the intensity and hatefulness of harassment. Complain? Oh sure. A 17-year study of all such cases before the federal Human Rights Commission shows that 75 percent of the women who complained were no longer in their jobs. No wonder that only 10 percent of the women who suffer the degradation, anxiety, and shame of continued harassment actually seek formal redress or protection....

● ● ● ● ● ● ● ● ●

FINALLY IN 2010, just before he was due to retire from the Legislature, MPP Pat Hoy's anti-harassment bill passed in the Legislature. This was fourteen years after Theresa Vince had been murdered. So many years to right an obvious wrong; so deep is male sexual entitlement, with all its unacknowledged privileges in the street, in the home, in the law courts.

Sexual harassment is to rape as battering is to murder: a promissory note, a threat, a statement that "I can do it; I have power over you; you can't stop me."

Rape itself is still a bitterly contested topic. American women recently had to beat back a Republican effort to limit abortion funding for assaulted women to only those who had been "forcibly raped." This is the very stance that the women's movement has fought for at least six decades: most rapes happen without bloody wounds and shredded clothing, and even without vaginal penetration by a penis – but it's all rape, and it's all forced.

Since my first days as a columnist, the toughest part of writing about this crime was to control my own gut-deep rage at the authorities who question it, especially the police.

BUMBLING OPP REPORT 'SMEARS ALL RAPE VICTIMS'
January 1979

The Ontario Provincial Police report on sex crimes is breathtakingly inept. It libels the victims of rape as "promiscuous" without a shred of evidence – (and, it seems, without knowing what the word means) – and implies, preposterously, that 71 percent of rapes are provoked by the victim. The bumbling would be comical if rape weren't such a hideous crime.

Rape, to the victim, is not sex but a viciously degrading assault on her being. After a decade of feminist protest, we thought that message was getting through. Though we still hear the snickers about women who "asked for it," and though rape is still glorified in pop culture from *Straw Dogs* to Mick Jagger to punk rockers, still we thought most adults were beginning to understand.

Now, with the police report, I'm not too sure. Casually, the two anonymous statisticians who wrote the report remark that "with the exception of 29 percent of the rape offences, or the rape offences that were unprovoked, the victims showed a great lack of discretion. Promiscuity is a predominant factor."

How do they conclude, in defiance of all known studies, that only 29 percent of the rapes were unprovoked? Simple. They list the six "circumstances" in which these 75 rapes occurred: "home environment, social occasion (dates, swimming, picnic, etc.), accepting a ride, hitch-hiking, runaways, and unprovoked."

This means if you're raped on a date, at a party, or when accepting a ride, in the eyes of the OPP you've provoked the attack. That's statistical analysis?

The accusation of promiscuity is even more staggeringly unfounded. Other than the flat statement, no evidence is given.

I asked Staff Superintendent Neil Chaddock, head of the OPP research branch which prepared the report, how he knew the victims were promiscuous.

"Listen, according to Webster's dictionary, that word promiscuous means indiscriminate. That's all we're saying – that these girls were indiscriminate."

"Do you mean they slept around with a lot of different boys?" I asked.

"No. Indiscriminate means indiscreet. We didn't ask these girls any questions about their sex lives. This report was compiled from statistics. Taking a ride from a stranger is indiscriminate."

"Then taking a ride from a stranger is promiscuous?"

"Yes. Indiscriminate."

As I once was?

Come on, Superintendent. It's too late now to back away from the damaging smear implied by that word.

It doesn't help to know that the name-calling wasn't based on any fact. It doesn't even help to know that major studies in the United States show that only 4.4 percent of rapes are "provoked," as opposed to 22 percent of homicides and 10.7 percent of armed robberies. What matters is that the OPP's careless use of that word will shore up the prejudices of thousands....

Chaddock couldn't understand my distress. He said he was a husband and the father of two daughters and he had asked for the report in order to help prevent rape, after a 46-percent increase in the number of rapes was reported over a four-month period last year.

Perhaps it's too much to ask the police to understand the sickened outrage, the sense of betrayal women feel when society conspires in the big lie that women invite, provoke, and enjoy rape.

It doesn't surprise me, and it isn't any defence, that one of the report's authors is a woman. Many women believe nice girls don't get raped. It's a self-protective mechanism in a culture that despises the rape victim as much as it blames the criminal.

I participated in the lie myself, as a teenager. Repelled by the image of woman as a cringing victim, I boasted that any woman could fight off a rape attempt if she were smart enough and strong enough.

Then it almost happened to me. I fitted perfectly into Chaddock's statistics. I was 18, and indiscreet. Innocent, but "indiscriminate" or "promiscuous" because I accepted a ride. Seven thousand miles from home, on an Israeli kibbutz, I accepted a ride on the watchman's horse. I even "abused alcohol," dutifully joining him in drinking arak at Arab villagers' homes because he told me they would be insulted if I refused their hospitality.

After all, I was a politely brought up girl. I also had never before experienced the effects of alcohol. We rode back across the fields, and when I slipped groggily from the horse's back, the man attacked.

I won't ever forget my stunned surprise, our long, squalid struggle as I fought back, or the way I lay exhausted and retching on the ground long after I had scared him off with my screams.

As shocked as I was, rage didn't come until the next day when I shakily told the story to my Canadian friends. I expected consolation, moral support, and maybe even protection from future attack.

Instead, one girl was aloofly silent and the boys were convulsed with laughter. "Great fantasy life you have!" they shouted. "Don't you just wish!" They slapped each other's backs in shared mirth and derision.

A moment like that puts iron in your soul; the humiliation you feel is nothing compared to the black frustration of trying to break through those smug assumptions.

It was years and years till I risked ridicule by telling the story again. But now a strange thing happened: The story was like a touchstone. Friends, colleagues, women of every ordinary kind, would suddenly unlock their own memories over coffee or notebooks.

The uncle or camp counsellor who secretly fondled them when they were children; the shame of it, the fear of "telling" on an adult and being accused of complicity. The rape and attempted rape by boyfriends, neighbours, landlords, a husband's buddy. Always, this story is told with gritting rage, not just against the criminal, but against all those who refuse to hear how it happened and what it felt like.

The OPP's report breathes new life into the old libel. No wonder more rape victims call the Rape Crisis Centre than call the police. No wonder only one rape in 10 is ever reported at all.

I wish, just for a moment, Chaddock could be in the shoes of those "promiscuous" teenagers who were so indiscreet; who took a drink or a ride; who were too naive or too polite to see the danger signals; who were, after all, very young.

You and I, as we once were.

Our daughters, as they will be.

• • • • • • • • •

THAT SAME YEAR, 1979, the first pebble in an eventual avalanche of legal change quietly came loose and started skittering down the mountain, a disturbance that began half a continent away, but reverberated tellingly in Canada. An Oregon man, John Rideout, beat his estranged wife in public, dragged her back to her apartment and brutally choked, beat, and raped her in front of their two-year-old daughter. Rideout never bothered to deny any of it. His lawyer argued that a man couldn't be guilty of raping his "own" wife. Furthermore, rape laws were unfair to men, since they protected only women, and gave women the balance of power in a marriage by giving them the right to say "no" to sex. Rideout walked away free, smirking.

I wrote about the case in a column advocating a law against marital rape. It was a concept that startled, not to say inflamed, many of my male newsroom colleagues, who came by to pound my desk in rage until the papers jumped in time to their hammering fists. "You're trying to destroy my marriage!" hollered the worst of them.

Anyone who touched on this subject had to prepare herself for a backwash of despair. The research at the time (and I doubt that anything has changed) showed that rape mythologies were so deeply embedded in our culture, and spread like viruses so rapidly through the toxic medium of pornography, that it felt hopeless to combat them. University of Manitoba psychologist Neil Malamuth had shown that glamorously violent films and popular pornography could make men measurably more callous to women's pain. Male students who watched *Swept Away*, a film in which a woman is first humiliated, starved, and injured, and then grovels adoringly at the feet of her gloating rapist, were aroused by her excitement and indifferent to her suffering. Indeed, these normal students showed a preference for women in porn films to suffer pain along with their orgasms. This appetite for cruelty, Malamuth wrote, "revealed a pattern that bears a striking similarity to the callous attitudes held by convicted rapists."

Women are by no means immune to this media brainwashing. Though the female students in Malamuth's study were repelled at the thought of being raped, a substantial number thought that *other* women might like it.

IS LEGAL SYSTEM SICK JOKE ON RAPE VICTIMS?
May 1981

How is it possible? One out of every five Canadian women, according to the Winnipeg Rape Incidence Project and the Advisory Council on the Status of Women, is sexually assaulted against her will: grabbed, fondled, clothes ripped, or the victim of attempted rape. One out of 17 is forcibly raped. (The study of Winnipeg rape incidents in 1978–79 was conducted by community health workers and researchers from the University of Manitoba and Simon Fraser University.)

Yet 94 percent of sexual criminals walk free, never to be arrested, say the same studies. And only 2 percent of all rapists will ever stand in court and hear themselves pronounced guilty. And for those 2 percent, the average sentence will be 2½ to 3½ years… though many, many, are let off with a warning or a fine.

This winter, a man in Toronto held up a grocery store and stole $50 and a carton of cigarettes and was sentenced to nine years in jail.

A man who grabbed at knifepoint, a 14-year-old newspaper delivery girl and raped her and committed other foul acts, was given five years, even though he had 10 previous convictions.

A man who lured two 16-year-old boys to his hotel room with a promise of liquor, and then attacked them, got nine years. A 15-year-old girl who took a ride from a friend of the family was raped and dumped on the road at 3 a.m., far from home. The judge lectured her about "using better judgement" (no one lectured those boys) and gave the man 2½ years. That man had 45 previous convictions.

I don't argue that longer sentences are the cure for crime.

But to compare the relative seriousness with which courts view different crimes reveals something to me: that the legal system is a monstrous sick joke, a joke of which we women are the butt.

Defence lawyers rant and rave about rape charges as though rapists are the aggrieved victims. And in two weeks of interviews, at least 10 experts, from psychologists to lawyers, made the same telltale slip in talking to me: They referred to the raped woman as "the accused."...

• • • • • • • • •

PICTURE A VICTIM of rape: a doe-eyed girl with clouds of soft dark hair, like the one I once wrote about, so quiveringly vulnerable and wounded that your protective instincts bubble to the surface, and you interview her with infinite delicacy. Now picture a coarser, stockier woman, with tattoos, a few missing teeth, and hair amateurishly chopped short. She swears casually and cackles in self-mockery. It's the classically self-protective working-class armour, and you know before I finish forming this sentence that your instinctive image, your automatic responses, are far less tender.

Now picture her as Caribbean, coming from one of Toronto's enclaves of immigrant life, complete with defiant bravado. Or, even more typically, think of a young aboriginal girl. The Ontario Native Women's Association reports that eight out of ten aboriginal women have been victims of sexual assault, according to Holly Johnson and Myrna Dawson's excellent 2011 text *Violence against Women in Canada*. Does their experience of rape instantly, in your mind, retreat behind an unbreakable glass wall, to some unknowable foreign land that you shrug off because you can't hope to understand it?

Class and race other than "middle and white" have always doubled and tripled the hazard both of rape and of official indifference to the crime. One of my earlier brushes with this truth was when I met with a group of the "Grandview girls" in the early 1990s. These were working-class women in their mid to late thirties who had been imprisoned in their early teenage years by their own parents, consigned to a "training school" in southern Ontario, most often for "uncontrollable behaviour." Read on to see how they were treated when they finally came forward with their experiences of being sexually assaulted in reform school.

Five of the Grandview survivors (there were seventy making claims for redress) came to be interviewed at my home, for the sake of greater anonymity. Just a few days before, one of Premier Bob Rae's aides had leaked some information about one of the women to the *Toronto Sun*, of all papers, in a clear attempt to discredit the claimants.

PROVINCE OWES HELP TO VICTIMS OF GRANDVIEW
November 1992

...[That day, they] were shocked, frightened and enraged by the reports of the dirty trick. Would they be next? Could they hope for justice from the same government that would try to discredit one of them? Judi Harris, the woman whose "rap sheet" has been bandied about, sat wordlessly shaken through our interview.

Try to imagine the many layers of abuse these women have endured. All five (like many, though not all, of the Grandview women) were emotionally and/or sexually abused at home. All five were considered "incorrigible" or "delinquent:" they had run away from home, skipped school, or acted out sexually. All five were sent to Galt Training School for Girls, later called Grandview, when they were only 11 or 12 years old.

I was a young reporter when the Grandview women were kids in jail. I wrote features about disturbed children in reform schools. I was shocked, back then, to discover that girls, unlike boys, were "sent away" without committing any crimes. Now that we all know why some girls behaved with such defiantly precocious and disturbed sexuality, the story is even more horrifying.

Once in the reform school, they were abused again by authorities, at least some of whom evidently saw them as sexually available young creatures, not as the hurt, violated, and angry children they were. Some Grandview women have told of being thrown naked into a concrete-floored, barred punishment cell, where male guards had access to them. These were 13-year-old and 14-year-old girls. At least one former guard has been quoted describing the girls as sexually tantalizing.

Almost 20 years later, as some of the women began to tell their stories to the press, new levels of abuse were added. A year and a half after the first complaint, Waterloo Regional Police have still not laid any charges. At least one officer was removed from the case when he made crude, sexually explicit remarks to one of the 64 complainants. And the OPP is now investigating former Waterloo police who might also have been implicated in the abuse of Grandview girls during the early '70s.

Worse still, it seems likely that the then-Tory government or its bureaucrats knew of the abuse at Grandview and covered it up. In the mid-'70s, government officials filed a secret report on improprieties at the "model" reform school. No charges were laid. The school was closed. The report is still secret. Why?

The women I met with are smart, tough, and explosively vulnerable. They lack the middle-class gloss to try to hide their hurt; their frankness is both scary and exhilarating. "We're low class and no class," Joyce Taylor, their president, once quipped to a reporter.

They're astute about the lack of public fuss over their childhood torment. The boys who were raped in Christian Brother reform schools are seen as innocent victims of stark horror. It's not the same for girls – "bad" girls are assumed to be complicit in their own rape. But the hard truth is that adults who exploit desperate children are committing a grave and unforgivable breach of trust.

• • • • • • • • •

THERE WAS ONE RAY of unintended humour to lighten our afternoon of tough truths. I learned later, from the lawyer who accompanied the Grandview women to my house, that the women were greeted by my husband at the door. "Congratulations," he told them, "I just heard on the news that the government is ready to give you access to your personal files from Grandview."

"How do you like that," hissed one of the women to the lawyer. "Even the goddam butler knows more than we do."

It was another year before the government awarded the women a grudging "healing package" (the sums ranged from $3,000 to $60,000, depending on a chart spelling out the various levels of violence done to them). And another five years passed before only two of the guards (of the many guards, superintendents, and professionals who were accused of extorted acts of sex) were sentenced to prison.

Rape is an inexpensive crime.

Over the last three decades, governments fiddled repeatedly with the rape laws, bending to pressure from the women's movement and responding to continuous legal challenges from accused rapists and their criminal lawyers. The revision in the works when I wrote a series of columns about rape was the one that expunged the word "rape" from the law books and replaced it with "sexual assault." I dutifully supported that change at the time, though inwardly, I regretted the loss of a word that, for women, had incredible negative power. All these years later, most of us still refer to "rape" rather than "sexual assault," the phrase that rightly was meant to emphasize the violence, not the sexual aspect, of the crime, but somehow leached the horror out of it.

NEW RAPE LAW MAY CUT THROUGH SEXISM
May 1981

...Rape is being seen more clearly for what it has always been: a violent sexual assault on the body, heart and soul of another person.

This year, Canadian law may leap forward to meet our new perceptions. Bill C-53, the long-awaited act to amend the Criminal Code, is due to be debated in Parliament next fall. Chief among its reforms, hailed by almost all women's groups, is the redefinition of rape as "sexual assault." It shifts attention to the violence, and away from the dangerously emotional and myth-haunted realm of sex....

The new terminology happily washes away accumulated layers of sexism currently built right into the laws: that only women can be raped, only by men, and only when the penis penetrates the vagina. Law historians say that this exaggerated concern for the vagina springs directly from male concern over property and legitimacy of inheritance.

Since C-53 throws out any distinctions between male and female aggressors and victims, some of this archaic silliness will vanish. Of course men can be raped, and that crime will be prosecuted under the new law.

The definition of rape as vaginal penetration also will disappear, and not a moment too soon. "The fact is that most violent rapists either can't hold an erection or can't achieve ejaculation," says Dr. Ruth Bray, psychologist and forensic consultant.

The irony is that since the rapist's aim is to dominate and humiliate the woman, he then resorts to greater viciousness. Rape with bottles, knives and tools, or forced oral and anal penetration are common. "Most of the rapes I've prosecuted in the last couple of years have involved forced fellatio," confirms Assistant Crown Attorney Mary Hall. "These acts are just as degrading, or more so, to the victim." But under current law, all these horrors are classed only as indecent assault (with a maximum of five years imprisonment)...

...All rape trials hinge on the issue of "consent." Until now, women have been caught in a double bind. According to a trenchant analysis of Bill C-53 by Toronto lawyer Rose Zoltek, women have always been counselled not to resist a violent rapist. But if women have appeared in court without evidence of violent resistance, juries have assumed that they have consented to the assault.

Bill C-53 takes a deep breath, vaults bravely over that hurdle, and then slumps back into the old pit. First, it says that when a victim submits to rape through fear or force, that doesn't mean she consented. So far, so good.

Then Bill C-53 loses its nerve for a moment and collapses back into Section 244 (4). "Consent shall not necessarily be inferred" if the complainant did not resist force, this section says. Zoltek, and most women's groups, argues that this confusing afterthought in the amendment "destroys any hope of reform" and should be dropped.

There are two other hot issues in Bill C-53. First is the crucial question of whether a complainant's past sexual conduct should be introduced as evidence.

Thousands of rapes have never been reported because the victims knew that the defence lawyers would attempt to discredit and smear them in court by making them look lascivious and wanton.

In 1976, Parliament tried to stop this abuse of the law by introducing Section 142 of the Criminal Code. It said that a victim could be questioned about her sexual past only if a judge ruled, in a closed hearing, that it was admissible evidence.

That amendment boomeranged badly. In a 1980 Supreme Court of Canada case, Chief Justice Bora Laskin ruled that the complainant, the rape victim herself, could be forced by the judge to testify about her sexual past – in effect, becoming a witness for the defence. Lawyers I interviewed say that this ruling has discouraged women from reporting rape and has given the accused an unintended advantage.

The new amendments, in Section 246, specifically rule out that interpretation. But the wording of the amendments, say lawyers, is just too vague. The only real protection for a complainant is to rule once and for all that her past sexual history has absolutely nothing whatsoever to do with the question at hand: Did she consent to this sex act with the accused?

This would bring equality into the courtroom. A man previously convicted of 10 sexual crimes can sit through his trial and no one in the court may know that he is a convicted rapist. Why shouldn't the victim's past also be considered irrelevant to the current circumstances?...

Bill C-53 proposes that husbands no longer will be automatically immune from the charge of raping their wives. "This 'spousal immunity' from rape (charges) derives from the traditional belief that marriage meant irrevocable consent to sexual intercourse," says a brief from the Justice Department.

"A change like that could open the floodgates," says Bob McGee, Deputy Crown Attorney in Toronto.

"Why should that be upsetting?" counters Toronto lawyer Mary Cornish. "If we find more theft, nobody's upset that we have to prosecute more theft."

I agree. All laws can be said to be open to distortion or to a deluge of misguided charges. But the law does not exist for the convenience of the courts. The law exists, surely, to spell out what is morally acceptable and unacceptable in this society. It changes as those perceptions change. And it is time now for the laws of this country to say that is unacceptable for a man forcibly to rape his wife....

• • • • • • • • •

IT WAS AN UNPRECEDENTED, almost incomprehensible event: Conservative prime minister Brian Mulroney was in power, and here was his minister of justice, Kim Campbell, summoning grassroots and front-line women's groups to a private conference table in Toronto; I was among the startled invitees. Never before had a justice minister asked the advice of women in reforming the rape laws. Campbell's legislation, known as Bill C-49, was probably the first rape legislation in the known universe to define "rape" from a woman's point of view. Of course, it has been under sustained legal attack ever since, but it was passed unanimously by Parliament at the time and still stands as a high watermark of feminist jurisprudence.

WILL RAPE LAW PROTECT VICTIMS FROM COURTROOM SMEAR TACTICS?
August 1992

Today, Canada's brand-new sexual assault law comes into force. "No Means No" is now the law of the land – and not a moment too soon. Rape has long been the least-reported and least-punished of all violent crimes, in part because the laws worked in favour of the accused man.

The new law not only redefines the meaning of consent, it also attempts to restore some dignity and safety for the victims of sex crimes. (Our previous "rape shield" law, intended to protect victims from aggressive and irrelevant questioning about their sexual history, was struck down by the Supreme Court last year.)

Let's hope that judges and Crown Attorneys take the new law seriously and study its intent – because, until now, victims (or "complainants") have too often been doubly violated, first by the rapist and then by the courts.

Fascinatingly enough, tactics for "destroying" a rape victim before the case ever comes to trial were spelled out in a 1988 article in *The Lawyers Weekly*. Women's advocates and rape crisis counsellors say that those aggressive tactics are being used by some defence lawyers in a way that offends every principle of fairness.

Federal Justice Minister Kim Campbell appears before the Commons committee studying gun control on October 8, 1991.

The article described a workshop for defence lawyers, Crowns, and judges in which lawyer Michael Edelson of Ottawa is quoted as saying defence lawyers should "whack the complainant hard" at the preliminary hearing in hopes of getting her to drop the charges.

"If you destroy the complainant...you cut off the head of the Crown's case and the case is dead.

"My own experience is (that) the preliminary hearing is the ideal place in a sexual assault trial to try to win it all. You can do things... with a complainant at a preliminary inquiry in front of a judge which you would never try to do for tactical, strategic reasons – sympathy for the witness, etc. – in front of a jury.

"Unfortunately," said Edelson, "it's slice-and-dice for the complainant."

Unfortunately? Pardon me, those crocodile tears are getting my shoes wet. Nor does my heart break over Edelson's lament that it has become so faddish to lay sexual assault charges that "Every time I turn around there is more sperm and pubic hair in some file on my desk."

Rape crisis workers say that in the past few years, and especially since the rape shield law was struck down, more and more defence lawyers are enthusiastically following Edelson's blueprint.

Preliminary hearings are supposed to be brief proceedings where a judge determines whether there's enough evidence to send an accused person to trial. But in sexual assault cases, some defence lawyers are turning the "prelim" into full-scale attacks on the victim's credibility and sexual history. Some of these gruelling "slice-and-dice" hearings are dragged out for as long as a year.

In several recent Ontario preliminary hearings, defence lawyers have succeeded in isolating the rape victim completely by subpoenaing everyone she's ever confided in or asked for help, including friends, rape crisis counsellors, witness support workers, and medical personnel. (Once they're compelled to be witnesses for the defence, they may not discuss the case with the victim or remain in court during testimony.) A complainant's private life has been stripped bare as some judges have allowed lawyers to subpoena the victim's disgruntled ex-lovers, or her complete medical and psychiatric records, private diaries, and even personal notes.

One recurring tactic is the fanciful accusation (often based on no evidence whatever) that the victim suffers from multiple personality syndrome, and that "one of your personalities agreed to have sex." Courtroom observers say it's a blood-chilling experience to sit in a public courtroom and hear a defence lawyer declaim at an already upset rape victim that she's an unreliable witness because she "may" have been sexually abused as a child, or that she's "sexually insatiable," or "loves the taste of sperm."

Criminal lawyers say they have an obligation to defend their clients to the hilt, and that these wolverine tactics are simply part of their duty. Maybe so. But our system also expects judges to curb abusive excesses. And sometimes that doesn't happen.

When the Supreme Court struck down the rape shield provisions last year, it expressed its confidence that judges would not permit "demeaning and abusive conduct by defence counsel."

I've got news for the Supremes: their confidence was misplaced....

• • • • • • • • •

IN THE LATE 1980s, a startlingly vicious chain of rapes began to be reported from the Toronto suburb of Scarborough. In the early '90s, two young schoolgirls were kidnapped and murdered in the town of St. Catharines, one year apart. In 1993, Paul Bernardo was arrested, and then his estranged wife Karla Homolka, for the murders. Lurid rapes and twisted sexual tortures inflicted on beautiful young girls – the media were wild with excitement.

When I wrote the following passage, I had already been secretly approached by some of Bernardo's rape victims, who were re-traumatized by the constant sight of their torturer's face on the front pages, the spewing of his sick fantasies. I met with the young women for several long and excruciatingly painful sessions, hearing their stories and holding back from reporting until they told me they were ready – some two years later.

HOW TO EASE THE HORROR STILL STALKING BERNARDO'S VICTIMS
November 1995

...The memories are so jagged, so raw. He raped all of them at knifepoint, forcing himself anally and vaginally into the slender, virginal bodies of young teenagers.

He degraded them with the same sick demands he made on Kristen French and Leslie Mahaffy. They were forced to fellate him and say they loved him.

He ran his knife over their bodies, lacerating their genitals. He taunted them that their friends would mock them. In one case, he coldly broke the arm of the young woman as she lay helpless on the ground.

His emotional cruelty was viciously calculated. He would leave them bound and bleeding in the dark behind a house or a school – and then he would come back unexpectedly to rape them again and again. Most of the attacks lasted an hour or more.

"Please God, let me die," prayed Elizabeth (not her real name) before she passed out. He let them know he had stalked them and he stole their I.D. so they would live in terror that he would find them again.

Elizabeth was amazed she didn't die from indescribable fear that night she was raped. When her parents arrived at the hospital, "I cannot express the look on their faces when they first saw me covered in blood, clothing torn. My father, normally a pillar of strength, fainted...watching my parents and family cry because of what I endured makes my heart ache with pain I'd never felt before."

Elizabeth lives with a "depression so deep and despair so gnawing that I do not feel I can go on." She has been unable to have a successful relationship with a man.

Anne, 25, (also a pseudonym) has had the same experience. "He took away my innocence...my dignity and will to survive. I can't keep a stable relationship with anyone because I fear if they find out what happened they'll walk away...Actually, they all have."

Then we in the media had our turn. Everyone, in fact, enjoyed ample free speech except the victims – three of them were dead; the rest were not allowed to speak to each other or to the press, lest they compromise Bernardo's eventual trial...

When I asked two of the survivors what was the most painful after-effect of the attacks, they each, separately, named the media coverage.

Daily, the victims had silently to absorb the hurt of office gossip based on "sensationalized" TV and tabloid news.

Their complete lack of control over what was said about them in the media triggered the same rage and humiliating helplessness that they experienced during the rapes.

Anne feels that some media peddled sexist stereotypes about the victims. If the public could do anything, says Anne, it would be to "educate themselves and stop blaming the victims of rape. Stop the violence; help the women across this country."...

THE FOLLOWING YEAR, Judge Archie Campbell was appointed to investigate the "systemic failure" of the police investigation into the Bernardo rapes and murders – a repulsive saga of mountain-goat egos battling over turf and glory, while at least four rapes and two gruesome deaths could have been avoided.

What the Campbell report stupidly failed to highlight was how completely the police investigation was warped and thwarted by the police force's ingrained sexism. The details revealing the bias are all there, but Campbell did not seem to understand what they implied – that young women continued to be raped and murdered by Bernardo because the police dismissed all the evidence that came from the women themselves. Police did not bother to test lab samples, ignored three separate, accurate descriptions of Bernardo and his car from young women who had been terrifyingly stalked, and refused to follow up tips from women who recognized him from the police artist's portrait, drawn from the description supplied by one of his victims. Police failure and ineptitude due to gender bias continue to be a menace to women everywhere. Campbell missed his chance to try to rectify that catastrophic flaw.

In 1986, a woman, later known only as Jane Doe, was awakened by a rapist holding a knife to her throat. He had climbed through her window, open on a hot summer night. The Balcony Rapist slipped out of her window after attacking her, and Jane immediately called the police.

Jane Doe was extraordinary – a professional woman, feminist, supremely articulate and self-controlled, attractive, her fierce intelligence matched by unstoppable determination. Jane waged a breathtakingly arduous battle for twelve years to hold the police to account for using her (and other women) as bait to lure and trap the rapist.

POLICE OWE EXPLANATION ON JANE DOE

July 1998

Break out the champagne and raise a glass to Jane Doe. Every Torontonian owes her thanks; every woman and girl is a little bit safer because of her sheer, gutsy determination, through 12 long and painfully difficult years, to hold the cops to account for the way they failed to protect her from the Balcony Rapist.

Now that Toronto City Council has voted (51 to 1) to apologize to Jane Doe and to veto any possibility of an appeal, we can truthfully say that police and politicians have gone through a grassroots, anti-sexist educational experience.

The women on council spoke up with such concerted energy and focus on Jane Doe's behalf that most of the men who wanted to appeal backed off, thought a bit, and changed their minds.

The decision by Madam Justice Jean MacFarland, as most readers know by now, roasted the Toronto police for discriminating against Jane Doe because of their sexist biases, and using her as "bait" to catch the Balcony Rapist.

Take a moment, in the midst of celebrations, to remember two other brave "Jane Does" who paid a heavy price for fighting police wrongdoing. Robin Gardner Voce was pulled over for drunk driving at the age of 19, ordered into a police cruiser by two officers, driven to an underground garage, and raped. She died by hanging at the age of 24, two months before her abusers were found culpable and fired from the force.

Fiona Stewart, a respected Toronto housing activist, was forced into sexual acts by then-Sergeant Brian Whitehead, who is still on the force. He pleaded guilty under the Police Services Act to "corrupt practice and deceit," was chastised for his "totally despicable abuse of power" and demoted. Stewart died an untimely death at the age of 36.

Both Stewart and Voce had endured years of emotional abuse, stalling, and efforts to make them look "crazy" by the very people to whom they turned for redress. It's a frighteningly lonely struggle when you confront the arbitrary power of the police.

The word "arbitrary" comes to mind when I contemplate police Chief David Boothby, who swaggered his defiance ("I'm my own person.") when city council suggested last week that he apologize on behalf of the police.

In fact, much more than an apology is required here. For 12 years, through the reign of Police Services Commission chairs Clare Westcott, June Rowlands, Susan Eng, Maureen Prinsloo and now Norm Gardner, and mayors Art Eggleton, June Rowlands, and Barbara Hall, a series of police chiefs (Jack Marks, Bill McCormack, David Boothby) was telling the commissioners they had to battle Jane Doe in the courts – at great cost and damage to Doe – because the insurance company insisted. But there was no insurance company. The city is self-insured. Boothby and his predecessors must surely have known this. What did he know and when did he know it? What did the police commissioners know – or fail to ask?

Who's in charge here?

It's ludicrous for Boothby to claim, in view of such ineptitude, that the police are "on the cutting edge" in dealing with issues of violence against women. He would do far better to read the judge's decision in silence and humility before he speaks again.

Madam Justice MacFarland sets out a clear chronology of all the internal reviews, back as early as the mid-70s, in which the police admit they mishandle rape cases, abuse, threaten, and disbelieve the victims, and fail to pursue the criminals, all because of sexist prejudice. Over and over again, the police swear they have changed their ways, or are going to. But in each successive review, further examples of sexist harm are sheepishly admitted.

Look at the investigation of Paul Callow, the serial rapist who attacked Jane Doe. Although these cops had been trained in handling sexual assault cases, their sloppy investigation was fraught with every sexist idiocy in the book. They were upsettingly prurient about the victims' sex lives. They didn't believe one of the victims because she was "too calm," but they didn't warn the targeted women because "they might get hysterical" and warn off the rapist. Too calm or too hysterical – seems like no woman is as believable, or as worthy of protection, as a man.

Rape is not a crime of sex, the judge stressed, but one of terror, dominance, control, and humiliation. But police go on thinking it's all about sex. That's why they record sexual assaults separately from domestic violence crimes.

Had the police the wit to cross-file all crimes of violence against women, they might have interviewed Callow's battered ex-wife sooner, learned about his previous four-year sentence for serial rapes in B.C., and nabbed him in time to save some of his victims from attack.

These cops had been taught about "rape mythology," and yet they relied on a U.S. pamphlet called "Oliver Zink's Rape Cookbook." They decided that Callow, who raped women while holding a knife to their throats, fit the Zink definition of a "gentleman rapist" (is that oxymoronic or what?) who "didn't use profanity" and was "sorry afterward." That's why they felt so little urgency in pursuing him as he went on his rounds of wrecking the lives of five Toronto women.

The justice system shines today in a rare moment of understanding what sexual assault victims endure, and what the real world is like for women. City council can be proud of its role – belatedly.

And Chief Boothby should not only apologize, he should explain, promptly and fully, how those entrusted with management of the police of the city were so ill-informed for so long.

• • • • • • • • •

JUST IN CASE we were too intoxicated by the victory that Jane Doe won on behalf of all women, just in case we thought we had finally made measurable progress, we heard the old, bigoted message coming from the west. Justice John McClung in Edmonton defied the "no means no" rule and upheld the acquittal of a rapist. Yes, the name resonates: McClung was none other than the grandson of the great Nellie McClung, one of the Famous Five women who won the right for Canadian women to be regarded as persons under the law.

BRACE YOURSELF FOR BACKLASH: DOES NO MEAN MAYBE?
October 1998

Brace yourselves, if you care about women's equality rights and our entitlement to equal protection of the law. The whole concept of "no means no," enshrined in the sexual assault law since 1992, is under heavy fire. It's not just the Ewanchuk case from Alberta – we always knew they had a lot of dinosaurs there – but also an accelerating campaign by defence lawyers, relayed to you by your local newspapers, talk shows, and radio ranters.

To sum up the sorry chronicle of the Ewanchuk case, now awaiting a ruling in the Supreme Court of Canada: On a hot June morning in Edmonton in 1994, a slight 17-year-old girl dressed in shorts and a T-shirt was lured to a trailer parked at a mall to apply for a job. The young woman, at 105 pounds, was half the age and half the size of the looming Ewanchuk. He locked the trailer door behind her, immediately stating that he was "a nice guy and wouldn't hurt her." The frightened complainant, who testified that she thought showing fear might provoke him to brutality, remained impassive but repeatedly said "No" and "Please stop" as he massaged her back, tried to touch her breasts (she protected herself with her arms), thrust his hand up her leg and finally lay on top of her and ground his exposed penis against her crotch.

Explaining why she didn't resist more aggressively, the complainant said, "I barely even could mouth those words, never mind do something that was an action."

As soon as Ewanchuk unlocked the door, she left, went home, and reported the assault to the police.

Ewanchuk did not testify at his trial, but nevertheless the judge acquitted him on the grounds of "implied consent." The court was not told Ewanchuk had three previous rape convictions, served 10 years in prison, and had another conviction for sexual assault.

The Alberta Appeal Court upheld the acquittal: after all, said Alberta Justice John McClung, "the complainant did not present herself to Ewanchuk...in a bonnet and crinolines." (How quaint: wear a bonnet or risk rape.)

He dismissed the idea of "No means no" as mere "sloganeering," described Ewanchuk's actions as "far less criminal than hormonal," and then went on to revel in the oldest myth of them all – that if a woman is in the same place as a man, she is necessarily in a relationship with him and therefore she has automatically consented to have sex with him.

In the old days, said Justice McClung, "going too far in the boyfriend's car was better dealt with...by a slap in the face or...a well-directed knee."

Notice how the girl (who was frozen with fear in the stranger's trailer) has now become a "girlfriend" rejecting a too-bold advance. McClung even went so far as to describe Ewanchuk's "pelvic grinding" as "three clumsy passes" rather than a sexual assault.

Meanwhile, as we await the ruling of the Supreme Court, the din of an anti-woman media campaign fills our ears. Just the other day, *The Globe and Mail* devoted an extra-long editorial to the case, fretting about whether the "equality rights" of men were jeopardized in the courts. Their revoltingly sly language spreads a slime of innuendo over the complainant, referring to "consensual body massaging," "a couple in the back of a trailer on a hot afternoon" and "murky mating rituals."

Evidently, neither the Alberta court nor *The Globe* believes in a woman's right to bodily integrity. Neither understands the threat, harm, and violation of sexual assault – unless, of course, it involves a young hockey player.

Just weeks ago, Dr. Ed Renner of Carleton University released a study of 58 sexual assault court cases showing how these prevalent rape myths prejudice women's equality and safety. According to Renner's analysis of Statistics Canada figures, fewer than 1 percent of self-reported sexual assaults lead to a jail term. The court cases he examined in detail were filled with "outrageous examples" of false stereotypes that led to obvious injustices: only 30 percent of those convicted of sexual assault were sentenced harshly (i.e., more than two years), compared to 53 percent of those convicted of robbery.

"Women and children are fair game to male sexual violence and the courts are an accessory after the fact," Renner told the press.

Based on Renner's evidence of a less than 1 percent rate of imprisonment for accused assailants, *The Globe*'s panic about the rights of male defendants is preposterous. In fact, when judges can voice such primitive prejudices, unchastised, it's not a moment too soon for women to begin to panic. Hard-won equality rights are swiftly melting in the hot, fetid breath of the backlash.

● ● ● ● ● ● ● ● ●

THE SUPREME COURT briskly overturned McClung's decision in 1999, and he proved as sore a loser as he was inept as a judge. Supreme Court Justice Claire L'Heureux-Dubé, a beacon of feminist jurisprudence, castigated McClung for relying on sexist myths. He lashed back with an intemperate letter to a right-wing newspaper, declaring that she must contribute to the rising rate of male suicide in Québec. He apologized, but it's doubtful that many women concluded his record of misogyny was now clean.

AS PAINFUL AS the rape stories are, they continue to be a universal affliction. Rape is now recognized – after Rwanda, after Bosnia, after Zimbabwe, and during the ongoing horror of the Congo – as a strategy as well as a weapon of war, inflicted as brutally and as systematically as possible on entire populations of women by conquering armies, in order to demoralize, crush, and disperse their subject populations. We have not bestirred ourselves to stop the ripping apart of the women. Maybe we can try to aid in the aftermath – especially when we take a closer look at the horrors of the past.

WHY WE MUST HELP WARTIME SEX SLAVES GET REDRESS
May 1996

They appear like sad ghosts, wearing formal white robes as they make their deputations: grey hair, spectacles, haunted eyes. Fifty years after the end of World War II, the women who were forced into sexual slavery by the Japanese military have just begun to speak out, to demand justice, before their halting voices are silenced forever.

There were an estimated 200,000 of them: girls in their teens, though some were as young as 11, kidnapped from their schools or lured by promise of good jobs or, like one youngster, snatched by soldiers as she skipped down to the village stream to fetch water and then taken away to the front lines.

About 80 percent of them were Korean. The rest were Asian girls from the Philippines, China, Malaysia, Burma, India, and Taiwan – and 200 Dutch women captured in Java and reserved for the use of officers.

In January, the United Nations' Special Rapporteur (investigator) on violence against women, Radhika Coomaraswamy, reported her gruesome findings about the sufferings of these women. And now a touring photographic exhibit has arrived at the Metro Reference Library, in a bid by a volunteer support group to publicize the women's campaign.

The Japanese called them "comfort women." Usually it is the victors who invent the names, write the history, twist our perceptions to their own comfort levels. Although the Japanese army was defeated, it succeeded for almost half a century in concealing its shameful secret.

In this silencing, of course, it had the co-operation of nearly every culture in the world. We all project some shame and guilt on to the victims of sex crimes. None do it more thoroughly than the victims themselves.

Only in 1991 did the first "comfort woman" come forward publicly. She had waited until all her family members died and there was no one left to be ashamed.

"I was raped on that first day (at age 17) and it never stopped for a single day for the next three months," testified Kim Hak-soon in her landmark lawsuit against the Japanese government. "I was born as a woman, but never lived as a woman...I suffer from a bitterness I do not know how to overcome."

Emboldened by her courage, 200 more women have come forward. The Japanese government has made a few tepid apologies and offered to set up a Japan-Korea youth cultural exchange program in some cockeyed version of "redress." No. The survivors want clear, public apologies, the crime acknowledged in Japanese history texts and specific reparations.

It is their lives that were stolen away; it is they who suffered unthinkable war crimes, and it is they to whom the debt is owed.

It hurts to read their testimonies. What is clear: the Japanese military organized the so-called comfort stations and the widespread abduction of young girls to service its soldiers from 1932, in China, until the end of World War II.

Conditions varied. In some places girls were penned in rooms little bigger than cages – three by five feet – or even shackled if they were rebellious.

On average, all the sex slaves were forced to service 40 to

50 soldiers a day, one after another, with no break but moments snatched for food. One photograph shows the soldiers lined up outside, waiting their turn in the sunshine, grinning like yokels. Poor sods, they were cannon fodder themselves, deriving some fleeting sense of power and safety from brutalizing the defenceless girls the army provided.

Disease was rampant. So were cruelty, contempt, and casually inflicted horror. Women were tortured with cigarette burns, bamboo slivers, beatings, bayonets, heated pokers. Ribs, arms, teeth were broken, organs ripped. They began as virginal children, most of them, and ended as women whose lives were permanently ruined.

Frequently, they were made sterile by repeated infections. Most endured three or four years of these daily rapes. Some survivors say that they cannot bear the touch of men, or even foods or drinks that remind them of semen. At the end of the war, many were killed – herded into caves or ditches and blown up.

The Japanese government hoped that its crimes were buried forever with the broken bodies of the raped girls. The truth, however, survived, and began to leach up to the surface.

The organizers of the Canadian Coalition for "Comfort Women" Redress say they are frequently asked why Canadians should care about this issue.

Why?

Because our Korean Canadian sisters and their many supporters, including Japanese Canadian women, ask us to care. Because the same horror keeps being replayed, in Bosnia, in Rwanda, wherever there is war.

Because the women who survived are still suffering and it is our human duty to them to help. Because wherever women are sexually abused and the powers deny it, every woman is made vulnerable.

Because it goes on and on, and Asian women – in the Philippines and Thailand and, more recently, Nepal – are now pressed into servicing Japanese sex tourists.

Because the U.N. Commission on Human Rights in Geneva, just two weeks ago, passed a resolution insisting that violence against women "impairs or nullifies the enjoyment by women of their human rights and fundamental freedoms" and asked us all to become aware and active.

Because the Beijing Women's Conference called on us to join hands around the world to try to protect the girls and women in war zones.

Because the Special Rapporteur has demanded that the Japanese government offer full disclosure, apology, and compensation to its victims.

Because if we don't care, we are on the side of the criminals.

An affirmative action poster produced by Canada Post Corporation in the 1980s advised workers to contact their divisional human rights office if they had been sexually harassed. Unfortunately, in many workplaces, women who made such complaints were often belittled or dismissed outright.

SEXUAL HARASSMENT IS NOT A COMPLIMENT

LE HARCÈLEMENT SEXUEL, CE N'EST PAS FLATTEUR

IT IS OFFENSIVE AND ILLEGAL

C'EST BLESSANT C'EST ILLÉGAL

**Affirmative Action
Making Up the Difference**

For further information, contact your Divisional Human
Rights Coordinator or the Head Office Human Rights/
Affirmative Action Division (613) 992-1921

**L'action positive
peut rétablir l'équilibre**

Pour plus de renseignements, contacter le coordonnateur
des droits de la personne de votre division ou le gestionnaire
principal, Droits de la personne/Action positive du
bureau chef (613) 992-1921

 **Canada Post
Corporation**   **Société canadienne
des postes**

14 women died
in Montreal
December 6, 1989.

97 women died
in domestic violence
in 1988 in Canada.

First mourn.
Then work for change.

Sponsored by:

Black Women's Collective

Canadian Auto Workers Union

Canadian Labour Congress

Canadian Union of Public Employees

CKLN staff and volunteers

Education Wife Assault

Labour Community Services

National Action Committee
on the Status of Women

United Steelworkers of America,
Canadian National Office

Ontario Federation of Labour

Ontario Institute for Studies in
Education, Department of Sociology in
Education

Ontario Public Service
Employees Union

OXFAM-Canada

Public Service Alliance of Canada

Regards de femmes, Programme
français de l'Office National du film du
Canada

S.O.S. Femmes

Studio D, the Women's Studio
of the National Film Board

Toronto Women's Bookstore

Women's Committee of the United
Steelworkers of America - Peel/Halton

Women's Press

Statistics from the Canadian Centre for Justice Statistics. Concept and design Joss Maclennan. Produced by Standard Fine Printing.

Chapter Four

WOUNDS AGAINST SOCIETY: VIOLENCE AGAINST WOMEN

IT HAS NEVER STOPPED. Our first cartoon image of prehistory is a caveman holding a club and dragging a woman by her hair. It's so deeply ingrained, across almost all known cultures, that men hit women and have a right to do so, that the first question thrown at battered women is "Why don't you leave?" rather than the more relevant "Why does he hit?" Judges still shrug off brutishness with the explanation that the abuser "just lost it" or "he blew his fuse:" impersonal, predictable glitches in the male mechanism.

Hitting hurts, of course, and not just the body and the soul of the woman; it hurts the fabric of the family and wounds the larger society. There is no such thing as a blow dealt by one human, received by another, that stops right there. It goes on and on, not like ripples, which diminish as the circle goes wider, but more like bacteria that swiftly multiply into a festering boil. The beaten child grows up suffering, or makes someone else suffer, and sometimes the violence goes even further – to murder.

On December 6, 1989, a young man entered Montréal's École Polytechnique with a semi-automatic rifle and went from class to class, demanding that the male students leave the rooms. He then shot and killed fourteen young women, thirteen of them engineering students, and wounded a dozen more, while screaming "I hate feminists!" and "I want the women!" Then he turned the gun on himself.

REMEMBERING THE MASSACRE POINTS THE WAY
TO PROGRESS
December 1999

Tomorrow pause and force yourself to think about 5-year-old Gamil Gharbi, clinging frantically to his father's pant leg as blow after blow rained down on him till he bled from his nose and ears. His mother, a former nun and then a nurse, was forbidden to console him. She, too, was constantly cursed, insulted, humiliated, smashed up against walls and beaten. Gamil, with his little sister, was locked in his room for hours at a time so his father, a high-flying Algerian mutual fund salesman who believed all women were chattels, could have a leisurely brunch.

Gamil grew up brimming with rage and primed to hate the only creatures lowlier than himself – women. In his teens, he changed his name to Marc Lepine. If his father metaphorically loaded the weapon, our violence-saturated society showed him where to point it: at the "feminists" so vilified in macho culture for encroaching on male entitlements.

Because of Lepine and the promising young lives he snatched away, we may be the only country in the world with an official Day of Remembrance for women. Instead of poppies, our lapels sprout the now-familiar button with the red rose to commemorate the 14 women engineering students who were gunned down, in blood, shock, and horror, on that ordinary afternoon at l'École Polytechnique 10 years ago.

We need the candlelit vigils and concerts for Dec. 6 just as we need the solemn bells and silences of Nov. 11. We need the cleared space, the stopping of time's relentless clock, the ceremony, and the heightened words that will unlock our feelings and make us remember.

It takes an effort of will to bring to mind the blows and the ugliness that lie just beneath the surface of so many lives around us. We must make the effort, because even as you read this, other hands are raised against other children who will grow up to take vengeance on those who never harmed them. The National Day of Remembrance is for all women killed by male violence – not in battle, not because they were criminals, but simply because they were female.

As usual, when we gather tomorrow, only the willing of heart will be present. Willing or unwilling, however, no Canadian had an option 10 years ago when the blurred, urgent, news crackled into our consciousness. We had to hear; we had to feel the sting of hatred's poison.

I didn't hear about the massacre until the next morning. I was cocooned in the welcome warmth of bed, waking slowly after a happy public event the night before – the Toronto debut of a feminist documentary that had played to a huge, exuberant crowd. The glow of pleasure still wrapped me as my eyes opened to my husband bursting out of the bathroom, his razor still in his hand, relaying in shocked tones what he had just heard on the radio: "Somebody killed a lot of women…" he exclaimed. "Montréal…it's a slaughter…"

Within moments, it was clear that the young women had been cold-bloodedly separated out and executed solely because of their gender. The pain of that news was physical, like an arrow of ice stabbing my heart. Only equality – full, rich, deeply entrenched equality of respect, dignity, and human worth, for all people of all colours, reflected in laws, popular culture, and social mores – can ever heal that wound.

Our posters and banners for Dec. 6 all read: "First mourn. Then work for change." In these 10 years, thousands upon thousands of Canadians, women and men, have done both. The mourning was and is painfully real. For women who were activists, working at low pay or as volunteers in the front lines (a telling phrase) of the war against women, staffing the clinics, the rape crisis centres, the women's counselling centres, the incest recovery groups, the battered women's shelters, that bleak day was the final unbearable crisis. All the stifled rage and despair at the useless violence welled up and spilled over in tears, angry speeches, boiling words.

For myself, I regret now that the *Star* asked me, only hours after I heard the news, to write a front page reaction piece. Along with many others, I felt that at this raw moment, of all moments, I could say, without being misunderstood, how enraged and defiant we felt about the constant stream of blows and wounds inflicted on women simply because of their femaleness.

I was wrong.

Based on the angry reaction to our words, it apparently was still taboo to speak about male violence against women. As a learned man once explained to me, such blunt speech violates "men's right not to know" what their buddies are doing and what their male culture permits and even fosters.

Instantly, our hot tears and painful grief were dismissed as "political." The story, in countless broadcasts and news columns, became not the dead women but the outrage of "innocent" men, in a fury at being linked by their maleness to Marc Lepine. It was all about them – were their feelings hurt, were they being discriminated against because a few all-female vigils were planned. I regret that many of us spoke up so honestly only because it gave the backlash an opening for attack that served as a distraction from the real issue. (Sometimes it seems that anything will distract the public from the dead bodies of murdered women – 40 women a year in Ontario killed by male rage.)

Now, 10 years later, I'd rather draw people's attention to lessons we might learn from the life of Gamil Gharbi. His brutal, control-freak father – one of the real root causes of the Montréal Massacre – sued for custody, although he never bothered to visit or pay for his children after the divorce. Today, there are angry and violent men, some of them slick and plausible, who insist that they are entitled to custody of their children, and there are parliamentarians dedicated to promoting their cause.

Most men, thank heaven, took a different path. Patrick Quinn, chair of the Professional Engineers of Ontario, swore on the spot to make a difference, and he tells me that today not only have the number of women engineering students doubled, but attitudes have changed: "The young men are used to equality in their relationships now, and many, including older men, were awakened to different values by Montréal."...Tomorrow, on the National Day of Remembrance, let each of us think of those who died and what we can do to stop the killing.

• • • • • • • • •

BEATING, BATTERING, BURYING...they are inextricably and gruesomely linked. When evasive words wrap the reality in cotton batting ("spousal abuse"), hard truths slide away into the fog.

But to give a name is often to shine a spotlight on a previously unnoticed reality. In 1973, when Interval House, possibly Canada's first shelter for women, had opened in Toronto, we all learned to call the crime "wife-battering." At the time, I was working at *Chatelaine*, and Doris Anderson assigned me to interview the shelter's founder, Trudy Don. I remember the vague picture I had in my mind of a "battered wife" as I drove to the shelter: a woman with bruises; a working-class woman; a disorganized woman, maybe a drinker; nobody I would ever know. It didn't take long for Trudy to divest me of my class prejudice. As a journalist, I'm a quick learner. I never again thought of battered women in this uninformed way.

The message had trouble penetrating the walls of Canadian denial. In 1982, when NDP member of parliament Margaret Mitchell raised the issue of one in ten women suffering from violent abuse, the House erupted in raucous male laughter, guffaws and jibes, mostly from the Conservative benches. It was a landmark moment for feminists.

That year, the Liberal minister of health, Monique Bégin, enclosed a little red-and-white leaflet entitled "Wife Battering: A National Concern" in the envelope containing the baby bonus that was sent to every mother in Canada. (Introduced in 1945, the "baby bonus," or family allowance, put money directly into the hands of women; it was Canada's first universal social programme.) Within two months, three women sought refuge at Interval House because of that leaflet.

BEATEN WOMEN FIND A DOORWAY FROM HELL
December 1982

...[F]or untold numbers of bruised and frightened women in this country, that leaflet may have stirred the first shaky awareness that there is a doorway out of hell....

At first sight, Georgie, 35, is something of a waif: a tiny 98-pound woman with wide blue eyes under a frizz of natural blonde curls. The first policeman who learned about the beatings she had suffered took one look at her and said, "Lady, I can't believe you didn't die." But take another look: there's strength in those high East European cheekbones, and the bitter humour of a natural survivor in that sardonic grin.

Georgie's second husband was so tender, so devoted, so dotingly possessive, that she could hardly believe it herself when his ardour slowly became poisonous, pathological, turning their country home into a prison cage. And when, shortly after their marriage, he began to batter her with his fists at least once a week, she was dumbfounded.

Stranded in their isolated home with two children, no car, and no job, she twice tried to run away when Bruno was away from the house. Both times he caught her and dragged her back, threatening her with death if she tried again.

The day after the leaflet came ("He saw me reading it and grabbed it away from me – I only got as far as the sentence about how it's a crime for anyone to beat another human being.") he brooded, accused her of planning to leave him, then abruptly ordered her to leave, then began hitting her when she angrily and eagerly agreed. She felt the sharp crack of one of her ribs. He refused to take her to the hospital and accused her of wanting to seduce the doctors.

The next beating came when her rib wasn't yet healed. She ran from the house in terror and crouched in a nearby cornfield. It was after midnight. For the rest of the night, Georgie scrambled and staggered through mud as she saw his car criss-crossing the country roads, his headlights searching for her.

Just before dawn, she reached the highway and began to walk to Toronto. "I was crouching because it was so hard to breathe with my broken rib and finally an old lady stopped her car and asked if I was all right."

In Toronto, Georgie climbed onto a bus and, mud-caked and battered, fell asleep. Later that day, she found refuge with a friend. That's where Bruno found her; he came with her children who were crying for her return, and a policeman in a cruiser, who told her, "You can be charged with deserting your kids."

Georgie went back with Bruno that time. But, emboldened by the leaflet she made her plans. Then Bruno broke her wrist, systematically and deliberately, and when she tried to make a cardboard splint, he sneeringly grabbed the broken hand and twisted it. One morning, when she was able to use her hand again, she waited until he relaxed his fanatically jealous vigilance; when he went to the bathroom she snatched his car keys from the table and ran from the house, collected the children from school, and drove straight to the nearest police station. Today, Georgie and the children are recuperating at Interval House....

• • • • • • • • •

ALL THROUGH THE 1970s and 1980s, women worked doggedly, passionately, and sometimes desperately to create and sustain rape crisis centres, women's shelters, and women's centres. Provincial and federal funding was almost always trivial. Some town councils devoted years of strenuous scheming and slander to prevent a shelter from opening. Men in power cast slurs, indulged in mockery, put women petitioners through fiery hoops of bureaucracy. They managed, in many cases, to destroy not only the authenticity of the shelter's feminist work, but also its power to help battered women change their lives – simply by imposing social service codes, rules, and conditions. For decades, municipalities would pay only the minimal daily "bed" rate for homeless shelters, cheating the women of funds for counsellors, children's services, and all kinds of emergency supports.

Interval House, founded by Trudy Don in 1973, may have been the country's fist shelter for women.

Meaningless requirements, like providing one parking spot for each bed, were used in some areas to prevent shelters from opening.

A younger generation of women had been shocked into anti-violence work on campuses immediately after the Montréal Massacre. University students, including one survivor of the Massacre, threw themselves into the campaign for better gun control and partly achieved it, and true to their youth and daily preoccupations, they made date rape and sexual freedom two of their top issues.

Governments, too, were pressured into doing something,

finally, about the daily toll of violence against women. The federal Parliament produced a committee report called "War on Women." Declining to follow that with a full-fledged Royal Commission on Violence Against Women, as recommended, they instead came up with the "Canadian Panel on Violence Against Women." By this time, in the early '90s, the feminist movement was roiling with internecine struggles over race and class; the Panel ran into crisis after crisis, all internal.

Still, the movement went on naming, reporting, and documenting the staggering amount of harm done to women by men, often with impunity. It was violence winked at by the police, sanctioned by courts and judges, dismissed casually by governments.

LITTLE IS BEING DONE TO END WAR ON WOMEN
July 1991

The "War on Women," a stunning report just released by a parliamentary committee, is emphatic about "the overwhelming and terrifying problem" of violence against women. A deluge of recent studies all confirm that grim assessment.

Sixty-two percent of women killed in Canada are killed by their male partners – often after the women have attempted to separate.

Hospital emergency departments generally identify only one in 25 cases of woman-battering. But once medical staff have been instructed to look for tip-offs like perforated eardrums, internal bleeding, wounds to breasts and stomachs of pregnant women, acid and cigarette burns, and fractured teeth, their identification rate has been known to jump by 1,500 percent.

A woman is beaten up 35 times, on average, before she even reports the violence to the police. Think about that.

Yet there isn't an institution in our society that hasn't colluded in denying, shrugging off or minimizing this pervasive crime. Judges, for example, regularly make excuses for the most savage and brutal batterers.

"Neal Ellis is an intelligent man from a good family but for some unknown reason he just went haywire," said Mr. Justice John O'Driscoll a couple of weeks ago, sentencing Ellis to 10 years for torturing, raping, beating, and terrorizing his former girlfriend while holding her and her 11-year-old son captive for three days.

Kenneth Taylor, an engineer, who fractured his girlfriend's skull when she was eight months pregnant (his wife was pregnant, too) explained to a jury how he simply went berserk and "wheeled around and hit her on the back of the head really, really hard." The jury found him guilty of assault causing bodily harm instead of attempted murder. And Mr. Justice John Hamilton sentenced him to 90 days, to be served on weekends, so he could continue to support his wife and children.

When judges and juries are so compassionate about a man's unfortunate "loss of control," what are the police to think when summoned to a crime in progress?

The highly regarded Assaulted Women's Helpline, which takes 300 to 400 calls a month from assaulted women, carefully studied the 10 percent of their callers who had previously called police. Only half the women felt their calls to police had been taken seriously. In fact, the police threatened to charge one of the women because she was holding a knife to defend herself. Police refused to lay charges against batterers even in cases where a woman's nose was broken, or when a child called them and they arrived while the father was still beating the mother....

• • • • • • • • •

WHEN CONFRONTED WITH a grievous problem, North Americans love to see the solution in the individual. Men battering women? Give that guy some therapy! The path of individualism usually leads quickly to a dead end.

So did the therapeutic approach to the batterers.

WIFE ABUSERS RARELY GET THE TREATMENT THEY NEED
July 1991

...Lots of people lose their temper, but there's a difference between normal anger and criminal behaviour. A man assaults the woman he lives with in a purposeful attempt to control her – to dominate and terrify her into a state of chronic fear in which she will tiptoe around his foul moods and stormy signals, eager to comply with his wishes in order to escape further violence.

His controlling tactics include psychological brutality (obsessive, jealous questioning, menacingly raised fists, pounding walls and smashing furniture, degrading insults, threats to seek custody of the children) to outright physical harms (kicking, biting, slapping, punching, coerced sex, assault with weapons).

As women's advocates insisted that the public pay attention to the epidemic of battering, we looked for answers and found them in "treatment." Such a man, we reasoned, must be sick and in need of help.

But many of the therapy groups that mushroomed in the '80s are now being criticized as misguided. Some actually encouraged the men to "express their anger," or enabled them to transfer the blame on to their victims. Meanwhile, many of their spouses, lulled into a false sense of security by the promise of their partners' treatment, may have been placed in the direct line of danger.

A confidential 66-page report done by the federal justice department recently reviewed the research on battering men's programs. Its conclusions are frightening. Only a tiny percentage of violent men ever attend such groups, wrote senior criminologist John Fleischman. Of that small number, 50 to 60 percent drop out before completion, two-thirds continue to be psychologically abusive, and the research is so half-hearted and contradictory that we really don't know what works and what doesn't.

Fleischman concluded that results of therapy so far are "discouraging," that some researchers "falsely indicate that more males have made changes than actually did," and that treatment as a "diversion from prosecution" is "ill-advised...and worrisome." Distressingly, many of the victims stay with their batterers, believing therapy may end the violence. "The results...give little hope for this ultimate goal," Fleischman wrote.

I think he's right. Violence isn't a symptom; it's a crime. And like most criminals, batterers commit their crime to gain a benefit – a frightened, submissive wife.

• • • • • • • • •

BY THIS TIME, all of us in the women's movement were tired of telling individual horror stories to shake the public out of its drowsy indifference. But then I came across a case in which the justice system spectacularly failed to do justice on behalf of one gruesomely murdered woman, and I had to take up the cause.

MOTHER FIGHTS FOR NEW TRIAL IN KILLING OF DAUGHTER
November 1992

"Justice for Debra!" the banners will plead, when women demonstrate in front of the Ontario Legislature on Monday. "Justice for Debra!"

But there will never be any justice for Debra. She is dead. Her three boys, aged 5, 7, and 9 when she was killed on Feb. 5, 1989, will never have their mother back. And Guy Ellul, the estranged husband who admitted to stabbing her 21 times on that fatal night when he had come banging on her door, is a free man. He said it was self-defence, that the stabbings came after Debra grabbed him by the hair and cut his arm with a knife.

He was pronounced innocent (even of woman slaughter) by a jury.

Attorney-General Howard Hampton immediately announced that he would appeal the 1990 acquittal. But a year later, on the eve of the deadline for such an appeal, he tersely announced he was abandoning the attempt. There had been no error in law, he said.

And that was that.

No further legal steps are available.

But the case of Debra Ellul simmers on, like a low fever with no cure. Every day, Debra Ellul's mother, Ruth Williams, demonstrates with her "Justice for Debra" sign in front of the Hamilton courthouse where Guy Ellul was tried and exonerated. The Women's Centre of Hamilton has helped Ruth Williams gather 10,000 names on a petition calling on the attorney-general to re-try Ellul.

And even though the Crown Law Office has told me that there is no remedy available in law for what seems like a great injustice, I, too, find it impossible to let the case go.

Guy Ellul never denied the evidence about his behaviour in his 13-year marriage. He was an intermittent labourer; she was a Tiger-

Cat cheerleader who married him when she was 19. After she got a good job, he was obsessively jealous. She once came home to find he'd sold her furniture and absconded to Malta with the three small boys; he returned three months later, after extracting a promise that she wouldn't tell police of his actions. He threatened to kill her and the children countless times, but, as Ellul told the judge, "that was just an expression." Really, he loved her desperately.

After the separation, he obsessively spied on her, peered in the windows of the new house she had bought, and phoned her home and her office five or ten times a day, demanding to know "who she was with, where she was."

For an hour or two every day, for two weeks before he killed Debra, Ellul openly sharpened knives at work. When co-workers asked him why, he said, "Would you f- with me when I have this in my hands?" He discussed with them how the tip of a sharpened knife would slide in easily.

The evidence showed that Debra Ellul's torso was pricked with the sharp point of a knife many times, as though she'd been "threatened." And then there were the deep stab wounds, six driven through her right breast when, according to a pathologist, she was immobile or unconscious. Her lungs, liver, and vagina were also pierced. Some cuts were 6 inches deep, the knife driving right into the bone.

After the stabbing, Ellul went home and slept. He did not call police or an ambulance. Debra lay dead on her hall floor until her mother came looking for her.

When police arrested Guy Ellul 17 hours later, he said it was self-defence. He had argued with Debra, hit her, yes, but then she attacked him and he defended himself. He had some superficial self-inflicted knife wounds on his arms that were, he said, from a botched suicide attempt, and two cuts that a doctor testified probably were not self-inflicted.

Ellul said that after he arrived, he and Debra argued and that he slapped her after she uttered a hideous obscenity at him. He said that as he turned to leave she grabbed him by the hair and stabbed him in the upper arm. A fight for the knife ensued and Ellul stabbed Debra 21 times.

To confuse matters more, police (according to the Crown, defence, and judge) failed to do a thorough investigation of various knives and blood stains. Ellul's contention that Debra stabbed him first could not be disproved.

The trial was the usual blame-the-victim sexist circus that has made many women deeply cynical about the possibility of justice in the courts. Defence lawyer John Rosen painted Debra as promiscuous; so did a neighbour of Ellul's who happened to be a Hamilton police officer. Later, the Justice for Women Coalition of Hamilton complained publicly about the Crown's failure to confront this sexism. [The prosecutor later became a Tory MPP.]

Judge Walter Stayshyn stressed to the jury that they must not draw any inference "adverse to the accused" from his having taken the three boys to Malta: "I think it is clear he was a loving and concerned father."

As for the spying: "Were his concerns...about her being a fit and proper mother justified? Did these suspicions, therefore, not give him a reasonable reason to call, attend at work, and watch at work?" Judge Stayshyn asked the jury.

The judge asked the jury to consider whether Debra Ellul might have provoked Guy beyond endurance by allegedly using foul insults. Judge Stayshyn constantly repeated the most obscene of these insults in his charge to the jury. Besides, said the judge, Ellul "never once over the years" showed "any hate or violence" to Debra Ellul.

As for the fatal knifing, the judge instructed the jury that a man protecting himself from a perceived attack on his life cannot be expected to "weigh any niceties."

Ellul, rejoicing that he was "reborn" and that the verdict was a "dream come true," promptly sued for custody of the boys. He lost, but he is still trying to claim Debra's estate.

• • • • • • • • •

SEVEN YEARS LATER, Judge Walter Stayshyn, on the eve of his retirement, told Barbara Brown of the *Hamilton Spectator* that he had been "surprised" by the Ellul verdict and "thought Ellul was guilty of manslaughter, and so when the jury acquitted him, I thought 'Thank God the jury was there,' because they heard the same evidence I did and 12 of them thought he was not guilty. And if I had convicted him, he would have gone to jail for a long time."

I'm not surprised by their decision, though, because I have read Judge Stayshyn's 160-page charge to the jury. He appears to accept as perfect truth everything that Ellul said, and repeats Ellul's words over and over to the jury. He also makes elaborate excuses for Ellul's actions – wouldn't anyone wash blood off his hands after stabbing someone, just to clean up? – and goes even farther in excusing the most hostile and violent of Ellul's documented actions, repeating the palpable nonsense that Ellul was "a loving and concerned father." In other words, the most generous, forgiving, and respectful consideration was given to every violent and domineering action of the accused. Excuses were offered even for his repetitive stalking ("Did he not have the right to see that his children would be entrusted to proper parental supervision? Did these suspicions…not give him a reasonable reason to continually call, attend at work, and watch…?")

It seems that Judge Stayshyn was willing to overlook a flagrant violation of the criminal harassment law (not to mention first degree murder) in his concern for this "devoted father."

By 1993, we had reached the peak of attention, demand, fury over the violence against women. Statistics Canada issued its first-ever study on violence against women (hard to believe it came this late!), and public attention was riveted. As the different levels of government issued one report after another, the women's movement gathered itself for one more attempt to force actual change.

The National Action Committee presented "99 Federal Steps Toward an End to Violence Against Women," a tough, pragmatic, deeply informed report based on decades of front-line work and serious intellectual struggle.

Lee Lakeman, one of the most stalwart pioneers of the movement, writes in her preface to the report: "In 1973, it was possible to believe that ignorance on the part of politicians was our main problem. Surely, we said, if they knew how women were being treated, things would change....We used to believe that once Canadian politicians knew…they would stand up for the 52 percent of citizens who are women. They would surely stand with the feminist civil rights workers."

The bitterness is unmistakable – and earned.

CAN WE NOW ACT ON WOMEN'S VIOLENCE?

November 1993

Now that Statistics Canada has nailed down the truth of women's lives in hard numbers, perhaps we can, at long last, begin to take violence seriously.

And by that I mean: no more passive hand-wringing, no more disingenuous whining about "anti-male bias," no more utterly puerile slanging matches about who gets hurt more, men or women.

One married woman in every six is experiencing criminal levels of violence from her spouse. Many have feared for their lives. Half of all divorced women were assaulted in their first marriage, most on a continuing basis. And half of all Canadian women have experienced violence from men known to them.

For the purpose of the survey, StatsCan chillingly informs us, "violence" was defined as behaviour considered an offence under the Criminal Code.

"A significant number of women," says the survey, "reported being beaten up, sexually assaulted, choked, hit with something, and having a gun or knife used against them."

It's now almost the norm for threats and blows to go along with love, marriage, and the baby carriage.

Let's face the fact that it is no longer possible to talk about "the family" or the pros and cons of daycare, or the costs of Medicare, without factoring in, first and foremost, the ongoing social, emotional, and economic costs of unreported male violence.

What does it mean, for example, to insist that schools' success depends on tough discipline, standardized tests, and back-to-basics – when the documented reality is that countless numbers of our children are coming to school after trembling nights of listening to the screams and thumps on the other side of the wall?

If 27 percent of young women in the full flower of their youth and sexual power – ages 18 to 24 – have been victimized in the last year, how real is our much-vaunted boast of equal opportunity?

When you've decided to accept a certain level of pain, fear, and humiliation in your intimate relationships, how does that make you feel about yourself? Do you feel dulled, hopeless, and helpless about your own future? What do you communicate to your girl

99 FEDERAL STEPS

law has found a very safe
elter for battered women.

*Toward an end
to violence against women*

children? Your sons? Do you push for a promotion at work? Or settle for anything?

Are you liable to call yourself a feminist and speak up assertively on women's issues – or are you more likely to avoid controversy and non-conformity, and go along passively with your spouse's point of view?

Recently, there's been a spate of articles and books by men expressing deep concern about the future of the family, threatened – as they see it – by feminism and the working wife. But if half of all women who get a divorce have experienced ongoing abusive assaults, shouldn't we cheer their escape?

The family, so solidly nurturing when it works, so poisonous when it is the hypocritical hiding place of brutality, needs tough new scrutiny. And this time, no crocodile tears, please. Lives are at stake. How can we change the frightening fact that only 6 percent of sexual assaults and 26 percent of wife assaults were reported to the police?

99 Federal Steps Toward an End to Violence Against Women was a well-researched, hard-hitting report produced by the National Action Committee in 1993 in yet another attempt to instigate changes in the law, programmes, and policy. Instead, the women's movement encountered increased resistance.

If 2½ million Canadian women have experienced violence at the hands of a partner, what is the greater threat to a child's well-being – daycare or the spectacle of mommy being beaten up? And what price all that societal sanctimony about mothers and infants – when 21 percent of the assaulted women in this survey were beaten or attacked by a partner during pregnancy?

The StatsCan report, the first of its kind anywhere, is a world-shaker, an icy splash in the face of Canadian complacency. It must directly change the way we think about education, children, marriage, divorce, crime, availability of weapons.

Start now. What bedtime story are you going to read to your little girl tonight? Will it end with marriage as a "happily ever after"? And what will you teach your son about how to be a man?

• • • • • • • • •

INSTEAD OF A FRESH START based on the startling new evidence, the women's movement ran straight into the powerful and icy tidal wave of the backlash. For twenty years, and despite the steady undertow of resistance, we had built powerfully toward a public conversation that increasingly recognized the harms and injustices inflicted because of gender.

At the moment when Statistics Canada itself investigated and acknowledged the truth of our claims, the resistance set in with ferocity. I think at this point our success in making ourselves heard on rape, harassment, femicide, wife battering, pornography, and reproductive oppressions had created such a threat on so many fronts – to men who cherished their freedom to use pornography, to religionists who claimed the right to rule our bodies, to legal systems that ruled from an exclusively male perspective, unchallenged until now, to academics and professionals who now had to shuffle to one side to make room for women, and, above all, to so many of those women whose social, economic, and moral comfort rested on their alliance, real or potential, with a successful man – that it was impossible to avoid a very harsh and concerted backlash.

It was the start of the downward slide in the struggle to raise awareness and compassion for our battle to end violence against women. The conservative media – the TV conglomerates and their national chains of newspapers, featuring in-house conservative women who could be relied on to denigrate feminist causes – all rallied with one voice to decry the wife assault statistics.

The favourite weapon, the juiciest "man bites dog" angle, the freshest lead on a news story, the most joyful counter-attack to the women's movement, was the newly-minted conservative cause: husband-battering. Ambitious female freelancers literally lined up to get this "scoop" into print; newspaper barons rewarded them with endless bylines and feature play.

The story was false from beginning to end and premised on flimsy tales worked up by some of the most pathological miscreants I've met in my long career in journalism: the fathers' rights activists. Almost all of the most vocal among them were hiding behind a sob story of broken paternal hearts and concocted complaints of female aggression as cover for their rage against the women who had the nerve to leave them.

Wife battering is a strategy of domination, and it is not available to women. No man cringes around his house in a numb depression, aching from unhealed fractures and multiple bruises, afraid to leave because he might be killed. No man endures constant fear, physical pain, and degradation in his own home because he is afraid of losing his children. No man is raped nightly by his wife. No woman seeks to control her husband in every tiny action (the way coffee is made, the type of underwear he buys) with the constant menace of clenched fists, flaring temper, threats, and physical tantrums (punching walls, kicking the cat across the room).

The slightest imaginative effort would rip away the lies about "equal gender violence." Intellectual and emotional laziness, however, are bolstered by propagandists in the press, and few newspaper readers stop to question something so frequently repeated as the lie about women's violence. It became such a dominant story, washing out the reality of battered women in the public consciousness, in the media, and in the courts.

THE MALE MYTH OF "BATTERED HUSBANDS"
December 1993

Why would men's rights advocates, in this newspaper and others, keep raising the spectre of "battered husbands"?

A "battered wife" is, by now, a sadly well-documented and well-understood phenomenon. To quote a scholarly article: The beatings are "persistent and severe, occur in a context of continuous intimidation and coercion" and are "inextricably linked to attempts to dominate and control women."

Women get trapped in such horrifying relationships because they're primarily responsible for the children, are economically dependent, have been systematically isolated from family and friends by their batterers, and have been emotionally pounded into self-doubt and self-loathing profound enough to prevent action. [Realistically, they also understand what statistics proved only a decade later: 81 percent of femicides occur during or after separation.]

In our culture, men can never find themselves in this vicious trap. A man may indeed be hit, but he is always free to leave.

Why then do some champions of manhood claim that there is a serious unacknowledged problem of "battered husbands"? Is it because they're pursuing the novelty of a "woman bites dog" story? Do they envy the moral righteousness of victimhood that they imagine clings to the beaten woman? Or, as I sometimes suspect, are they merely closet misogynists, seeking to minimize and deny the harm that too many women suffer at men's hands?

I looked into this "battered husbands" claim recently and came up with a meticulously documented study by four of the world's leading researchers in the field of spousal violence: Russell and Rebecca Dobash of the University of Wales and Margo Wilson and Martin Daly of McMaster University.

Their article "The Myth of Sexual Symmetry in Marital Violence" in the journal *Social Problems* (February, 1992) demolishes those U.S. studies that are constantly cited by the men's activists as proof that wives are as violent as husbands.

The 30 studies in question all use Conflict Tactics Scales (CTS), a method in which interviewees are asked how they settled domestic arguments in the past year, by choosing from a list of 18 different acts, ranging from "discuss calmly" to "beat him/her up."

The survey-takers have already assigned each act a "violence rating" according to its potential for injury. A kick, for example, is judged to be "severe violence." But here's the flaw: the survey-takers never ask about the context, intention, meaning, or consequence of the "acts." This is supposed to be scrupulously objective. But in fact, as Dobash, Dobash, Wilson, and Daly stress, the method leads to massively mistaken and exaggerated conclusions.

In effect, they say, these "conflict" studies equate a wife's playful slap of her husband's hand as he reaches to take a bite of her dessert, with a husband's "tooth-loosening assault intended to punish, humiliate, and terrorize."

Every time the CTS study is repeated, the results are the same: husbands are said to be victims of severe violence more often than wives.

Unfortunately for those who greet these CTS studies with fervent joy, nothing else bears them out. National crime studies, court records, police statistics, hospital files, and scholarly research all show that only about 4 to 6 percent of domestic assaults are committed by women against men, almost always in defence of self or children, in response to the threat of imminent assault by the man.

The men's rights types usually claim that husband-battering is under-reported only because men are too ashamed or chivalrous to report to the police. Not so, say Dobash, Dobash, Wilson, and Daly. Police records show that the few men who are assaulted by their wives are far more likely than battered women to call police, and then to press charges.

The CTS method, when tested in other areas, has been shown to lead to similarly false results. So the next time a men's advocate starts moaning about "husband-battering," question his material and suspect his motives. He sure isn't operating from a basis of reality – and he probably knows it.

• • • • • • • • •

AS CONSERVATIVE POLITICAL strength deepened its hold in North America, ever more determined efforts were made to wash away the accumulated wisdom and evidence amassed by the women's movement. Taking the cue from U.S. neo-conservatives, Canadian ultra-conservatives have worked tirelessly to obliterate the advances claimed by feminism. Laws, approaches to crime, and even language, have all changed in lockstep with the Americans.

Never again did Statistics Canada produce such a strong and clear survey on violence against women as it did in 1993. Over the years, the terminology began to melt away into vagueness, like ice cubes puddling and dripping off the table. Wife battering turned into "spousal violence" or "family violence" at the same time as fathers' rights activists were making the case that men are victims of female violence. By the twenty-first century, the battle of words over "equal gender violence" had escalated substantially.

SPOUSAL ABUSE SPARKS BACKLASH AGAINST VICTIMS
July 2003

Statistics don't always lie, but they can seriously distort reality by offering a narrow peephole perspective on complex subjects. When the public gets hold of that skewed version of the truth, we can end up with crazily dangerous policies.

That's exactly what has happened with wife battering. I believe that if you asked any person on the street about "spousal violence" (note the reality-obscuring gender-neutral language), many would now tell you that women and men in relationships are equally violent.

This is not only false, but perilously false. Thanks to a decade of propaganda, this distortion is so widely accepted and acted upon that women and children are now exposed to cascading new dangers and harms.

If you feel sickened and angered every time the papers report another wife murder, please remember that the murder is often the culmination of years of emotional or physical violence. Battering is a systematic, purposeful exercise of power. A batterer humiliates, terrorizes, and hurts his partner in order to control and dominate her.

However, even now when misleading statistics have obscured the terrifying reality of battering, it's easy to get back to the human truth. Just ask a man who complains to police that his wife has "battered" him whether he is afraid of her.

Ask her if she is afraid of him.

You don't need statistics to know that she is the one living in fear and afraid to escape lest she be murdered or her children harmed.

If you think about it, you know that almost all her violence is a futile form of self-defence or pre-emptive striking back at her aggressor. Of course women are capable of violence – most often against children – but almost none use violence to maintain power and control in a relationship.

How did we come to think battering is gender neutral and equal opportunity? It took the women's movement at least two decades to get the public to recognize wife battering for what it is: a violent crime. And almost as soon as society at last began to insist that police get tough and arrest the batterers, the backlash kicked in with a vengeance.

Mandatory arrest policies provoked a counter-campaign by men's activists and defence lawyers. At the same time, it began to dawn on some violent men that "sauce for the gander was sauce for the goose" and they began to counter-charge their partners. They were greatly aided in the '80s and '90s by U.S. sociologist Murray Straus, who did pioneering – but strictly quantitative – studies of violence in families. In essence, he measured "hits." He slapped, she slapped. His "Conflict Tactic Scales" seem to show men and women as equally violent. In fact, these studies omit any analysis of unequal power, severity of harm, and long-term coercion.

Nevertheless, Straus's methods are widely copied, and studies like the Statistics Canada "Family Violence in Canada 2000" have increased the backlash hype. Like Straus, it reported an almost equal level of violent acts by men and women. "One problem with these research tools is that they count a man slapping a woman as one incident of minor violence, and a woman attempting to hit a man with an object as an incidence of severe violence," said sociologist Mavis Morton, a domestic violence expert.

Few of the headline-writers bothered with the details in the Family Violence study: overwhelmingly, it is women who are afraid for their lives (40 percent) and who report suffering isolation, multiple beatings, chokings, kidnappings, stalking, sexual assault, violence with weapons, threats to their children, hospitalizations.

Published in 1985, this was the first Canadian book to argue that there were connections among the various issues of violence against women and children.

Still, as the backlash view of women's violence began to take hold – avidly popularized by less-than-scrupulous conservative media – police began to follow suit. Not trained to understand the dynamics or assess the evidence, they often solved their bewilderment by arresting both partners and letting "the judge sort it out."

The steep rise in arrests of women fed right into the concept of equal violence.

From 2000 to 2001 in Toronto, the number of women charged with domestic violence rocketed from 16 to 93. The Elizabeth Fry Society suddenly had to create 72 spaces for court-ordered anti-violence counselling for women who had pleaded guilty. And startlingly, there were more and more women who were charged while their partners weren't. [Aboriginal women, immigrant women, and women of colour were exponentially more likely to be charged.]

"Almost all of the women were long-term abuse victims," Elizabeth Fry executive director Leslie Kelman said in an interview. "Unfortunately, women who are charged will often, almost naively, admit to having kicked or hit back. They often have no access to a lawyer. And they'll plead guilty to anything to get out and get back to their children before the Children's Aid takes them.

"Meanwhile, more men than women are reporting domestic incidents; they've learned to work the system, they deny everything, and more of them can afford lawyers."

The fallout is frightening. Women who plead guilty are automatically cut off from the counselling, support, and shelter offered to other female victims. They are more drastically isolated, trapped with ongoing violence, and afraid to leave their abusers lest, with that record of violence, they lose their children.

Surprisingly, and encouragingly, despite the many reporters who go on peddling the lie of equal violence, both the government and the higher levels of the police have done an about-face.

Since 2000, the Ontario solicitor-general has directed police to determine the "primary aggressor" in each case, and not to arrest or charge those who used violence in "defensive self-protection." As of last winter, the ministry told police to collect clearer statistics on male and female violence and dual charging.

Very slowly, word is trickling down to street-level cops. Slowly, the tide will turn. After all, this is about public safety and about preventing violence and murder. You can't do that by acting on badly warped assumptions.

● ● ● ● ● ● ● ● ●

IN ONTARIO, the far-right Conservatives under Mike Harris had moved hard against the battered women's movement. Funding was cut off completely from advocacy organizations and all of "second stage" housing, which had successfully been supporting battered women to move toward a normal and productive life.

All available anti-violence resources were poured into law-and-order structures like "domestic violence courts," which fell far short of their objectives. Other remedies, like providing free cell phones to women suffering from violence, were simply silly.

HUSTLING IN 'HARRISLAND' TO SAVE WOMEN'S LIVES
April 1998

If you're a worker in human services in Ontario, or even just a committed volunteer, cleaning up after Mike Harris' tax cuts is like walking behind the horses in the Santa Claus parade. Santa may be up there grinning and waving, but you're down on the ground where reality is pungent, and you're shovelling faster and faster.

Two years ago, with a fine flourish of their pens, the guys in suits at Queen's Park eliminated all funds – every cent of the $2.6 million – for second-stage housing in Ontario....

Women fleeing violence are entitled to just six weeks in a crisis shelter. After that, many find they have no choice but to return to their batterers. If they refuse to go back, this is the frightening moment when they are most likely to be stalked, threatened or killed by ex-partners.

Phyllis Lonsbary is the program director for Quetzal Family Homes in Simcoe. Her litany of frantic fundraising efforts says it all. "In the last year alone, we held a bake sale, garage sale, plant sale, 50/50 draw, brunch with Santa, golf tournament, two fashion shows, and rode in a monster bike challenge, took collection at a Sunday Gospel show, and kept our Friends Of Quetzal campaign (barely) alive."...

• • • • • • • • •

THE MOST STRENUOUS PUSH was against understanding and information. The women's movement had struggled for twenty years to make the crime of violence visible. Now the forces of backlash were single-mindedly determined to attack the language, the meaning, the knowledge, the statistical information, and the hard-won structures that underlay the movement to end the violence.

Under heavy pressure from fathers' rights activists in Parliament and the Senate (notably Senator Anne Cools), and under the ill-informed derision by *Globe and Mail* editorialists and columnists, Statistics Canada nervously backed away from its previous progressive approach and focused now on gender-invisible "family violence." By 2010, scarcely a scrap of information about violence against women was to be found in the thickets of StatsCan graphs.

The Conservatives' determined suppression of public knowledge and information is effective: once the statistics vanish, once the words for crimes like wife battering vanish, the energy and ammunition to combat them evaporate as well.

Some shelters survived with their feminist idealism and collectivist zeal still burning. Most settled into a polite and depoliticized social service model. By 2008, there were 550 battered women's shelters across Canada, and more than 100,000 women and children seek safety in them every year.

During those backlash years of the 1990s, astonishing cruelties to women piled up, even in the supposedly enlightened legal arena. Injustice takes many jagged shapes. One that goes on hurting, even decades later, is that the murdered woman's true story vanishes with her – like the story of Debra Ellul. Like the story of Gillian Hadley.

WHERE IS GILLIAN'S VOICE?

November 2001

Who speaks now for Gillian Hadley?...

Since the inquest began two weeks ago, I've been filled with a rising disgust at the way these horrific events play out in the public.

The killer gets to spew his sick ramblings – written and audiotaped – all over the headlines and in lengthy reportage.

The murdered woman is silent forever, her life and her story snuffed out by her husband. Gillian's infant son, Chase, whom she handed to safety seconds before she died, will never again know his mother's love. Now the child's inheritance will be to hear her story from the twisted murderer's – and the murderer's doting parents' – point of view...

So, once again, the obscenely repulsive Ralph Hadley – stalker, harasser, abuser, murderer – gets his "pain" front and centre.

Gillian, of course, had no chance to leave tape recordings and grandiose notes.

The inquest is already proving itself a morass of confusion in which Gillian's death seems to disappear. The coroner, inexplicably, granted official standing to a fathers' rights group. What on earth can these men contribute to making our world safer for battered women? Merely by accrediting them, officials have validated the preposterous idea that Ralph, as a father, was somehow the aggrieved party.

Let's make it clear: A man who murders his child's mother does not act out of love and concern for that child. Short of actually slaughtering the child, he has committed the most bitterly injurious and unforgivable crime possible against his own offspring...

But the press coverage slides into ambiguity. Over and over, we hear of Ralph's "concern" that Gillian was "a bad mother."

What garbage: There is absolutely no trace of "bad mothering," whereas Ralph himself was barred by the Children's Aid....

Why was Ralph released into the custody of his parents, including a father who repeatedly talked about "shooting Gillian's head off?" Are there no consequences to such a breach of responsibility, solemnly undertaken in the court?

"Ours is a culture of reinforcement, colluding with and supporting an abuser," said Eileen Morrow, co-ordinator of the Ontario Association of Interval and Transition Houses. One of the province's most informed and tough-minded commentators, Morrow is sickened when these inquests turn into festivals of victim-blaming.

If we look for causes, if we want the 40 femicides a year in Ontario to stop, look no further than inequality....Causes? They're all around us, especially in the inequities that entrap single mothers into social isolation, helplessness, and poverty.

Gillian has no voice now. We must be her voice.

• • • • • • • • •

THE INQUEST INTO Gillian Hadley's death seemed, at first, a victory for the abusers, the liars, the venal – and the media types who smugly supported them. And yet, when all is said, a pattern of victory is slowly, slowly forming, like a shape gathering in the clouds. After all these decades of struggle, and the ensuing effort to suppress the emergence of truth and justice, the femicide rate is gradually declining. To understand the reasons will take more studies and more scholarship – a dubious prospect in these conservative times – but the overall picture is getting clearer.

Battered women have more understanding of the danger they are in, and the options that may be available. People are marrying later, and therefore, perhaps, a little less recklessly. And one of Gillian Hadley's legacies is the Ontario Domestic Violence Death Review Committee, which includes experts from government, law, and civil society, and which examines each death in order to draw lessons for further prevention.

I recently called Ellen Pence, a brilliant innovator in violence prevention in her home state of Minnesota, to ask her about the time she spent in Toronto, working on her doctorate at the Ontario Institute for Studies in Education under the tutelage of sociologist Dorothy Smith. That was in the early '90s, when the whole anti-violence movement had reached a crescendo. The Montréal Massacre had made stingingly clear the prevalence of a culture of anti-woman violence. Governments had scrambled to look as though they were doing something. Reports piled on reports.

In Ontario, an NDP government had been elected just about the time Ellen had arrived in Toronto. The time was promisingly ripe for real action.

"Well, nothing much happened," Ellen recalled. "In some communities, individual police or prosecutors took up the banner, but in Toronto – no one. There was no charismatic figure to push it forward. The prosecutors were terrible. They played so close to the vest with information. There was no inter-agency approach – and really, with police, prosecutors, and judges all frustrated with and blaming each other, nothing happens. They all have to strategize and write policy together with the women's groups."

Although Pence went on to great success in her home state (and, in fact, throughout the United States), her template was never fully adopted in Canada.

The model still stands, however, as one that any government of good will and clear purpose could adopt. Meanwhile, we grind along with a resignedly minimalist approach to stopping the beating and the slaughter of women. Back in the 1990s when Phyllis Lonsbary listed off for me the desperate account of pitiful fund-raising done yearly by Quetzal Housing, I asked her to tell me some of her success stories as well. She paused before answering. "More than 130 women and 250 children are alive because of our services. They are alive. That's our success."

Duluth, Minnesota, does better.

COMMUNITY MOBILIZES AGAINST WIFE ABUSERS
July 1991

One out of every 23 men in Duluth, Minnesota, has been arrested for and convicted of wife battering.

This stark little statistic is a testament to what a community can do to protect women from violence if it has the will and the energy to mobilize.

When Duluth police are summoned to a "domestic dispute," and they have reason to believe the man used or threatened violence, they're under orders to handcuff him at once and take him to jail overnight. No victim-blaming is allowed. Officers may not ask the woman what she did to "provoke" the beating; they are not allowed to coax, mediate, or act as referees.

The Duluth Domestic Abuse Intervention Project is run by a feminist collective linked to the local battered women's shelter. The collective co-ordinates and monitors – on a daily basis – the response of police, courts, probation officers, and therapists to every single occurrence of battering.

That's why the system works so well: every cop, every probation officer and therapist, is accountable, finally, to women with front-line experience of wife abuse.

From the moment of arrest, a clearly defined plan swings into action. A women's advocate is called by beeper to visit the victim and offer her help, ranging from shelter to legal advice in getting a strictly enforced restraining order against her abuser.

When the cases come to court, more than 80 percent of the men are found guilty and are immediately ordered into an education and counselling course. If a man skips more than two of the 26 sessions, he automatically goes to jail.

Meanwhile, the battered woman is invited to regular group meetings and helped to take control of her life. She may well choose to leave her abuser while he's still safely under probation surveillance. The tragedy is that most women who are murdered by their partners are killed when they are trying desperately – but without any support or protection – to separate.

"We aim to protect the victim, not to fix the batterer," said Ellen Pence, a founding member of the Duluth collective. She emphasizes that battering men use violence deliberately as a tactic of domination. A woman who refuses to testify against her batterer is a good example of the extent to which an assailant can control his wife through physical and psychological terror. That's why, in Duluth, the onus is on the police to lay charges, and why women aren't sent to jail for refusing to testify.

New Brunswick's Hestia House has been sheltering women since 1981 in Saint John.

Arrest, even without conviction, is a sharp deterrent to wife abuse. Beyond that, the collective also created and oversees a tightly structured, no-nonsense education and counselling course administered by local social service agencies.

"Our research shows that about 40 percent of the men in our education programs really do stop battering. Another 40 percent moderate their behaviour. They hit less frequently, or establish fear another way, through threats about taking the kids away, for example. But at least the women are much safer," Pence said. After two years, 81 percent of the women report that they are not being battered.

Metro Toronto and the provincial government announced last week that they're embarking on a two-year project to develop a "protocol" similar to the one in Duluth, where every local agency dealing with batterers signed a written agreement to abide by a coherent plan of response.

This is the most hopeful move in years of mounting crisis and near-criminal neglect. Every day, the papers are filled with ghastly stories of women injured or dying at the hands of brutal partners. Yet our system is so fragmented and sloppy that most batterers are never arrested or punished.

We'll have to work furiously, with concerted government effort and unrelenting public pressure, to nail down a Duluth-style protocol in Toronto. Police intransigence may be our biggest stumbling block. Hierarchical male organizations, after all, do not easily agree to be monitored by outside, woman-run community groups. But that accountability is the vital key to the success of the Duluth project.

Maybe we can learn from the clever grass-roots organizing techniques of the Duluth women. "We persuaded police to co-operate with us by showing them that we could drastically reduce the number of repeat calls, injuries to women and injuries to police. Also, we got legal advice showing that police arrest records are public information. And we monitor. Every officer has to file a written report on every domestic call. We check

The Northwest Territories Society Against Family Abuse produced this button to draw attention to the issue.

the dispatch records daily. If an officer didn't file a report, he has to go back and do it or, eventually, be suspended without pay," Pence explained.

After 10 years of co-operating to stop men from battering, the police, court system, social agencies, and the women's collective enjoy a unique working harmony. In fact, said Pence, "We're having an inter-agency Fish-a-Thon next week." The prize won't go to the one who catches the most fish, or the biggest – but to the one who lands the fish with "the most character."

"The girls made the rules," chortled Pence.

Chapter Five
IN DEFENCE OF CHILDREN

ONE OF THE MORE surprising achievements of consumer capitalism has been to "white-out" our society's concern for the future and to re-focus our attention on the immediate gratification of every material desire. The collateral damage: our collective dedication to the well-being of children. This, of course, does seem to be in direct contradiction to the evidence. Our media, after all, overflow with stories about the neurotically excessive attention of "helicopter" (over-protective, hovering) parents. I'm referring instead to our society's collective priorities, as expressed through government decisions.

A society's deepest values are seen in its political choices and expenditures. It seems obvious to me that children – the most vulnerable and powerless among us, and yet also the ones who will inherit and nurture all that we work and strive toward – should have priority on our consideration and resources. We know so much about how to ensure that they thrive; we have more than enough money to prevent the shrivelling of any child's health and happiness due to poverty and neglect.

Why don't we prioritize childcare and education? Our society is increasingly swayed by the powerful American example of individualism, rather than the earlier Canadian model of working for the collective good, as well as individual stability. Nothing illustrates the perils of the new approach better than the drift to privatizing education. Every family feels the pressure to get (or buy) the very best educational start for their child to enhance her chance to succeed in the competition of life, and the devil take the hindmost.

Our anxious focus on "my child first" allows us to push out of mind and conscience the children who have been cheated, starved, and shunted aside by all of us, through our governments: the poor, the aboriginal youth on reserves, the immigrants in suburban ghettoes. And, of course, the damaged....

IT'S HARD TO STAY ANGRY AT THESE KIDS
August 1980

...I spent most of a day last week inside the maximum-security Juvenile Observation and Detention Centre at 311 Jarvis St, for youths who are likely to be "a danger to themselves or society." The occasion was a performance (for the inmates) of the play *Juve*, a pastiche of real-life adolescent musings enacted by a volcanically energetic troupe of high school kids on tour from Vancouver. In the bleakly modern corridors and locked bedrooms of the centre, children of an appalling criminal sophistication have pasted up their innocent drawings of Eeyore and Superman.

"The children here are ages 9 to 15, and they are being held pending trial for murder, arson, rape, break and enter, armed robbery, or assault," says John Kennedy, the superintendent. John Kennedy would make a wonderful TV cop. He looks hard and fit, with glinting blue eyes and a salt-of-the-earth style. For the past 10 years he has worked in adult prisons and training schools. If he walks with the brisk stride of a classic tough warden, he talks as though experience has made him humane.

"I knew some of the fathers of these kids when I worked in prisons," he says. "I think society is getting more conservative, don't you? They want to punish more. They say, 'Give these kids a boot in the ass.' If they could see the files on these kids, what they've been through, so much punishment, so many boots in the ass, they'd say 'Forget it.'" Kennedy, four months at his new post, is moving quickly to marshal community and preventive help for the kids once they are out of custody. "The girls especially are so taken advantage of. Someone's always trying to pimp them. They've been assaulted by their own fathers. It's pathetic."

Down in the gym to watch *Juve*, my eye is caught by a 14-year-old waif in the audience – call her Debby – whom I've seen before on the street. She's just been brought in on serious charges involving violence and had her stomach pumped after a prolonged Valium binge. The victim of years of sexual assault by father and stepfathers, she looks as frail as a 6-year-old, as big-eyed and spacey as an orphan painted on velvet.

"I'm glad Debby's in again, frankly, because she needs some rest and some food," says Kennedy. Debby lives by shacking up with anyone, male or female, who will take care of her. She wears a provocatively styled red dress that hangs shapelessly over her skinny form. In her arms she hugs a big, fluffy rabbit doll with red eyes. If a Hollywood director cast her in the role of a street kid, he would be accused of exaggerating.

There is not a kid in the audience, including Debby, who isn't dangerous, and not a kid who isn't the product of parental beatings, licentiousness, indifference, craziness, or cruelty.

There is Cliff, 15, who lived for five years in group homes, in on a concealed weapons charge. All he wants in life is a private room with a door.

Cliff loves the half-satirical hymn to dope performed with wild zest by the *Juve* crew. "That's so true," he tells me earnestly. "Trouble and the dope scene. That's how I solve all my problems. With dope, y'know."

There's a tall, tightly contained boy who has been deliberately left in here for an extra few days by his parents, who wanted a long weekend free for a dope and booze party. There's the adorable little kid whose home life is so sexually bizarre that he sets fires.

The two scenes in *Juve* that get the biggest response are the bitterly jocular account of prison homosexuality (hoots of nervous laughter) and a scene in which a weeping girl breaks down (shuffling and nail biting in the audience).

"They respond because they know that's their future," says Kennedy.

Afterwards, the kids shyly press the teenage actors: "Were any of you, like, criminals yourself, once?"

The faintest gleam of wistful hope shines on their faces.

The truth is, only a minority of these kids will succeed in putting criminality firmly in their past. And they know it.

•   •   •   •   •   •   •   •   •

LOOKING BACK OVER my columns of the last four decades, I can almost chart the rise and fall of the stock market by the frequency of snarling anti-child news or opinion pieces, a sure beacon of hard times. Very often, of course, these impulses are disguised as reasoned arguments about the role of women in the work force.

In 1978, when a third of Canadian women with preschool children were employed outside the home, childcare was in crisis. In 2011, it still is. By the first decade of the twenty-first century, UNICEF ranked Canada last of twenty-five developed countries for its early childhood care and education. Of mothers with babies under the age of two, 70 percent are in the paid workforce, and 77 percent of mothers of toddlers are working for pay. In most provinces, fewer than 20 percent of those children were in regulated childcare.

Even economically speaking, this criminal level of governmental neglect is equivalent to throwing away all the minerals mined in Canada, or letting other countries help themselves freely to all our fresh water. Our richest resource – our youngest people – are left to languish, resulting in hundreds of thousands of blighted lives, while billions are lavished on wealthy-beyond-avarice corporations.

WE'LL PAY DEARLY FOR TODAY'S ANTI-CHILD MOOD
June 1978

...Daycare is in a mess. Recently, the Social Planning Council study of Metro's daycare situation showed that 40,000 preschoolers are left daily in unsupervised daycare, and even the 116,000 in supervised care often spend their days in haphazard, emotionally barren, or downright unsafe conditions.

Now the Social Planning Council has come out with a list of recommendations that reads like a woeful litany of children's unmet needs. Once again, the people who care about children are begging for money to provide decent adult-child ratios, for lunch-time and after-school supervision, and for a central registry for daycare centres so parents can locate the kind of care they need.

You can glimpse the unspoken crises behind the recommendations. Daycare workers are grievously underpaid, handicapped children are too often excluded from nursery programs, families need all kinds of preventive in-home support, night shift workers are out of luck when it comes to supervised child care, and there is no long-term planning for daycare, or research about its effects on children....

• • • • • • • • •

NO MATTER WHICH male government has assumed power, the situation for working parents and the satisfactory care of their children has never changed substantially. I now believe that until we have a federal government led and at least partly dominated by enlightened women, we will never have adequate care or early education for our children.

INVESTING IN YOUNG KIDS ITS OWN REWARD
June 1998

New York author Mary Gordon, in town last week to give a triumphantly hilarious Harbourfront reading from her new novel, adjourned later to a nearby pub with a group of young 30-something men and women who had been in the audience.

"Right," she said, when drinks had been ordered. "What are we going to do about child care?"

Everyone instantly knew exactly what she was talking about.

"Two things we know for sure," Gordon said, ticking them off on her fingers. "Tobacco kills, and early childhood education works. And yet we can't seem to squash the tobacco lobby, and we can't get governments to do the right thing for children."

Agreement was lively, vocal and unanimous – which got me thinking about this subject again.

Overwhelmingly, science and sense tell us that investment in young children is its own reward. The latest evidence, a study

Though a 1998 survey showed that two-thirds of Canadians supported a national childcare program, demonstrations and protests against the lack of daycare continued to grow.

by two University of Toronto economists, says that every dollar spent on high quality daycare will bring $2 back to the public purse in savings and benefits. It would cost, they said, about $8,500 per child to create daycare facilities for all at the highest standard of skill, attention, and care.

As we lurch toward the end of a century in which women have fought for liberation from suffocating gender roles as well as from procreative and household slavery, the crisis of "the children" is on everyone's lips. No week passes without the announcement of another major study devoted to the plight of the modern (disintegrating) family.

The media play their part with a steady drumbeat of stories

about "working mothers." Usually, these stories confront mothers with a stark either/or decision – "going to work" or "staying home." The inference is almost always that the woman should feel guilty about her choices, whatever they are, and that if their children start hanging out at the mall, piercing their nostrils, and specializing in break-and-enter, it will be the fault of the mother who made the wrong choices.

Hogswallop.

The hypocrisy-soaked phony war between stay-home and employed mothers is the most lying, reeking, rotten red herring that ever created a diversionary stink.

All mothers work; almost all will work for pay outside the home at some time in their mothering lives. And no mother, no woman, created this ridiculously inefficient, human-hating social structure that plops all responsibility for children on the frail shoulders of individual families.

It was not a mother who invented a 9 to 5 work day and a 9 to 3:30 school day, but of course mothers take the rap for the resulting "latch-key child." No woman devised the economic structure that rewards leveraged buy-out jackals with mountains of gold, while condemning the most essential people in the country – child-minders – to lives of grinding poverty.

The quarrel is not between mothers who work for pay and mothers who don't. The quarrel is between those who care about children's future, and the (mostly) men in government who just don't get it.

Premier Mike Harris, who slashed welfare payments to single mothers and contemptuously insulted them, said, when told that the number of children living in poverty has soared, "I don't quite understand what that has to do with us."

No? Well, how about cancelling employment equity; firing tens of thousands of nurses, teachers, and civil servants; bankrupting non-profit daycares with higher property taxes; cutting welfare by 21 percent; cancelling all new social housing; devastating women's agencies, shelters, public health, counselling – not to mention imperilling libraries, recreation, parks, and innovative school programs.

Cuts in services take their toll: single mothers' incomes have slid backwards in the '90s; the teen pregnancy rate is rising for the first time in 40 years; the $2.9 million that Toronto budgeted for the "healthy babies program" looks sickly compared to the $5.9 million for "animal control."

Meanwhile, two-thirds of Canadians support a national childcare program – but the Chrétien-Martin government high-handedly reneges on its promise to provide one.

A universal, enriched, flexible, education-focused child-care service, available to every child (working mother or not) would turn the country around, heal the division among haves and have-nots, boost the economy and build a strong future – and be cheap at the price. There is no higher priority.

Do mothers have to riot to win what is needed for children? For that to happen, women would have to resist the divide-and-conquer routines of the conservative media. For once, women would have to make common cause.

· · · · · · · · ·

WE HAD A REVOLUTION, all right – the thuggish "Common Sense Revolution," an early Ontario-made version of the U.S. Tea Party that romped into power on no-brain slogans and, just like the invading Huns of history, proceeded to lay waste to our civilization. The wonderful parent centres I wrote about disappeared under the Harris-imposed amalgamation that threw urban Toronto into the wide and damaging embrace of surrounding suburbia and spelled the end of the progressive city. The proud Toronto school system has not been able to, and never will, recover.

Finally, even I, grasper at every rhetorical straw and stick that might whip foot-dragging governments into awareness about the plight of children, even I became sickened by the financial lingo we had all been using. Not that it was wrong. It was simply useless. We could use a hydrogen bomb and it still wouldn't make the kind of men who govern take notice of, or care about, children not their own.

CHILD POLICY DOUBLETALK WON'T HELP KIDS
October 1999

We're all guilty of child policy doubletalk. All of us in the scribbling trade who write about children keep falling into the same trap: we crank up the bond-trader rhetoric, we trundle out the criminal-justice bluster.

Children are an investment, we say. Pay now or risk declining returns later. Increase the value of your (human) stock by value-added programs; the economic profits will come rolling in.

Pony up for daycare and more resources, others of us threaten, or you'll find yourself at the pointy end of a knife in some parking lot one dark night, at the mercy of a pierced and tattooed teen who didn't get enough love and orange juice.

As the Chrétien government does fancy footwork on a "children's agenda" in its new budget, and the Harris regime fails to respond to the child care crisis, we're bound to hear ever more plaintive public cries about "investing now or paying more later."

Why do we do it? Not one of us who raised children, with enormous effort, trouble, and pains, did it as an "investment." We weren't banking love in hopes of compound interest. We weren't making intellectual down payments on future honours degrees.

We raised our children as best

Women have made progress on reproductive choice but child care remains a problem. By the late 1970s, one-third of Canadian mothers of young children were employed outside the home and daycare was lacking. In 2011, close to 80 percent of mothers are working for pay and there is still a daycare crisis.

we could out of sheer devotion to their well-being.

Why, then, do we resort to the language of the stock market when making our public plea for better child and family resources? I guess we do it because we feel we're talking to men (and some women) in power who don't care about children as human beings.

We want to woo them by using their own sterile language and appealing to their own materialistic values.

I think we make a serious mistake when we use language inauthentically. We don't really believe that a child is a promissory note. And those who inhabit an emotional desert of profit and loss calculations aren't about to be moved by our pose of sharing their assumptions.

Children are a "hot" topic right now. Both federal and provincial governments are trying to capitalize on the public's unease about the well-being of children in our smash-and-grab culture. Chrétien dangles vague promises while making it clear that there will be no universally accessible daycare, and Harris boasts about "early childhood development" initiatives, while distancing himself from anything real.

Harris did have something substantive in hand: he had Fraser Mustard and Margaret McCain's Early Years Study. What that report showed was that love, nurture and brain development are inseparable, and the preschool years are critical. Not only that, but we have a brilliant example right here in Toronto of how we can, as a society, help all children achieve their full potential. The Toronto District School Board's 34 parenting and family literacy centres – warmly welcoming, informal centres in neighbourhood schools – are admired and emulated around the world. Mothers, fathers, babysitters, and grandparents can drop in daily with their infants or toddlers for stories, games, toy-lending, crafts, group play, songs, multilingual books – and lots of support for parents learning the importance of stimulus and emotional responsiveness.

Couple those programs with high-quality daycare, available and affordable for all working parents, and you have the ideal foundation for a vigorous society.

Dream on, as the young would say. The Harris government, like the wolf in granny's nightgown, remains its own hairy, unregenerate self under the pastel disguise of election promises. Margaret Marland, Harris's minister responsible for children (hah!), recently explained to the media that "the government believes that child care and child development are unconnected. These are separate issues," she said.

That's beyond embarrassing; it's idiotic. Think about it for a moment: surely Margaret Marland understands, even if her government doesn't, that nurture and development are inseparable in a child's first years. Have these people even read the Mustard-McCain report? Instead of acting on its straightforward recommendations, the government is whiffling on about a few "demonstration projects" in some conveniently Tory ridings.

Enough nonsense. We already know what children and their families need. The evidence, the examples, the proofs have all been marshalled by every prominent social agency, non-profit group, and policy think tank in Canada, excluding (of course) the most rabidly right-wing. If governments are still refusing to act on that collective wisdom, then at least we know what their real values are, and we can stop trying to ape their desiccated and soul-shrivelling vocabulary.

Those who care about children because they are children, and because this is our community, will have to start thinking about a social revolution.

• • • • • • • • •

LIKE MARRIAGE, procreation, and divorce, the issues around childrearing are ultimately political. What we think is "common sense" or "second nature" often reveals itself later as a cog in the larger political machine of the times. Nothing exists in isolation; everything is interconnected.

This is certainly the case with our acceptance of corporal punishment, for example. In his nasty little book *Dare to Discipline*, James Dobson praised the infliction of pain on very young children as a wonderful mode of punishment.

At first I thought Dobson was merely, earnestly, misguided. How could I have gotten Dobson's motives so wrong? His supposed concern for bringing up "good" children, which I then took at face value, was the cloak of invisibility he wrapped around his fanatical need for masculine dominance. All of Dobson's purported philosophy – including his advice to let a beaten child cry for two minutes and then beat him or her again to stop the "wilful" crying – was in the interests of a violently controlling patriarchy.

PARENTAL BACKLASH HURTS KIDS
October 1978

For a few years there, having children seemed almost trendy. Grown-up flower children were settling down to raise families with a new fervour of commitment. Backpacks were everywhere, co-op nurseries sprang up like daisies and innovative playgrounds were the rage.

Now, suddenly, the talk is all of discipline versus permissiveness. Time to slap on some controls, say disgruntled adults. Right on the brink of International Children's Year, it seems, Canadians have gone sour on the kids.

The backlash has gone farther than we may imagine. Parents in their thousands are snapping up *Dare to Discipline*, a Bantam paperback (four printings last year alone), which proposes that we use pain to control our children.

"The shoulder muscle is a surprisingly useful source of minor pain, actually, it was created expressly for school teachers," chuckles author James Dobson, explaining how to squeeze the muscle hard to force a child into obedience.

Approvingly, Dobson tells how his own mother "cracked him with a shoe, or a handy belt," and once thrashed him with a buckled corset. His pièce de résistance, though, is description of a "desirable" incident when the mother of a 15-month-old girl ordered the child not to step outside the door while the mother went out to get firewood.

"Suzie decided she didn't want to mind her mother," says Dobson, so mother "stung her little legs a few times with a switch."

Dobson sees children as a "Now Generation" out of control, spoiled rotten by "too much love." His imagery is revealing. Kids, even babies, are described as "brazen, defiant, stiff-necked, rebellious." A parent will draw a line, says Dobson, and the child will "flop his big hairy toe over that line." Any show of defiance by a child under 10, he says, should be met instantly with the application of pain, a "marvellous purifier."

The other night, Dobson's book was being promoted (though he underplayed the "pain principle") by a Thunder Bay high school teacher on a TV talk and phone-in show in which I participated. The viewers voted, by a narrow edge, that Ontario should continue to use the strap in the public primary schools. Caller after caller wanted to bring corporal punishment [back into daily use]. A policeman vowed that my approach of loving attention "scared him to death." He had been strapped in school, he said, and he wanted his 6-year-old son to have the same experience.

What's going on here? I have the glimmering of a theory. Dobson and his followers are frightened and angered by youngsters whom they see as sullen, rebellious, ungrateful, and immoral little vandals.

Well, nobody's arguing with their revulsion. Who can warm to a pot-smoking schoolyard bully of 12? Where Dobson gets muddled is in his definitions. These spoiled kids, he says, are the products of "permissive" parents who give too much love and not enough discipline. These "too-loving" parents, he says, let their kids run wild, indulging them one minute, screaming at them the next.

Since when is this the hallmark of a loving parent? These are lazy, unloving parents who have emotionally abandoned these kids. They're not "permissive," they're plain inadequate....

It's tough work responding to every cry of a newborn infant. It's hard to hear the fright or anger in your 2-year-old's tantrum and not to respond with a tantrum of your own. It's hard to tune out your own concerns and listen to a pestering 3-year-old with such concentrated attention that you suddenly understand his behaviour isn't defiance...it's despair about being left at a strange babysitter's house....

The best children I know – the most self-disciplined, creative, alive, and affectionate – have had this kind of "permissive" attention. The most successful children in school are those whose teachers respect them, listen to them, involve them in planning and rule-making, and treat them as worthy human beings.

The whiners, the obnoxious kids, the sullen little despoilers... maybe they're the ones with self-absorbed parents who didn't try hard enough, who veered sloppily between emotional neglect and angry attempts at control.

Maybe the parents who lust after simple answers (strap, discipline, control) are counsellors of despair. Perhaps they failed to love early enough and intelligently enough.

Parental devotion isn't measured out in absent-minded indulgence or in blows. It's measured out in concentrated hours of serious attention being paid. And, as heaven is my witness, the rewards are more joyful and more glorious than the child-swatters will ever know.

• • • • • • • • •

IN THE DISCOMFITING LIGHT of hindsight, James Dobson was the herald of the Reagan era, still four years away from its leader's first presidential win in 1981. Few of us in the mainstream media had any idea that Reagan would inaugurate a new era of unholy matrimony between fundamentalist religion and active politics. Unused as we were to detecting the political motives behind so many "religious" sentiments, Canadians were easily suckered by the sly innuendos and manipulations that swirled around straightforward public policy concerns.

With their iron determination to retain the traditional, heterosexual nuclear family as the bedrock institution of capitalism, religious conservatives were tireless in their efforts to prevent, among other things, the creation of public and non-profit childcare. The connection between those who oppose public childcare and those who believe in corporal punishment may be subtle, but both groups rely on the same instincts and political philosophy.

In 1995, I wrote about the need to repeal Section 43 of the Criminal Code, a law exonerating and justifying physical assault on children. In 2011, Section 43 is still in effect, despite mountains of evidence that show how astonishingly effective corporal punishment is in producing adult criminals. The more and the harder they're physically hit, the more violent the adult criminal.

REPEAL LAW THAT LETS PARENTS SPANK KIDS
May 1995

Honestly — if you were angry with your 5-year-old daughter's misbehaviour, would you deal her four hard blows, throw her over the trunk of the car, yank down her underpants in full public view, and then hit her hard, eight times, on her bare buttocks while she screamed?

That's what U.S. tourist David Peterson did in London, Ont., last year. A witness reported him to the police, who held him overnight. But a judge recently acquitted him, noting, "A judge applies the law. Parliament makes the law."

Too true. So if you are not one of the many vociferous callers to talk shows who applauded and rejoiced at Peterson's acquittal, take a moment now to think about the law. Section 43 of Canada's Criminal Code says that "a schoolteacher, parent, or person standing in the place of a parent is justified in using force by way of correction toward a pupil or child...if the force does not exceed what is reasonable."

Well, just what is reasonable? Over the years, and right up to the present day, courts have ruled that hitting with straps, belts, sticks, extension cords, and rulers is reasonable; that beatings causing bruises, welts, abrasions, swelling, nosebleeds, and chipped teeth are reasonable; that kicks or blows – even one that left the imprint of an 8-year-old boy's sweater on his skin – are reasonable.

When I listened to a discussion of the London spanking decision on CBC's *Radio Noon*, I was riveted to hear parents speak of the need for corporal punishment to "instil respect" for authority. My experience of human nature suggests that violence and the threat of violence instil contempt, fear, hatred of authority, and a surly conviction that "might is right." "Respect" is merely the grim code word used by authoritarians; perhaps they really can't tell the difference between true respect and sullen, inwardly mutinous compliance.

But most of us can. Most of us will blush to admit that in the years of bringing up children, we occasionally swatted the bottom of a toddler who sprinted into traffic or otherwise made us momentarily frantic. Most of us were ashamed of our lapse and tried not to repeat it. When we think about Section 43, and the way it explicitly justifies the use of violence, let's remember that it's not talking about the occasional swatter. Section 43 is, on the contrary, the shelter and refuge of the determined violent assailant.

Corinne Robertshaw is a retired lawyer and co-ordinator of the Repeal 43 Committee. "A University of Toronto study last year reported that 'discipline' was involved in 85 percent of substantiated reports of physical child abuse," she told me, "and there were 5,000 such cases in Ontario in 1993."

This is the proverbial tip of the iceberg, as we know to our sorrow from the very low rate of reporting of wife assault, which is widely agreed to be a crime.

People who sympathized with David Peterson, the London spanker, may be defensive; they're average parents who are ashamed of their occasional loss of control and therefore rationalize that spanking is normal and no one's business. But wake up: there is a hard core of aggressive parents in our midst who believe in their right to inflict frequent pain and humiliation on their children, in the name of "discipline."

It is to reach and educate such people that the Institute for the Prevention of Child Abuse, among many other organizations, believes in repealing Section 43. And no, that wouldn't mean police would be snooping into everyone's living room. "The well-established rule is that the law does not take account of trifles," points out Robertshaw. The serious hitters who are charged may rely, like other citizens, on sections of the Code which allow for reasonable force in cases of necessity, emergency, or self-defence.

This coming week, Canada will appear before the United Nations Committee on the Rights of the Child in Geneva. According to committee member Dr. Marta Pais of Portugal, Canada's Section 43 is quite clearly in contravention of the U.N.'s Convention on the Rights of the Child, to which we are a signatory.

When you're finished with gun control, Allan Rock, bring us into line with civilized nations. Repeal Section 43.

• • • • • • • • •

AN EVEN MORE sinister form of violence against children is prevalent and has been equally ignored: incest. I first became aware of it as a very young 23-year-old reporter at *The Globe and Mail*, when I was sent to do a feature on inter-racial adoption, a hot new topic in the early '60s.

I remember sitting across from the very respectable and esteemed Lloyd Richardson, director of the Toronto Children's Aid

Society, discussing the assigned topic, when he suddenly leaned across the desk with a desperate expression and burst out, "If you want a story, I'll give you a real one: What on earth am I supposed to do with the hundreds and hundreds of little girls in this province whose fathers are interfering with them? Am I supposed to take them out of their homes? Where am I going to put them?"

I was stunned. I barely comprehended the nature of that "interference" – had never heard of incest or contemplated its existence. Richardson offered to put the full resources of the CAS at my disposal if I would write the story. I raced back to *The Globe* newsroom bursting with a mixture of excitement and loathing and incredulity. I was met with flat-out resistance, of a kind I would come to recognize over the years. The editor in charge was a small-minded, small-town conservative. He burst into sneering laughter when I told him my scoop. "C'mon," he scoffed. "Maybe hillbillies are up to that sort of thing, but not here in Canada!"

The story died unwritten. It was another ten years before the story about incest could appear in print – in *Chatelaine*, the women's magazine.

Hillbillies, like my former editor, are still omnipresent, however, still sneering, still covering up for other men – and still repressing the news when they can.

INCEST: STOP THE NONSENSE AND GET TO THE DIFFICULT TRUTH
February 1996

Over and over again in this century, the truth about incest has broken through the public silence, only to be savagely throttled again. Freud, faced with the rage of his colleagues, hastily repudiated his discoveries about incest and instead labelled his female patients "hysterical." Jeffrey Masson, the author who documented Freud's betrayal of women, was personally vilified.

There's a pattern here: those who have the most credibility in exposing the hidden crime of incest will be targeted most viciously.

Dr. Jennifer Freyd is a rising star of academe: a professor of psychology at University of Oregon, a much-honoured researcher in the study of cognition, memory, trauma, and dissociation.

In 1990, happily married, pregnant with her second child, Freyd entered therapy at a respected clinic with a well-established psychologist. After her second visit, she went home and began to experience terrifying flashbacks of her father's sexual abuse. When her husband privately confronted Freyd's parents, Peter and Pamela, they responded in a bizarre manner.

Within months, Pamela had sent a thinly veiled, scurrilous attack on Jennifer to her academic colleagues. She then created the False Memory Syndrome Foundation, which now has about 2,500 members, mostly accused parents. Weirdly, she invited Jennifer to sit on the board.

Pamela and her husband relentlessly publicized the story that their happy family, like "countless" others, had been destroyed by an irresponsible therapist who had "implanted false memories." Nothing of the sort had actually happened. And it was Pamela and Peter Freyd themselves who made the whole thing public.

Here are some less-well-publicized facts – not including the alleged acts of incest – about this "happy family:" Pamela and Peter are step-siblings who married in their teens. Peter boasted to his small daughters about his sexual experiences as an 11-year-old boy, calling himself a "male prostitute." He had his daughters, at ages 9 and 10, dance naked, adorned with Playboy bunny tails, in front of his friends. He encouraged Jennifer, as a child, to read *Lolita*. He would sit around the house with his genitals exposed. He was later hospitalized for severe alcoholism. He kept a model of his genitals on display.

Peter and Pamela Freyd are estranged from their two daughters and from Peter's brother, who has said: "There's no doubt in my mind that there was severe abuse in the home of Peter and Pam."

As Jennifer Freyd said in a rare public comment: "My parents have exhibited...a pattern of boundary violation...invasion and control...inappropriate and unwanted sexualization...intimidation and manipulation."

Why did the media leap to accept so blithely the hoked-up idea of "false memory syndrome?" Their deference is all the more disturbing when you take even a cursory glance at the quality of the foundation's board members and scientific advisers:

Dr. Elizabeth Loftus, the most prolific, respected, and plausible "false memory" exponent, abruptly resigned from the American Psychological Association two weeks ago, after 20 years of active involvement [and before a complaint about her alleged false reports on a case could be investigated].

Harold Lief, Pamela Freyd's personal psychiatrist, who once told Jennifer that her father couldn't have molested her because he had only "homoerotic fantasies," recently told a McGill University audience that black men suffer from psychological castration by the "uterine unit" of grandmother, mother, and daughter. Lief estimated that 25 percent of incest allegations are false "but I don't know where I got that figure. Sometimes I make up a number just to get reporters off my back."

Ralph Underwager was forced to resign abruptly from the board after he gave an interview to a Dutch pedophile magazine praising pedophilia as "an acceptable expression of God's will for love."

Dr. Ralph Ofshe, recently interviewed – very gently – by the CBC's Pamela Wallin, writes powerful, hair-raising anecdotes about real court cases in which "false memory" was to blame. But at least one incest survivor claims he falsified details of her case in his written account....

Dr. Richard Gardner attributes "false" accusations to anger fostered by feminist "zealots" who want to "destroy every man in sight." Angry women scapegoat their fathers because they are projecting their own sexual desires on to them: "Little girls have to learn that their fathers are off-limits when it comes to gratification of sexual feelings."

So! It's little girls who want to commit incest! [Gardner's self-published, and non-peer-reviewed works, are filled with seriously deranged views about sexuality.]

"False memory syndrome," backed by such dubious advocates and cardboard evidence, has not been accepted in any Canadian court. Serious scientists repudiate it utterly. The horrific anecdotes of suffering dads and crazy daughters – detailed most effectively in *Divided Memories*, a documentary saturated in bias, now showing on CBC Newsworld – almost never stand up to careful scrutiny.

...But the media rarely provide that critical analysis. And so therapists are maligned, harassed, and threatened with lawsuits, incest survivors are labelled as brainwashed lunatics and the public can go on denying the seriousness and pervasiveness of the crimes.

But the "false memory" saga, as I wrote last Saturday, is beginning to unravel as scientists show ever more conclusively how traumatic memories can indeed be buried and then recovered.

Now when will we stop the nonsense of believing perpetrators and their apologists and start dealing with the difficult truth?

• • • • • • • • •

THE "RECOVERED MEMORY" wars raged on in the media for most of the '90s. The "false memory syndrome," a rickety and non-scientific theory that could never stand up to serious analysis, was accepted unquestioningly by the huge majority of North American journalists and repeated as solemn truth in courtroom after courtroom.

Behind the noise, a steady stream of devastated women called, wrote, and even came secretly to my office at the *Star*, many of them unable to let their stories see daylight (father still alive and in a powerful position), but desperate to tell their stories to someone who would hear them out and not deny their truth. Stalwarts of the False Memory Foundation in Canada proved as bullying and frantic with me – trying to force me to recant – as they certainly were with their own daughters. Years later, I had a quiet and polite letter from one daughter herself, thanking me for telling her truth.

Even more unnerving than the stories of adult women struggling to overcome early abuse were the haunting stories of children who sometimes found redress, but were much more often utterly betrayed by the legal system.

YOUNG BOY FEELS ABUSED AGAIN – BY THE COURTS
February 1996

It's all antique oak and marble, stained glass and leather, hushed voices and an aura of high dignity at the Ontario Court of Appeal. The air hums with importance and power.

It's a world away from the neat little suburban apartment

where 8-year-old Gregory still needs the night light on, still asks anxiously why his Uncle Guido isn't in jail, and still doesn't know that the Appeal Court has decided that Uncle Guido should go free. Technicalities. Legal errors by the trial judge. The Crown may re-try if it so pleases.

The Globe and Mail breathlessly reported that this "gripping" Appeal Court judgment showed how trial juries can believe allegations of sex abuse "even in the absence of anything approaching hard evidence."

Eddie Greenspan, the defence lawyer, exulted that his client would now be free, the poor guy. "His life has just been completely turned topsy-turvy."

Gregory (I've changed all the family's names), a music-loving, friendly, freckled kid who blanches in terror when anyone says the name "Guido," and who struggles constantly to control his bowels in the wake of long-term anal assault when he was a toddler, will always have a life turned "topsy-turvy." When other kids were outside playing, he was agonizing through court, therapy, and long nights of fear. His mother knows. The jury knew. The clinician who supervised his treatment calls it a "classic case – beyond a doubt."

But somewhere in the relentless machinery of the legal system, between the trial and the dry abstraction of the appeal court, the vivid reality was lost.

Gregory's mother, Cathy, a 32-year-old high school teacher, is still stunned by the verdict, and by the way her son's suffering was so gleefully misreported.

"The judges were so flippant," Cathy told me, still bewildered and hurt. "They were chuckling about how they doubted the child was even abused at all." She brushes away quick tears of shock. Prosecutors and therapists alike tell me that she is one of the bravest, most caring, and scrupulous of parents they have ever dealt with.

I spoke to a respected clinician involved in Gregory's case. "He disclosed in the tentative, frightened way that children do," she said, sending up "trial balloons," calling his abuser "Dick Tracy" until he was reassured that it was safe for him to name the real perpetrator.

"Uncle Guido" was convicted after a two-week trial in which the boy, then 4, testified. The jury decided that the halting, elusive way a toddler discloses long-term abuse, collapsing many events into one night, backtracking in fear of being blamed, gradually spilling more and more details to trusted adults – all this added to the "hard" evidence. Indeed, what could be harder than the disturbing details, told in a child's language, of secret acts, whispers in the night, threats, bribes, fear, and sex.

Everything about this case hurts. All the loving encouragement Gregory received from parents and daycare workers is now interpreted by the defence as "leading" or "prompting" the child. But this is word play, juggling in air. People who have dealt with this little boy have no doubt about what he really suffered and who did it.

"One appeal judge made fun of some of the trial testimony: he asked how could you see terror in a child's eyes? Any mother could tell him," Cathy said. "It was like a horrible game." Other lawyers crowded into the courtroom, like ga-ga fans at a rock concert, when they heard that the great Eddie Greenspan was appearing for the defence.

The appeal court didn't declare the man innocent. It listened to legal argument and decided mistakes had been made by the judge. To Cathy, helplessly watching, it felt as though very short shrift was given to the Crown's brief rebuttal. "Half the time, the two male judges had their backs turned on her," Cathy said. "Then they interrupted her and just got up and walked out."

Cathy is heartsick at the prospect of a re-trial and the pain it may cause Gregory, now much stronger after four years of therapy. "But what will I tell him?" she asked me. "In the trial, he said he understood the oath; that you would go to jail if you told a lie. Now he'll know that Uncle Guido told lies – and he's free." Freer than Gregory may ever be. Free to become a trophy victory for the anti-victim backlash, now playing in a courtroom near you.

• • • • • • • •

"GREGORY" WAS, of course, a pseudonym and now I can no longer recall his real name. The boy himself, however, was and is excruciatingly real to me, and his suffering – both emotional and physical, as described to me in whispered detail by his horrified mother – stalked my nights for months afterward. The ugly, gleeful gloating by the right-wing media and by the peacocks of the courtroom made me physically ill as I contemplated their brazen, flaunting power over the life of a tiny child, the power to twist the truth, mock the wounded, and free the guilty.

DENIALS CAN'T ERASE STORIES OF SEX ABUSE
September 1996

...Denial is a quick and powerful mechanism and it takes a thousand urgent forms. For some, it's a wince of distaste and a quick turning away, banishing the painful images from consciousness. In others, hearing of another's woe seems to arouse hostility and resentment. An extremist minority greets every story of sex or domestic crimes with accusations of "male-bashing" media.

Let the sane majority, however, soberly consider the following stories, all printed within the last five weeks:

- A father released from jail for abusing his wife begins to attack his 12-year-old daughter. Evidently, he had intercourse (i.e., raped her) more than 100 times before he was arrested two years later.

- Police warn Parkdale parents to take their children to the doctor if they had any contact with Donald Mumford, who has been charged with sexual interference, anal intercourse, sexual assault, and exposing his genitals. He is HIV positive.

- A beloved Burnaby B.C. elementary school principal, William Bennest, shocks his community when he is hit with five charges of collecting and producing child pornography and sexual touching of minors.

- A Kingston man, Alan Emmet Simmons, is charged with sexual assault, drugging victims, and possessing home-made pornographic videotapes of girls aged 10 to 14.

- In Belgium, grieving families bury four girls who were kidnapped and hideously murdered in a child-sex ring.

- In Stockholm, an international conference concludes that every year, 1 million children worldwide are forced into prostitution, pornography, and sex slavery.

And that's just a sampling from the past several weeks. Dig deeper and you find the Christian Brothers, Grandview reform school, the 500 to 1,000 claims expected after 20 years of "savage physical and sexual abuse" of boys and girls in Nova Scotia training schools – not to mention the Jonestowns, Solar Temples, Branch Davidians, and all the other lunatic religious cults where children are drawn helplessly into their parents' sickness.

When the atrocities are first uncovered, most of us are appalled. But what happens 10 years down the road?

That's when the person who was once a frightened and abused child comes forward seeking redress and telling horrifying stories. Sometimes the memory is confused, because the child was deliberately lied to at an impressionable age ("Mickey Mouse wants you to do this"), or because the adult, having survived things none of us wants to imagine, is scarred and traumatized.

And what's our reaction, now that the victims are no longer tear-stained kids but angry adults?

Out comes the army of deniers: the criminal lawyers, with their accusations of "false memory;" the cynical reporters; the organizations of men's rights activists and accused perpetrators masquerading in the guise of righteous victims. The deniers are loud. The real victims – the survivors of incest or sexual violence – are very quiet. They are struggling to keep their sanity, see justice done, achieve some happiness.

The deniers know how to make the survivors look like pathetic fools. They cleverly stick the label of "satanic" on every report of ritual abuse. Instantly, the survivor is made to seem like a ludicrous Oprah wannabe, as nutty as UFO believers. But most survivors of ritual abuse never mention the word "satanic." They talk instead about weird offshoots of mainstream religions. (What do you think happened to those children of the Branch Davidians – Sunday school lessons?)

These things are done in secrecy all around us, and there are among us thousands of survivors of rape, incest, pornography, and child-sex rings.

How can we stop the damage? I don't know any one answer. But I try to have faith that the flippant cynics, the cunning perpetrators, and the paid propagandists will have to answer one day, somehow, for the suffering they caused, the crimes they helped – and still help – to conceal.

• • • • • • • • •

WHY WERE THE MEDIA so unthinkingly unanimous, rushing into such a dangerous minefield equipped with almost total lack of research or understanding? They are certainly culpable for the lasting impact of certain villainous ideas. "Parental Alienation Syndrome (PAS)," for example – another scientific orphan of a syndrome, without a shred of scientific backing – has become a regular presence in divorce courts, where it is a sharp weapon against any mother who raises the spectre of child abuse.

PAS was invented by the late and discredited Richard Gardner, who postulated that all child sexual abuse allegations in divorce cases are false, that little girls seduce their fathers, that adult-child sex is natural and not necessarily harmful, as well as many more bizarre sexual theories. He served as an expert witness for hundreds of accused men. His anti-woman bias and bizarre beliefs were so pronounced that it astonishes me that he was ever taken seriously. It does not surprise me, however, that he eventually committed violent suicide with a butcher knife, stabbing himself in the throat and heart.

Dr. Connie Kristiansen, from Carleton University, was one of the scientists who helped to debunk what she wryly dubbed the False Innocence Belief Syndrome (FIBS) of perpetrators. Her own studies show that the greater the violence, the longer the delay in recovering memory. Kristiansen's research has also produced some revealing clues as to why so many are ready to believe in the existence of "false memories." These believers, she learned, are also notably more negative about women, more authoritarian, and more hostile to women's equality. "Belief in False Memory Syndrome," concludes Kristiansen, "is ideologically motivated...."

Over and over, for a century and a half, society has insisted on burying the truth about crimes against children. Harvard psychologist Judith Herman, a profound analyst of trauma and memory, helped me to understand the appalling human capacity for denial of terrible truths: "To study psychological trauma means bearing witness to horrible events. It is very tempting to take the side of the perpetrator. All the perpetrator asks is that the bystander do nothing. He appeals to the universal desire to see, hear, and speak no evil. The victim, on the contrary, asks the bystander to share the burden of pain. The victim demands action, engagement, and remembering."

In the 1990s, the era of the most intense backlash against feminism, the militant fathers' rights movement rose to the surface. The conservative media, especially *The Globe and Mail*, welcomed them like wounded soldiers, and sometimes tried to paint the most violent and meretricious of them as martyrs and heroes.

The movement reached its crescendo at the end of the century. Due to some political twists, turns, and manoeuvring, as the federal Justice Department tried to juggle the combustible issues of joint custody and child-support payments, Parliament agreed to set up a joint Senate-Commons committee to study the issues.

One participant was Senator Anne Cools, named to the Senate by Pierre Trudeau in 1984, as a reward for having twice run as a Liberal in firmly Conservative Toronto ridings. Volatile, vehemently anti-gay, and sonorously verbose, Cools crossed to the Conservatives in 2004, but was booted from their caucus in 2007.

The Joint Committee on Custody and Access convened in 1998; by all accounts, it descended into a crazed hate-fest.

LUNATIC RHETORIC DISTORTS CHILD CUSTODY DEBATE
May 1998

...[M]ost divorcing parents in Canada do not engage in a legal slugfest for custody of the kids. About 80 percent of them settle those issues out of court.

And when fathers do petition for custody, they end up with sole or joint custody of their children more than 50 percent of the time.

Yet the fathers' rights lobby and its female spokespersons (girlfriends, second wives, grandmothers) have mounted such a high-decibel barrage of disinformation, and the media have repeated their claims so uncritically, that many people like my recently divorced pal have a totally distorted picture.

That's frightening. A misinformed public is the worst possible basis for democratic change.

On April 18, after I wrote about the hostile fathers' rights shenanigans at the committee hearings in Toronto, some men wrote to me to complain that I hadn't mentioned the good and loving fathers.

That's true, and that's part of what is so frustrating about the way the agenda has been commandeered by the fathers' rights activists. The tenor of their attack is so extreme, and their allegations are so far-fetched, that the whole debate gets shoved to the far end of the scale. In tackling all their misrepresentations, I couldn't afford to spend a word or a line of column space to acknowledge those loving and responsible fathers I believe to be in the majority.

Consider the Hansard accounts of the two days the committee spent in Toronto. In that little, closed, temporary world of the hearing room, the level of venom and hatred toward women rose to a pitch of hysteria. The few MPs and senators who began in neutral soon revved up to match the heat of the prevailing rhetoric. Eventually, even they were eagerly throwing little sops to the witnesses, condemning "radical feminists" for all the misery in divorce.

Sensible or dispassionate witnesses were mercilessly badgered by Senators Anne Cools and Duncan Jessiman, while the ignorant and the clearly unbalanced were incited by them to greater and greater heights (or depths) of folly.

Cools, who spoke often in transports of overweening humility, thanked the men "very, very personally...for the anguish and suffering you have endured." And she was moved to wonder aloud, evidently shocked to her core, about the fact that women may be as "violent...evil...deceitful" as men. This, she said, is a "massive" philosophical debate with "enormous" moral overtones. Above all, she wondered, "What is this fear that grips?" The fear that grips and "silences the country" is, apparently, fear of feminists.

Wendy Dennis, author of an article called "The Divorce From

Hell," about her boyfriend's custody battle, agreed. Feminists, she said, had "vilified" her boyfriend, an ideal dad. "The feminist position offends me as a woman, a citizen, a mother, a human being," she declared.

Senator Cools suddenly took the occasion to muse about women killing their newborn babies.

Walter Fox, criminal lawyer, then advanced the debate, first comparing feminism to McCarthyism, and then noting: "The current form of feminism is really a replay...of the side that lost the Second World War, where we're sort of refighting that ideology in a different form...I don't want to equate feminism with Nazism..."

Wendy Dennis interjected that men get convicted of assault for no reason. "When a woman says, 'That man hit me,' that notion is sold. You don't need evidence..." An award-winning *Star* series on domestic violence last year documented, in gritty and painful detail, the exact opposite. But reality had no standing in the committee hearing room.

It was left to seasoned family lawyer Michael Cochrane to puncture the bizarre balloon of hot air. "Having to listen to that frankly lunatic discussion about feminism is kind of tough," he said, pointing out that, with all the "disturbed passion" thrown around "supposedly in defence of children...the children's emphasis tends to fall off the table."

With rare exceptions like Cochrane, the committee hearings so far have been an insult to reason. You don't have to be pro-feminist to be revolted by the hate-mongering and ignorance on display. And this same committee will be recommending new custody laws to Parliament. That's why I have so little room to speak in praise of good fathers.

• • • • • • • • •

OF COURSE, it's not only in the divorce courts that defenceless children become political footballs. It happens in the wider arena of public life as well. One small boy became a pathetic plaything of the American right wing.

CUBAN BOY NEEDS FATHER AND FREEDOM TO GRIEVE

March 2000

Just before dawn last Nov. 24, in a gray, swelling sea off the coast of southern Florida, the flimsy motorboat from Cuba finally capsized after drifting all night with a conked-out motor. The 13 passengers clung to the capsized vessel briefly and then took to two oversized inner tubes.

Dawn. Elian Gonzalez, age 5, a cute little boy with round eyes and a shy smile, is lying on the inner tube in the sea. With him are his 28-year-old mother, formerly a maid at a Varadero beach resort, his stepdad, and several women. One by one, as the day wears on and turns into night, the exhausted adults slip into the water and drown. The other raft, with two passengers still alive, drifts away in the dark. The child is alone – except for the corpse of a 60-year-old woman tied by rope to the inner tube.

In that company, and in that vast darkness, abandoned, Elian clings on.

Dawn again. Two Florida fishermen decide to cast their lines under a floating inner tube. Coming closer, they spot what they think is a doll or a dummy – until a small hand moves.

Elian Gonzalez, plucked like an infant Moses from the terrible loneliness of the ocean, became an instant pawn in the U.S.–Cuba cold war. From his quiet life in a Cuban town (where his father, a Varadero security guard, and his four grandparents all helped care for him), he was catapulted into the hot glare of Miami exile politics at their most extreme: crowds, demonstrations, television cameras, photographers crouched and running backward in front of him, boom microphones thrust into his face, reporters shouting questions in English and Spanish. He was the focus of press conferences, parades, and a lavish funeral for the seven recovered corpses of his boat-mates. In photographs, Elian's face is blank, his eyes wide in shock. He whispers answers when forced to: "Yes, I want to stay," as he numbly clings to a girl cousin's hand.

As I write this, a federal judge is deciding whether to grant the request of Lazaro Gonzalez, Elian's great-uncle, to overturn the U.S. Immigration ruling that the boy must be sent back to his surviving parent.

Miami's rich, fanatically anti-Castro and politically powerful Cuban exiles are orchestrating this crazy horror show, but it's the American government, and its monstrously hypocritical war of attrition against Cuba, that stands indicted.

Economically, the U.S. is forcing Cuba to its knees, while at the same time weeping crocodile tears of sympathy for the "fugitives from Communism" that the U.S. itself lures out to sea in fragile boats. Instead of handing out U.S. visas safely and sensibly in Havana, according to existing agreements, the U.S. decrees that any Cuban who can set foot on the Florida shore is automatically granted admission — unlike any other truly desperate refugees.

Why the war on Cuba? What possible threat does it pose to the mighty U.S.? None, of course. But corrupt politicians rely on and pander to that useful bloc of Cuban exile votes.

Elian, now 6, is their hostage. The exiles claim they can offer him freedom and "the good life." But if Elian needed anything, after watching his mother drown, it was to be folded into the arms of his father and drawn back into the healing familiarity of his village life.

What he didn't need was to be pounced on by grandstanding great-uncle Lazaro Gonzalez, who is erratically employed, has several convictions for drunk driving and whose extended family boasts an impressive criminal rap sheet. Lazaro's brother is another convicted drunk driver; his twin nephews, 32, have served long terms for assault, concealed weapons, robbery, and grand theft.

Cuba, under the tyranny of Castro, may be poor, but I've never heard of a 6-year-old there shooting his kindergarten classmate, or living in homeless shelters — or like a 6-year-old boy in Michigan recently, living with his mother's corpse for three weeks before anyone noticed anything wrong.

Freedom and "the good life," for a grieving and shocked 6-year-old, is not TV fame, toy cars, and free bicycles, or posing for a photo op with a military helmet and submachine gun, or being dragged off to Disney World for a boat ride ("Will it sink?" Elian asked anxiously).

Freedom is the steady, comfortable love of his family, the chance to grieve in a child's way, and the hope of being quietly nurtured past the nightmares, the rage, the loss.

• • • • • • • • •

THE LAST TIME I CHECKED, a couple of years ago, Elian was a handsome and apparently happy teenager whose father had gone from humble security guard to an elected parliamentarian. Many other children whose hard stories preoccupied me probably did not enjoy such an untroubled adolescence.

It's impossible to discuss the protection of Canadian children without sparing some thought for aboriginal children who, on most reserves, lack even the most basic means to survive and to thrive. What happens to those in the cities – especially to the girls – can be equally grievous, as the following story illuminates. The story of "G," a young aboriginal woman, was part of a long, slow learning for me that every law passed for the "protection" of women or their foetuses turns out, on closer examination, to lead to a severe and counter-productive abuse of their human rights.

DO WE NEED A NEW LAW FOR THE PREGNANT?
May 1997

Test yourself on how quickly your rage rises at the following story: "G." is a glue-sniffing addict, a bone-thin 22-year-old who looks more like an emaciated teenager. She's already had three babies, two of them brain-damaged from her solvent abuse and all three of them taken into care by the Winnipeg Family and Child Services. Now she's pregnant again – and still sniffing. What would you do?

Yeah, that's how I reacted, too: with an angry impulse to stop the mess and shape "G." up, by legal coercion if necessary.

It's amazing how predictably that response is deeply, tragically wrong, immoral, and useless.

The Winnipeg and Family Child Services did in fact go to court and, at lightning speed – "G.'s" lawyer had barely a day to prepare – got her ordered by force into a treatment centre. Soon after, the Manitoba Court of Appeal overturned that ruling. Now the Winnipeg agency will ask the Supreme Court of Canada, on June 18, to rule that women like "G." have "a duty of care" to their unborn children and can therefore be coerced into treatment.

Here's some sobering detail about this horrible story. "G." was orphaned as a little girl, staggered through serial foster care, and was virtually abandoned to the streets at the age of 16. "Sniff," as it's called in Winnipeg, is the drug of choice for people like her, desperate, hurting, and hopeless women, because it's the cheapest trip to oblivion.

In fact, three times "G." tried to get treatment for her addiction, each time when she was pregnant. But there were no spaces, or she didn't qualify, or she was put on a waiting list. Treatment help barely exists for native women in Manitoba and there is none for women with children.

What happened when the appeal court sprang "G." from the hospital? Ironically, the Winnipeg Family and Child Services was forced to do what it should have done in the first place: provide "G." with round-the-clock help, support, and nutrition.

"Mother the mother and she'll mother the child," say the midwives, wisely. In fact, a successful program in Seattle has shown that addicted pregnant women can transform their lives when given a mentor – a woman like them who has overcome addiction – who encourages, befriends, feeds, and teaches life skills. Costs? About $4,000 per year per woman, compared to $40,000 for prison. And it works.

It's sadly unsurprising that a gaggle of religious groups should be supporting the legal action to coerce pregnant women into various kinds of behaviour. It's shocking that the Winnipeg agency should initiate it. And it's sickening to think that the Supreme Court would even contemplate such an extreme violation of women's human rights under the Charter, subjecting all women to a separate, unequal, and punitive law.

Feminist groups like LEAF, the Women's Health Clinic of Winnipeg and several aboriginal women's groups will argue, as well, that such a law would artificially pit mothers' interests against the foetus', and would inevitably discriminate against native women, who would be disproportionately targeted.

Authorities in both Britain and the U.S. have concluded that forced-treatment laws have one certain result: the women most at risk shun prenatal care for fear of being detained and punished.

Haven't we yet slaked our thirst for such punishment? Canada spent a century fighting the native people of this land, robbing them, poisoning their water, killing them, banning their languages, stealing their children en masse and wrenching families apart. Now we want to go on punishing them endlessly for the destructive aftermath of what was done to them.

All women, not just the poorest, are endangered by this rash court action. If the "duty to the unborn" is enshrined in law, authorities would be able to force-feed the pregnant anorexic, imprison the smoker, confine the too-ardent cyclist, perform caesareans on the at-risk mother. In the U.S., such things have happened – but only to the poor and racial minorities.

But any legal argument pales before the simple human truth. Listen to the women, give them the help they ask, feed them, treat their ailments, protect them from violence, teach birth control. Their babies will be healthier. The world will go better for them and for all of us.

● ● ● ● ● ● ● ● ●

G'S CASE WAS APPEALED all the way to the Supreme Court of Canada, where the arguments, pro and con, swirl around the "legal rights" of a foetus. Later that year, the Supreme Court ruled that courts cannot force a pregnant woman to get treatment, and that a foetus does not have its own rights. Rights arise only after birth.

I've watched these surges of "concern" for maltreated children for decades, and I know one thing for sure. Ours is not a culture that values other people's children. Those of us who have enjoyed the profound privilege of loving and caring for our own children and grandchildren have drunk deeply of life's riches. When will we collectively extend that generosity of spirit to those who need it the most?

The year after 9/11, I entered my dotage – the era of my life in which I have doted madly and beyond reason on one grandchild after another and all of them together. Just to look at their lovely faces made the endorphins go zipping around in my brain.

What made this first "grandbaby" column significant for me was my casual mention, midway through, of our daughter's lesbian community. We had all travelled so far from those first days in the movement when "difference" seemed so challenging. Maybe that progress should give me hope that one day we'll acknowledge all children as our shared responsibility.

GRANDBABY HAS ALTERED LIFE'S RHYTHM
March 2002

He was born within spitting distance of the Hudson River in midtown Manhattan, and when he was lifted up by the doctor, he seemed to be flying into this world – arms flung wide, face crinkled with effort, and lungs heartily announcing ("Laaaaaaaa!") his safe arrival. I can't begin to imagine the future thinking of a person to whom the millennium and 9/11 will be ancient history. But it's already clear how the birth of our first grandbaby has changed the world for this columnist.

The context of column-writing is constantly shifting with the writer's changing life, though the changes may not be immediately obvious to newspaper readers. Eons ago, when I began this gig at the *Star*, our three children were in primary school. Because my column appeared nearly every day, I frequently drew my insights and subject material from the richness, hilarity, and chaos of family life.

Over the years, as our three children grew up, and especially since I began to write in the news section, my focus shifted to the more solemn. Besides, if you're writing less frequently, you feel a responsibility to use your column space for pressing issues of public concern. My family life, which privately remained as lively and delightful as ever, seldom bobbed up in my Sunday column.

Grandbaby has imperiously changed all that. I had planned on all sorts of serious topics to be written about while I sojourned in New York for the last couple of weeks, hanging out with our older daughter before and after the expected birth.

I didn't reckon on what we came to think of as "babyheimers," a trance-like state of mind in which my husband, daughter, and I floated around the city, mentally on hold as the baby delayed his arrival. I forgot to pursue news stories, read the papers, chase down column ideas or even check on my return air flight to Toronto

– a deadline that escaped my attention until two days after I was supposed to fly home.

Meanwhile, we had a chance to remember just how warm and generous New Yorkers can be. Cab drivers pulled up mere centimetres from the curb so that our very visibly pregnant daughter wouldn't have to step down into the road. In a grocery store, a Bangladeshi clerk rushed over with a chair and an offer to fetch any items from the shelves for her. A cashier impulsively handed over a free ice cream cone. A street vendor swore to provide a year of free baby socks if the expectant mama would come back to tell him of the birth. A hairdresser promised that if the baby was born in his shop, he would provide a lifetime of free haircuts to the mother.

When Zev Nahum (named for beloved forebears, New Yorker by birth and Canadian by right) made his lucky debut, I was stunned by the force of my feelings. Not since the births of my own three had I felt such a surge of love, joy, and awe at the miraculous workings of nature. I was present at his birth – suited up in hospital scrubs and looking, no doubt, like a blue Santa – and got to hold him moments later. I don't have to tell any parents or grandparents about the beauty: skin as velvety as fresh apricots, hair finer than corn silk, the human body, so recently hidden inside his mother, minutely perfect, vivid and compact with energy.

Life can't hold many greater satisfactions than to see one's daughter as a grown woman, suffused with radiant tenderness, bending over her loved and wanted first-born as she holds him to her breast.

I've spent the last few days beaming so immoderately that every time I enter a hospital elevator, nurses glance at me and ask smilingly, "Grandma?" When I tell them how happy the mother and the grandfather are, they prompt, "And your son-in-law too, of course."

Well, no, actually. Our daughter may look like a shy pre-Raphaelite beauty, but her big blue eyes would blaze indignantly if I didn't say, gayforwardly (so to speak), that we don't have a son-in-law. We have a sperm-in-law.

We've been touched and impressed by the strength of her lesbian community in New York. The heterosexual couples on the same maternity floor seem to hang in together in a tight, time-honoured constellation, with friends and relatives orbiting around them at a slight distance.

Our daughter, on the other hand, is surrounded by friends who are intimately involved in making a community for this child. Already, they are doing shifts at the hospital, sleeping over to help her with the baby in the middle of the night, lovingly walking him up and down as though they were holding the most precious secret of the universe....

Michele places her first-born grandson, Zev, in the baby-carrying amautik worn by Elisapie Ootova of Pond Inlet, Nuvavut. Both women were in Ottawa to receive the 2002 Governor General's Award in Commemoration of the Persons Case.

Chapter Six
WOMEN WITHOUT BORDERS

THERE IS NO ONE FEMINISM. But it is safe to say that all schools of feminist thought have had a visceral impulse of sister-feeling toward women across borders. At the turn of the nineteenth century, young garment workers on New York's Lower East Side adopted the March 8 celebration that had first been observed among German leftists; soon International Women's Day was a global institution. No one pretends that the situation of women everywhere is the same, but we do affirm, every March 8, that we are on the side of women, wherever they are, who are battling the injustices of misogyny and sexist oppression.

I must have written hundreds of columns about the struggles and triumphs of women in far-flung corners of the globe; there was always a war somewhere, and the news reports always left out the anguish of the women. Over and over again, I found myself writing on behalf of women exiled or fleeing across borders toward uncertain destinations, women imperilled precisely because of their femaleness.

A column is a piece of writing that draws a bead on the reader's heart or mind – or both. Unlike news writing, it is intended to move, to engage, to persuade, to provoke, even sometimes to enrage. But although the privilege of having a column in a major daily newspaper gives you the possibility of tremendous power, there's a price the columnist must pay. You can't seize the reader's heart unless your own has already been seized. To move readers to a new understanding, and to move them to want to take action, the writer must genuinely (and not exploitively) open herself to another's truth, no matter how painful.

I learned, in the course of twenty-five years of writing columns, that my own life was both enriched and deeply stressed when I opened my heart fully to another woman's story. Those that affected me most strongly were often the stories of refugee women who arrived in Canada, desperate and frightened, and were not heard, not believed, and were cast back into the deep, dangerous waters of statelessness.

Dularie Boodlal's story not only seized me, but made me frantic. I remember that the story brought no response at first from immigration officials, and that I began to lay siege to the *Star*'s editorial board, begging them to lend extra clout to my plea by running a supportive editorial. I was ignored for several days until I waylaid Haroun Siddiqui, then chief of the *Star*'s editorial board, in the corridor and passionately argued the case with him. Haroun listened, looked exasperated, and then snapped at some nearby editorial writer to "see to it."

CANADA MAY SEND WOMAN TO BATTERER
September 1992

Only a week ago, I wrote critically about an immigration system so slapdash and inept that sometimes only media and public pressure can save a woman's life.

Now another woman is in danger of deportation, this time to a killer-in-waiting. Immigration Minister Bernard Valcourt certainly won't listen to me. Only you, the public, with your letters and faxes and unrelenting pressure, might be able to save Dularie Boodlal and her children from the probability of being murdered.

Dularie Boodlal was a shy and pretty 17-year-old in a village in Trinidad when her elderly parents arranged her marriage to a stranger – a man so terrifyingly violent that he entered the room where she waited on their wedding night and immediately beat her senseless.

For 17 years, Dularie's husband Kenrick Boodlal beat her frenziedly, at least twice a week. He slashed her with knives and razors, slammed her head in a car door, hunted her down in a rage when she fled to her parents or siblings, and then terrorized and beat them, too, till they no longer dared take her in.

Four times, local police brushed aside Dularie's complaints, refusing to intervene in "a domestic dispute." Beating your wife, said a local paper, is a way of life in central Trinidad.

By the time she had three children and no more hope or place of refuge, Dularie was planning suicide by poison. Friends persuaded her, instead, to run away to Canada.

Dularie arrived in Canada in 1988. A scant two weeks later, Kenrick arrived in hot pursuit. He continued as before, brutalizing Dularie and their children – a teenage girl (now hiding from him in Trinidad) and two boys in primary school.

After four months, Dularie escaped from Kenrick (he had locked her in a room, beaten her and urinated on her), took refuge in the Red Door shelter, and reported him to police.

Canada offered Dularie and her children the kind of protection and opportunity she had never found in Trinidad. She worked full time as a boutique manager at the Gerrard Square mall, supporting her children, and moving frequently to escape Kenrick.

But he was implacable. He stalked and harassed her at work until mall security guards had him arrested. He stalked her when she went to an assaulted women's support group at the Barbra Schlifer Clinic, and counsellors had to call police to have her escorted safely home.

Kenrick was convicted three times of assaulting Dularie, and convicted also on eight counts of uttering death threats.

"The police were always good and helpful," Dularie told me. "I would run to the police station at the corner of Coxwell and Dundas and they would come and take Kenrick away. But nothing would stop him."

He would serve his 10 days, his weekend sentence, his 30 days, and immediately return to savage her again. Officials at the Don jail would phone to warn her that Kenrick was being released and coming after her.

Only one police officer at the Coxwell station was unhelpful. He was the one who would do inestimable damage to Dularie's hopes for safety in Canada.

In October, 1990, as Dularie, with the help of the Parkdale Community Legal Services Clinic, was in the process of applying for refugee status, Constable Gordon Upson, a community relations officer at 55 Division, wrote a letter to Al Lewis of the Davisville office of Immigration Canada.

The letter attacked Dularie as a neglectful mother, a deceitful refugee claimant and a lying manipulator who had "a magnificent way of compelling tears." Unbelievably, Upson praised convicted wife-batterer Kenrick as a man "to be believed," who "has held up under extreme circumstances" and only wanted to "return with his children to his home and his own traditional values." He also praised Kenrick for wanting to alert Immigration Canada to "false refugee claims that Trinidadians are making."

Some weeks later, Parkdale Community Legal Services learned of the letter, with all its errors, and hastily phoned the Immigration Canada office....An officer there checked Dularie's file and swore the letter had never been received.

Parkdale persisted. In December, 1990, Parkdale's director complained about Upson's damaging letter to police Chief William McCormack and received a reply from Acting Superintendent Robert Fowler in January, 1991.

"I have investigated the circumstances in which this letter was issued by P.C. Upson....In hindsight, he regrets supplying this letter to Mr. Boodlal and realizes how best intentions can go amiss," wrote Superintendent Fowler. "P.C. Upson has contacted Mr. Al Lewis of Immigration Canada and he assures that this letter never reached him and has not been placed in Mrs. Boodlal's file."

Either someone lied or someone was incredibly sloppy. The letter most certainly was in Dularie's file, and was eventually used as the basis for rejecting her application to stay in Canada.

Kenrick, meanwhile, returned voluntarily to Trinidad in October of '91, after serving part of a two-year sentence. The very night he arrived, he phoned Dularie in Toronto. The death threats he left that night on Dularie's answering machine tape were pornographically foul and vicious....

He wrote her a letter, too. "I am waiting an tell you that I will chop off your hand an foot as you come back to Trinidad...I, Kenrick say so...I could say anything now. Trinidad never have a law like Canada."

In July of this year, Dularie's case was ruled on by the Immigration and Refugee Board in Toronto. They found that Dularie was credible – but that she did not fit the definition of "refugee" because she was fleeing domestic violence, not political violence. They turned her down.

Parkdale immediately appealed to the Refugee Backlog Review Unit in Ottawa to reverse that decision on humanitarian and compassionate grounds. The Ottawa officials were sent evidence of Kenrick's convictions and the threatening tape, as well as letters from employers and social workers who had witnessed Kenrick's violence and were sure "this deranged and dangerous" man would kill Dularie if she returned to Trinidad.

But, in August, our marvellously compassionate and intelligent immigration officials crisply ruled that "there are no compelling grounds to warrant favourable consideration."

Now Dularie can be deported at any moment. The children are terrified. One of the boys is desperately asking neighbours to adopt him so he can stay here.

But it gets worse. Under freedom of information rules, Parkdale then obtained partial records of this grotesque "review" and discovered, to its horror, that Upson's letter had been in the file all along…

The officials' wilful ignoring of overwhelming evidence is utterly reprehensible. And since Dularie's rejection was based in part on a repudiated letter that should never have been there, the decision is untenable, a mockery of the law, and must be overturned.

It's unbelievable that Canada would knowingly pass a death sentence on Dularie Boodlal and her children. And it's illegal. Canada has ratified and is bound by the International Convention on the Rights of the Child. By that convention, Canada is sworn to protect Dularie's children from harm.…

• • • • • • • • •

THE *STAR* CONTINUED to back my efforts in this case. *Star* readers in their hundreds sent me copies of the letters with which they jammed Immigration Minister Bernard Valcourt's fax machine, at my urging. It took another two weeks to change the course of Dularie's life.

READERS SAVED DULARIE FROM IMMIGRATION'S DEATH SENTENCE

October 1992

...At first, Valcourt was adamant in supporting the idiotic decision by his officials. Two weeks later, as the pressure continued, he relented.

I admit to a deep personal investment in this case. After studying Dularie's file and interviewing her in person, I was desperately convinced that her deportation order was a death sentence. I was frightened for her, and made frantic by feelings of helplessness in the face of stubborn official obtuseness and cruelty. I found myself compulsively repeating Dularie's story to friends and family, lobbying politicians, falling asleep with foreboding and waking with dread. When the call came at last with the astonishing news that Valcourt had relented, I spoke in pleased and adult tones, hung up the phone, and immediately burst into wrenching sobs of relief....

"I have found the constitutional debate bewildering and impersonal," wrote a Stouffville man, "but Dularie Boodlal's plight is one that rouses me to action. If we can have compassion for one woman who desperately needs our help, then Canada means something. If not, then Yes or No votes become irrelevant."

It was this sense of Canada's values that so moved me and made me feel that, in the snap and snarl of the letters, columns and phone-in shows, in the cantankerous debates of elected leaders, a deeper dimension of Canadianness is often unrepresented. Your letters to Valcourt were tart, furious or Swiftian. You "urged," "demanded," even "expostulated." Pleaded. Begged. Implored. You raged: "Why not save the plane fare and kill her here?"...

• • • • • • • • •

ONE YEAR LATER, in 1993, Canada became the first nation in the world to affirm that gender persecution is a valid ground for claiming refugee status. Like many honourable rules, this one is often ignored – but I still cherish its existence. It is there to be used as a lever when an aroused citizenry takes the trouble to act.

I lost track of Dularie after this struggle, but I think of her often, and hope that she made a happier life for herself and her children in Canada. The ferocity with which the *Star* readership rose to her defence showed me that there is often a gulf between our government officials and the views of ordinary Canadians.

• • • • • • • • •

THE YEAR I BEGAN writing columns, 1978, the apartheid regime was still firmly entrenched in South Africa. When I wrote about an anti-apartheid activist who had moved to Toronto, the fiery young woman took a moment in the interview to pour scorn on Canadian women who sometimes asked her if South African women were feminist. Freedom fighters, she exclaimed, were by nature liberated! I didn't completely agree with her certainty about this, but I kept her bristling sensitivities usefully in mind whenever I wrote about international issues thereafter.

The anti-apartheid fighter who was so fierce about white western attitudes actually did me a great service; she made me hyper-sensitive to the way white feminists could back women of colour into a defensive corner around issues of male violence – a corner where they felt both "matronized" and compelled to defend the men of their racialized group.

When I approached another African topic a couple of years after that interview, I trod warily – and then I wrote only because I'd been approached by an African woman who begged me to militate against female genital mutilation (FGM). It's possible that mine was the first description of FGM in the Canadian press.

A few days later, I heard that a man waiting for a flight arrival at Pearson Airport had suddenly fainted. When a police officer helping revive him asked his wife what had happened, she answered "Nothing! He was just reading Michele Landsberg's column in the paper!"

Sorry.

Well, not really.

GENITAL MUTILATION A CULTURAL BUT HORRIBLE PRACTICE
January 1981

This is not going to be a pleasant column to read, so put it aside if you're feeling squeamish or the kids are around.

It isn't a pleasant column to write, either. For more than a year, I've had a file crammed with papers about genital mutilation, routinely performed on tens of millions of African and Middle Eastern women and girls (30 million affected right now, according to a 1979 World Health Organization report). It may sound grotesque and frightening to us, but in at least 26 African countries, the cutting off of a young girl's clitoris and labia is so normal a part of life that it is unquestioned even by many doctors.

It's not a pleasant column to write because, along with the horror of the physical act I'm describing, there is the difficulty of writing about a custom that, to those who practise it, does not seem horrible at all.

Except, of course, to the little girls. "It took five people to hold me down and I was only 8," writes a Nigerian law student. "I screamed and screamed until I passed out," writes another. "It was sheer hell."

Typically, the operation is performed on girls, ages 4 to 8, by old women using razors and rags. The child may be prepared for a mysterious rite with elaborate ritual, or taken absolutely by surprise.

Though some of these so-called circumcisions now take place in hospitals, most are still done in crude circumstances and without anaesthetic. The girl's legs are forced apart, a din is set up to cover her screams, her clitoris and minor labia are cut off and, especially in Muslim countries, the edges of the major labia are cut off and the bleeding edges are forced together so that the scar tissue will eventually close her in "the seal of chastity." A matchstick or splinter may be inserted into the wound to leave a tiny hole for urine and menstruation. Then the child's legs are bound together and she is kept immobilized for 20 to 30 days.

There are, of course, variations across the length and breadth of Africa. Sometimes it's done in infancy, sometimes in adolescence; sometimes less tissue is cut off, sometimes more.

The more extreme excisions instantly and forever deprive

the female of sexual pleasure and orgasm. The reasons given for the ancient custom are always vague and always at variance with biological reality, but it is widely held that an uncut girl is "unclean" and certainly unmarriageable. It is said to "calm a girl down and make her manageable." Some tribes believe that a woman will be sterile unless her clitoris is removed.

The immediate medical consequences can include shock, bleeding, tetanus, infection, and death. Later, there is much suffering. The infibulated (sewn together) bride must be cut open, sometimes by her bridegroom. There are special little knives for the purpose, and she goes bleeding and in pain to her marriage bed.

A doctor who worked in Somalia in the late 1960s wrote, "Young Somali women, among the most beautiful in Africa, never smile. The little knife holds a central place in their lives." More than 90 percent of Somali girls still have the illegal operation.

Childbirth is the real horror story. Often the vulvar scar tissue is so massive and rigid that, without surgical cuts, the baby cannot emerge without suffering brain damage, or dying, or killing its mother, or ripping her grievously. Vaginal rupture, and damage to the urinary tract and the rectum, are not unusual.

Delphi Buchanan is a gentle Tanzanian nurse-midwife who works for Planned Parenthood in Toronto. Though her Christian family was always against the practice, she flinches to hear it called "mutilation." The parents who do it "think they are doing something good for their daughter," Delphi told me. Though some circumcised women told Delphi that intercourse was agony for them, many more did not complain, were not bitter and did not link their difficulties in childbirth to their genital scarring.

It was good for me to sit and talk with Delphi Buchanan because it forced me out of the easy path of western righteousness and made me try to see this through African eyes.

It has been 50 years since North American doctors ardently recommended clitoridectomy to curb the "evil" of female masturbation. But 50 years isn't so long that we can afford to sneer at Africans who have had independence, technology and public education for many fewer years than that.

The best we can do, I think, is to lend support to those African women's organizations who are out in the field, teaching and persuading, sister to sister. And to be aware that whether we're speaking of unequal pay, toxic shock syndrome, or genital mutilation, there is a common thread on which all these beads are strung.

• • • • • • • • •

BY NOW, well into the twenty-first century, hundreds of grassroots organizations in Africa are working against FGM with locally appropriate approaches. They often have the vocal and economic support of United Nations agencies, which uniformly decry the practice of "cutting" (its politer name, meant to spare the sensibilities of some apologists).

The columnist's role is to interpret and analyze events for the reader. In my case – fired more by a drive to advocacy than a dedication to simple reporting – I have wanted to arouse my readers to care about some distant rumble of noise in the news; that almost always meant embodying some complex foreign train of events in the story of one specific person. Readers often wrote me to say "Thank you for making me care." Caring is a form of connectedness; most people would rather be alive to the world and hurting on its behalf than to be withdrawn into a numbed apathy.

ONE WOMAN'S DAUNTING MISSION TO BEAR WITNESS TO HISTORY
May, 1987, New York

She haunts the hallways of the mighty, waits in outer offices, tells her story again and again. Government men groan when their secretaries say Rose Ndayahoze is on the phone. Rose, like some restless unwelcome ghost, is a witness to mass death, and is determined to be heard andacknowledged.

Rose Ndayahoze, now 41 and a Canadian citizen, is a Tutsi – an aristocratic African tribe of tall, kingly nomads. For 400 years, the small Tutsi minority ruled the vast (85 percent) Hutu majority of Burundi. The Hutu, a shorter and more thickset tribe of farmers, became serfs in their own land. In 1972, the long-simmering fear, intrigue and sporadic violence between the two tribes erupted in genocide. In a period of two months, the ruling Tutsi slaughtered at least 100,000 Hutu. Rose's husband, Martin Ndayahoze, an army officer [in the Tutsi-dominated government] and a Hutu, was among the first to be killed.

Now an exile, without money or political clout, Rose wants the Burundi Government to admit its past guilt and compensate the families of the victims. Burundi officials (ironically, her own tribespeople, who still rule) have brought considerable pressure to bear on her, and on those she petitions, to be silent.

But Rose Ndayahoze, persistent as a headache, refuses to be silent. Tall, gentle, with a beautiful, sculpted face, soft voice, and delicate gestures, she has a deceptively self-effacing presence. After a while, though, you can sense in her a muted but almost reckless resolve. Hers, after all, is a daunting task. Rose does not have the stature of an Eli Wiesel: the Burundi massacres of 1972, though well-documented, are virtually unknown in the West, and people almost instinctively resist awareness of distant atrocity.

Rose, however, cannot forget. Her last evening with her husband, one of the very few Hutu to have served in the mercurial Tutsi Cabinet, is still fresh. It was April 29, 1972, and the young couple was at home with their three little boys, eating supper, when they were startled by the rattle of machine guns somewhere in the town.

"The radio went off suddenly; nobody knew what was happening. There was a curfew, so we couldn't go out to see. At 3 a.m., Martin, my husband, an army officer, was called to go to the barracks. I never saw him again."

Confusion seized the capital, Bujumbura, during the next agonizing weeks. Former friends shunned Rose, doors closed, blinds were drawn. The houseboys ran away in the night. The bishop at the cathedral, a Tutsi, brushed off her pleas for help. When soldiers evicted Rose and her three sons (one a newborn) from their home, she saw that "the men had a large African basket half-filled with house keys. It was then I realized how many people had been taken away."

Western reporters and diplomats described trucks rumbling through the capital filled with tangled Hutu bodies, and raw mass graves where they were dumped. Tutsi soldiers systematically rounded up every educated or semi-educated Hutu in the country, from high-school students to officers like Martin Ndayahoze, and fatally shot them or clubbed them to death. A special rapporteur for the United Nations has called it "genocide."

Rose tells me all this while sitting in the clattering cafeteria of the New York YWCA, where she has been staying for four months, vainly trying to persuade the U.N. to take up her cause. She is on unpaid leave from her Montréal secretarial job, all her savings are used up, and this week she will have to go home with little to show for her exhausting efforts.

The Burundi Government, now stable, has always insisted that the massacres took place in the context of a civil war. (Historians disagree, though some say that a small Hutu uprising served as a pretext for the genocide.) Burundi officials have even hinted, though without advancing any evidence, that Rose Ndayahoze is not entitled to compensation because her husband was plotting to take part in an anti-Government coup. Rose is adamant that that is not so.

She shows me letters written by her French-educated husband, when he was still a Cabinet minister, gravely urging the Burundi president to stop the Government's paranoid anti-Hutu rumour-mongering, lest people be inflamed to "tackle the problems in a very un-Cartesian manner."

After the un-Cartesian happenings of that April, Rose fled with her children to Kenya, and eventually to Canada, where her conviction grew, over the years, that the story must be told.

The press alone has been responsive to Rose. Governments remain silent. There are skeletons restlessly tapping behind the locked cupboard doors of every nation in the world; no one wants to mention, let alone open, those doors. Canada, not having settled the claims of its Japanese-Canadian citizens or of native peoples, is no exception, nor is the United Nations. African or Western diplomats and officials tell Rose uneasily that "it's an internal matter" or "it's history – forget it."

Our century has been crisscrossed by lonely witnesses like Rose. Alone in foreign countries, they have desperately tried to make the powerful ones hear them. Escaped from the Warsaw ghetto, fleeing the nightmare of Cambodia, remembering Armenia, these survivors buttonhole us, like the Ancient Mariner, with unspeakable horror in their eyes. They have documents, details, frayed letters. They cannot believe that the world might just shrug....

• • • • • • • • •

ATROCITIES IN OTHER parts of the world continued to happen – and still do. I thought of Rose, safe in Montréal, I hope, just seven years later when the Rwandan genocide erupted in 1994. And in 2011, when one of the Guatemalan war criminals was arrested in Calgary, I remembered Alaide Foppa about whom I had written in 1982.

HELP KEEP A WORD, AT LEAST, ALIVE
October 1982

It was at noon, among the bright busy crowds of Guatemala City's finest shopping district when Alaide Foppa disappeared. A brilliant professor of Italian literature and women's studies, a lyric poet, and a celebrated intellectual in Mexico, Alaide was back in [her native] Guatemala to visit her aged and ailing mother. Suddenly, from the bustle of cars around her, a Toyota Bronco swerved to block her driver's path. Men in civilian clothes leaped out and dragged her from her car.

It took only a few seconds, in the noon rush hour of December 19, 1980, in full view of hundreds of startled witnesses, for Alaide Foppa and her luckless driver to disappear. Today, if she is still alive, she is 67 years old and an innocent prisoner of the military goons who rule Guatemala.

No crime, no charge, no word to her five grown children (most of whom have since been killed), no reply to the thousands of alarmed inquiries from governments, universities, and citizens around the world. From Guatemala, nothing but the silence of the grave, the silence of sound-proofed torture chambers.

It is an ironically well-timed coincidence that Thanksgiving and Prisoner Of Conscience Week came together this year. In my brightly lit kitchen, surrounded by the fragrant remains of our feast and the clatter of my family, I received the phone call I was waiting for: an Amnesty International translator was waiting to go with me to talk to a Guatemalan refugee who could tell me more about Alaide.

At first, I had to be taught even how to pronounce Alaide's name (Ah-lah-ee-dah). It struck me with an eerie force: at this moment, as I haltingly speak this woman's name aloud in my Thanksgiving kitchen her body may be lying with dozens of others in a Guatemalan ditch, or she may be panting for life and breath in a dank isolation cell in one of the many prisons of General Efrian Rios Montt, new ruler in a very old style.

Umberto, the 31-year-old refugee, told me more about her.

"She was a woman of great prestige, but warm and approachable," Umberto told us in rapid Spanish over cups of steaming coffee. "She had many friends from all walks of life. Her husband had been a cabinet minister in the democratic government of Guatemala that was overthrown in 1954. The Foppa family fled to Mexico, where Alaide became a leading feminist and critic." She was a member of Amnesty International there. "She always remained passionately concerned for Guatemala's Indian women."

And well she might be. Since 1954, slaughter has been the daily bread of Guatemalans. It was there that the sombre name *desaparecido* was coined, to describe the thousands (80,000, according to one observer group) of disappeared ones who have vanished into the prisons and the ditches.

Though General Rios Montt calls himself a born-again Christian, thus winning valuable allies in the Reagan camp in the United States, his actions are satanic. Just this week, Amnesty International released new reports of so-called anti-insurgent massacres that took place last spring in the Guatemalan countryside. In a series of 112 separate incidents, 2,000 Indians and peasants, including children, were raped, mutilated, beheaded or burned alive in their huts.

Alaide is (was?) a fine-looking woman in the one photograph I've seen, with beautiful eyes in an oval face, a face lovely with intelligence. As an artist, she believed in the power of the word. If she is dead, it is for free speech and for conscience that she died.

One of her poems, gropingly translated by Umberto, goes something like this:

A childhood nourished by silence,/A youth sown with goodbyes,/A life filled with absences,/Only from words do I hope for/The ultimate permanence.

Alaide disappeared in the bright busy noon rush hour two years ago, just two blocks away from the Presidential Palace of Guatemala. In that palace, there is a headquarters for the secret death squad. The room is called The Presidential Services for Communications.

So far, the silence of this communication service has swallowed up thousands of screams, thousands of lives. In passing Alaide's name on to you, I hope I am justifying a small part of her faith in the immortality of language. Tomorrow night, a benefit concert of song and satire at the Church of the Holy Trinity will raise money for Amnesty's work. If you can't go, at least pass on Alaide's name and story. Keep one true word alive.

• • • • • • • • •

A DECADE LATER, and still women were singled out as targets of brutality in small and distant wars.

ALGERIAN SLAUGHTER DEMANDS ACTION
January 1998

I try to imagine it: the yapping of skinny dogs in the evening quiet, the smell of smoke from cooking fires, kids getting cranky before dinner is ready – and then the attack, the shrieks, the shock of gunfire, doors crashing open, people roughly seized, blood spouting from gashed throats as small children watch in helpless terror.

I'm trying to imagine Algeria, where I've never been, because very soon, we'll all have maps of Algeria blazed on our TV screens, the names of towns will leap into our consciousness for a month or two – until they're blotted out by the next war and the next geography lesson – and we'll be chagrined that it took us so long to pay attention. And when the slaughter has risen to its crescendo and subsided at last like a bloody tidal wave, we'll be reckoning up the cost and our share of guilt again. Maybe we'll even greet the millennium by noting our century's special distinction: an unbroken record of genocides and mass killings, from Armenia to Nazi Germany to Hiroshima, from Cambodia to Argentina to Kurdistan to Rwanda to Bosnia.

On the other hand, now that Canada has a chance to send in a delegation to help end the crisis, perhaps we can re-shape that Algerian chapter before it's written in shame.

For the last decade, a new facet of war has come to our attention. It was always there, but until modern media could enter war zones, and until women began writing history as well as men, it had not been particularly noted. I mean the specially vicious sexual targeting of women and girls, and the cold, calculated slaughter of infants and children.

In Algeria, armed Islamic groups have resorted to terrorism since an election was cancelled by the military in 1992. What was a modern, secular state became an open prison for its women. Only 8 percent of Algerian women continue to hold paid jobs. Driven out of employment and off the streets by fanatic fundamentalists, women have been slashed, shot, and burned with acid for daring to remain unmarried, walk with uncovered heads, visit beauty salons, teach in mixed schools. One young judo champion was warned by terrorists to retreat and veil herself. When she didn't, they came to slaughter her family members, one by one, on separate visits – first her 16-year-old brother (his mouth taped, his throat slashed in front of her), then her second brother, then her mother.

Nor can Algerian women turn to the state for protection: the state is as indifferent to women's human rights as the fundamentalists, and nearly as repressive in its laws.

Human Rights Watch and Amnesty International say that 80,000 people have been brutally slaughtered in Algeria in the past six years. Since the tempo of murder has stepped up in the last month, the world is paying attention. But the world is stymied. The Algerian government rages against outside "interference," insisting both that it has everything under control and also that those who criticize its human rights abuses – torture, disappearances, arbitrary arrests, executions – are simply liars.

It isn't always clear who the killers are. According to Amnesty International's observer reports, the Armed Islamic Forces often disguise themselves as government militia – and vice versa.

Shocked survivors of recent massacres have told how they desperately phoned or ran to nearby military posts, where soldiers simply refused to intervene while the flames and screams of the massacres went on for hours, 100 metres away.

Meanwhile, the government has begun to arm roving bands of "Patriots," so now we'll have the classic aftermath of war – vast numbers of young men, raised up in hatred, permanently unemployed and hopeless, but equipped with Kalashnikovs, a religious zeal to enforce female "modesty," and a righteous entitlement to rape and brutalize any female they find.

In Mexico, a recent news photograph showed a group of terrified Mayan women crouching, hands bound, at the feet of armed soldiers. In Rwanda, Hutus killed a convent full of nuns this week. In Algeria, thousands of girls have been abducted and repeatedly raped by the terrorists until they are discarded, mutilated, or killed.

Rwanda is now populated by a traumatized population, 70 percent female, a huge percentage of whom were viciously gang-raped. This was not an accident of war: much of the "hate radio" propaganda that fed the Rwandan genocide was focused on targeting Tutsi women for sexual degradation and violence.

The International War Crimes Tribunal at the Hague has already failed abysmally to make rape a priority, to prosecute Bosnian and Rwandan war criminal rapists, or to offer even minimal protection to the raped women who are willing to testify.

Isn't it time, then, to snap out of this passivity? Isn't it time the United Nations pressured governments like that of Algeria to pass and enforce laws guaranteeing women's human rights? Shouldn't the War Crimes Tribunal live up to its rhetoric and prosecute the hell out of war criminal rapists? If Canadian MPs carry out an Algerian mission, surely they must insist on a searching examination of crimes against women and children, committed by the state as well as by the terrorists.

It's not hard to imagine a world in which armed men .of many different cruel factions deliberately single out women for their worst torments while spouting sick religious cant about women's purity. We live in that world.

It's a little harder to imagine – but I'm trying – a world in which the most distinguished and powerful leaders single out crimes against women and children for their toughest talk and strongest demands.

• • • • • • • • •

SEXUAL SUBJUGATION is the bedrock under our feet, wherever we stand in the world. There's always a substratum – easy to ignore, if we're among the lucky – buried just out of sight. Trafficked women, raped women, women prostituted through no will of their own, women held hostage to cultures that regard them as cattle. Human rights reports and investigations have, until very recently, ignored this mass torture. In a column in 1996, I wrote that when men are persecuted, it's political; what happens to women is "cultural" and therefore not the business of human rights agencies.

Canadian journalist Sally Armstrong is seen here in the Congo where she was reporting on the mass rape of women as a strategy of war. In Afghanistan, she reported on the treatment of women by the Taliban.

Today, thanks to the insistent campaigning by international and feminist groups, this limp excuse is more rarely heard. The horror of mass rape as a strategy of war in the Congo has stripped away the last barrier to recognizing crimes against women as crimes against humanity. But just twenty years ago, many of those crimes remained stubbornly invisible.

Easily forgotten now are the early days of the Taliban rule in Afghanistan, when the plight of Afghan women was resolutely ignored by the conservative politicos, who would suddenly discover them as a burning cause immediately after 9/11.

Within a couple of years of the Taliban triumph, Canadian journalist Sally Armstrong was bringing back the appalling story of their institutional woman-hatred.

AFGHAN WOMEN CRY OUT FOR SALVATION
March 1998

Tomorrow, more than 100 of the world's most distinguished crusaders [overwhelmingly male] will gather in Geneva to celebrate the 50th anniversary of the Universal Declaration of Human Rights....

I hope these bearers of the world's conscience will turn a

blazing spotlight on the worse-than-medieval darkness that fell on Afghanistan four years ago when the Taliban militia seized power.

In this short time, an entire population of women has been plunged into slavery. Afghan women now have no rights. They are forbidden to work, attend school or even leave home without an official permit and a male relative as escort. They are shrouded head to foot in heavy cloth, forced to peer like blinkered animals through a tiny mesh panel over their eyes. Women's faces, say the mullahs, are "indecent" and serve to "corrupt men" –

The mandate of Canadian Women for Women in Afghanistan is to advance education for women and girls.

so ground-floor windows must be painted over, new houses must be built without second-floor windows. Women must not wear high heels or white socks or let their footsteps make noise. Women have been beaten in the marketplace for letting a hand show when paying for food.

All females are caged creatures in Afghanistan. At the state orphanage in Kabul, the girls have not been allowed outside since September, 1996. (The boys, housed nearby, are free to play outside daily.)

The population of Kabul – a ruined capital after years of civil war – is 70 percent female. Widows and orphaned girls, without a male "shepherd," must beg or starve.

When Sally Armstrong, editor of *Homemakers* magazine, visited Afghanistan last year, she interviewed doctors, professors, and engineers – muffled in unaccustomed shrouds, under virtual house arrest – who seemed in a state of shock and terminal despair.

The Taliban men obsess constantly over new methods of controlling and humiliating women. As *Homemakers* reported last month, a badly burned woman was recently left to die because women may not be undressed for medical treatment. This cruelty is routine.

And this week, the mullahs issued a new command: all foreign women of Muslim faith stationed in Afghanistan (with international aid organizations) are forbidden to leave home unless escorted by a husband or male relative.

In a startling cry from the heart, the Afghan Women's Network smuggled out a plea to the world last week on International Women's Day.

"Is obsessive preoccupation with women's veils and men's beards going to remedy the…ills of our people?" the women asked. "The agonized women of Afghanistan are pushed ever further into the dark dungeons of degradation, ignorance…deprivation of all human rights…"

We luckier ones, north and south, celebrating our own phenomenal progress, must hear those desperate voices. Besides the duty of conscience, there is a stern lesson to be learned. Now, when women are making greater strides than ever before, the destructive fury of fundamentalism is everywhere on the rise, and, always, its driving motive is to drag women back, to control and subjugate them.

Israel is a prime example. Although ultra-Orthodox fanatics make up only 10 percent of the population, cynical governments of both the left and the right bought their votes by giving them inordinate and damaging power over the lives of the secular majority.

Now there are several public transportation routes in Israel where women passengers are directed by signs to sit at the back of the bus. [In 2011, the Israeli Supreme Court ruled in favour of "voluntary" segregation on public transit.] The fanatic ultra-Orthodox have attacked and stoned women on their way to work for wearing "immodest" dress. These crazed devotees of the faith have frequently hurled chairs, sticks, and even excrement at women and men who dared to worship together at the Western Wall.

In the United States, fundamentalists (including some openly defiant police officers) violently refuse to concede the legality of abortion. Fully 25 percent of abortion clinics last year suffered invasions, bombings, chemical attacks, death threats, arson, and stalking. This mania over abortion is historically recent. It was fanned to an out-of-control blaze by President Ronald Reagan in his successful bid to lure the traditionally apolitical fundamentalist movement into the ranks of Republican activists.

The Taliban, too, had their roots in cynical political manipulations. During the Soviet occupation of Afghanistan, the United States eagerly armed and supported the Islamic "freedom fighters" who ultimately did defeat the Russians – and then rolled into power with a crusade against women as vicious as the one they had waged against the Soviet army.

Now that they've inadvertently unleashed a misogynist terror upon the women of Afghanistan, the western powers seem to be shrugging off the harm they've done.

The United States is said to be joyfully deluded that the Taliban will help to curb Afghanistan's huge trade in opium. The U.S. is also a strong ally of the three countries that officially recognize and aid the Taliban – Saudi Arabia, Pakistan, and the United Arab Emirates.

And, sickeningly, the Taliban stand to gain $100 million in profits when a huge U.S.–backed oil pipeline is built across their country from Pakistan.

U.N. Secretary-General Kofi Annan flew to Iraq to stop a war and came home covered with glory. Canada's Lloyd Axworthy was crowned with world praise for his leadership against landmines. Now that the whole of Afghanistan is a sinister Soweto for women, we need another Mandela to ignite the world's outrage. Dare we hope that leadership will arise – this week – in Geneva?

• • • • • • • • •

PREDICTABLY, LEADERSHIP did not arise in Geneva in 1998 – but the feminist movement did. That same year, in the United States, the Feminist Majority Foundation mounted a huge campaign against any further support of the Taliban. In Canada, women responded to Sally Armstrong's reporting with an unprecedented degree of commitment to an international cause. Canadian Women for Women in Afghanistan is still, fifteen years later, raising money for schools, libraries, and girls' training in Afghanistan, and providing a pipeline for information.

The Afghan women I interviewed at the time were praying not for armed extinction of the Taliban, but for a chance to build a democracy. They have never had that chance.

COULDN'T WE BUILD, NOT BOMB, IN AFGHANISTAN?
November 2001

Today marks a double Remembrance Day; it is also the one-month anniversary of the World Trade Center catastrophe, and no one can be sanguine about where we are headed. After all these weeks of bombing and political posturing, I still can't see what shape a "victory over terrorism" will take.

John le Carré, the British author, writes in the current issue of *The Nation* that "the war is long lost. By us. What victory can we possibly achieve that matches the defeats we have already suffered, let alone the defeats that lie ahead?"

Indeed, the breadth and depth of the terrorist triumph was bitterly evident by Sept. 12. Thousands of lives were destroyed; the symbolic heart of capitalism reduced to rubble; stock markets reeling; tens of thousands of jobs wiped out and millions more imperilled; entire industries shaken to the core; long-cherished freedoms curbed in the name of the war against terror....

It would be one thing if we could really extinguish terrorism by the war in (or on) Afghanistan. But even if the Taliban are driven out of Kabul, what then? It's hard to believe that any surviving Afghans will be in the mood for a democratic election, or that there will be visionary contenders for leadership.

Even a massive United Nations presence – supposing the U.N. could marshal the resources, after years of being starved by a delinquent U.S. – couldn't guarantee a peaceful and constructive transition to a reborn Afghanistan.

Anyway, we're all being sidetracked here. Loathsome as the Taliban are, they did not create the terrorist plot against America. And the plot's very birthplace – Saudi Arabia, where almost all the criminals in the plot originated – is supposedly our great ally.

How would we regard the Saudis (think of them as Taliban in clean clothes, Rolexes and Mercedes-Benzes) if we didn't need their oil? The hypocrisy surrounding this anti-terrorism "coalition" reeks almost as foully as the burning oil wells in Kuwait during the Gulf War.

My prediction is that two seconds after the "end" of the bombing of Afghanistan, with the entire countryside reduced to a parched and emptied desert, Unocal will be building its long-lusted-after oil pipeline across Afghanistan, bringing Caspian black gold to the gas-guzzling West. Then the true meaning of the war will be made clear.

Remember, just last year the proposed Unocal deal with the Taliban was stopped at the last moment, and only thanks to the ferocious women's protest lobby led by the Feminist Majority Foundation. At that time, the Texas oil barons didn't seem very troubled by the Taliban's denial of all human rights to half their population. And just let me hazard the guess that, should the Northern Alliance replace the Taliban, the U.S.-led coalition will miraculously forget its recent dedication to the cause of Afghan women.

Everywhere in the world where fundamentalism takes hold, there is terrorism. Are we forgetting the Christian fundamentalist acts of terror against abortion clinics in the U.S. and Canada? Just to show their kinship with their Islamic counterparts, Christian fundamentalists mailed anthrax threats and hoaxes to 450 U.S. women's clinics and family planning organizations in the last few weeks.

How can we attack fundamentalism at its roots, if not by bombing?

...Even so soberly conservative a source as *The Economist* reported recently that "as the bombing of Afghanistan proceeds, the extremists are also gaining new converts."

In the years when the Soviets and Americans fought their proxy war in Afghanistan, they poured in a total of $45 billion in weaponry. Forty-five billion.

Just think if, instead, they had competed in pouring money into building schools, training agronomists and teachers, creating rural health services, and increasing food production.

Make dinner, not war.

Maybe, someday, we'll try it.

• • • • • • • • •

THE DANGER OF WRITING about Taliban oppressions, and about women of the developing world in general, is that we may tumble inadvertently into our own form of misguided imperialism, preaching our western dogmas from a privileged and narrow perch. Feminist scholar Cynthia Enloe pointed out, as long ago as 1989, that "male colonizers' success depended on some women's complicity," and some critics have urged that we recognize all white women's complicity in the triumphs of international capitalism. Aware of this difficulty, I sought and eventually found indigenous feminists, in Afghanistan and elsewhere, who could take the lead in defining the issues and telling their own truths.

MUSLIM FEMINIST FOCUSES ON ROOTS OF EXTREMISM

December 2002

Just mention 9/11, or the horrors inflicted on Afghan women under the Taliban rule, or the cruel flogging of young northern Nigerian teenager Bariya Magazu for the crime of having become pregnant, and rage flows easily through our veins.

Rage against the medieval cruelties of fanatical Muslims; rage against terrorism; rage against the male domination that dons a religious robe as a disguise for sexual sadism.

It's difficult, when daily headlines fuel our anger, to keep a reasoned perspective.

In fact, it was courting insult and verbal abuse for any journalist, after 9/11, even to wonder aloud how such extremist ideas and actions could have taken root.

Enter Dr. Ayesha Imam, who has just completed a speaking tour of Canada. (Her doctorate is in social anthropology from the University of Sussex.) Together with the Nigerian women's rights organization, Baobab, of which she was co-founder and executive director, Imam is the winner of the $25,000 John Humphrey Freedom Award from the Montréal-based Rights and Democracy.

Imam points the finger for some of the more recent outrages in Nigeria straight at an economic disaster engineered by the West.

Structural adjustment programs, or SAPS, were dictated to the African continent by the World Bank and the International Monetary Fund back in the 1980s and early '90s.

African poverty, they decreed, could be solved only by extreme capitalism. In order to qualify for loans, African leaders had to slash social spending on health and education and switch agriculture from subsistence farming to cash crops that would compete in a free trade world. It wasn't long before entire populations were, in Imam's words, "immiserated." As public programs vanished, and crushing burdens of hunger and sickness fell on the shoulders of the most vulnerable women and children, religious organizations stepped in to fill the gap.

By the time the World Bank and the IMF admitted the scope of their error, it was too late. Many African economies were hobbled, and medieval-style religious leadership had surged to local power.

Dignified and soft-spoken, her head decorously covered with a white scarf, Imam is a Muslim feminist who has worked tirelessly for women's human rights in her native Nigeria and across the Muslim world, relying on serious scholarship to make her case within Islam.

As I listened to her deliver a public talk, and then interviewed her privately, I had to admire her steely resolve – couched in the politest terms – not to be co-opted. Not by Western feminists, not by inflammatory media, not by eager Islam-bashers. For those willing to listen, she offered a rare, informed perspective that was both more difficult to hear and more enlightening to grasp than the usual fare.

Baobab, her organization, employs 15 full-time staff and has nearly 100 volunteers, all of them researching the impact of laws – Islamic, Christian, secular, and customary – on women's rights.

Right now, Baobab is actively appealing the case of Amina Lawal. The young woman was sentenced by a sharia court to death by stoning. Her crime: pregnancy outside of marriage. A first appeal court recently insisted that the death sentence be enforced once Amina's 8-month-old daughter is weaned.

In case you're astonished that Baobab relies on Islamic law to appeal such a case to a higher court, Imam will wryly remind you that Baobab has successfully appealed seven or eight such sentences in the last three years. One of its rare failures was the case of young teenager Bariya Magazu. The harshly extremist governor of Zamfara state pressured the court to hasten Bariya's flogging, precisely to show his contempt for Western protesters. For now, Imam prefers that Western supporters channel their protests through Baobab, which is knowledgeable about local attitudes, rather than acting independently and provoking a Muslim backlash.

Sharia law, Imam insists, is no different from Christian or secular law in this respect: it varies hugely, from era to era and from country to country, and always reflects the interests of the men in power who codify and enforce it.

Just think of the way U.S. President George Bush, in pandering to his evangelical supporters, has imposed fundamentalist Christian principles on millions of developing world women. As we recently learned from the United Nations, those women will be cheated of essential health care and safe childbirth funding because of Bush's blinkered view of reproductive rights. In Israel, even a secular Supreme Court has not being able to pry the grim strictures of Orthodox family law from the throats of Israeli women. And in "secular" Canada, anyone who has worked in the past to change outmoded matrimonial, rape, reproductive, property, and employment laws knows that the law has always entrenched hierarchical male interests.

When Imam grew up in northern Nigeria, the daughter of a Muslim doctor and granddaughter of a Muslim religious leader, there were no such extremes as the strict isolation of women, flogging, and stoning to death.

Now she thinks she knows why a reactionary form of sharia law has swept across 13 of the 19 northern states in the last four years.

"It's a question of identity politics – cynical politicians stir it up in place of party politics. Partly it's in order to lay claim to resources," Imam explained. "Who will get the best stall in the market, who will receive the fees, who will allocate the community lands?"

Structural adjustment programs shut down schools and clinics, drove up the child and maternal mortality rates, and condemned entire generations to illiteracy. The rewards for religious affiliation began to look tempting, as Muslim religious groups offered free schools and clinics.

"And then the service turns to coercion," Imam said. "A mother learns that unless she covers herself, her child won't be able to continue at school."

Hopeless economic misery doesn't just happen. It's often inflicted by the richest on the poorest. And, inevitably, the price for that misery will be paid by many hapless bystanders. If we're satisfied with self-righteous rage against obvious villains, rather than seeking out more complex understanding and solutions, we only sink deeper into the mire.

• • • • • • • • •

THEN THE MILITARY DRUMBEAT began again, as the United States rushed into a war against Iraq, a war (as everyone now knows) predicated on brazen lies about Iraq's possession of "weapons of mass destruction."

CHILDREN OF IRAQ LIVE IN TERROR OF U.S. ONSLAUGHT

February 2003

If you were a mother in Baghdad, how would you comfort your children as you tucked them into bed tonight? The children know from the media that the United States will launch a rain of fire upon them, possibly within weeks. You yourself, exhausted from the constant struggle to find enough food for the family, have no way to influence your country's destiny under an insanely cruel dictator. You, too, have heard that the U.S. and its righteously finger-jabbing president are now openly threatening to use nuclear weapons (another Hiroshima!) against you. What would you say to your terrified children tonight?

The answer, despairingly, is nothing.

There is nothing to say.

The children of Iraq are haunted by the fear of not getting to grow up, of burning to death, of crying for their dead mama amidst the rubble of their home, according to a report by the International Study Team.

"They have guns and bombs and the air will be cold and hot and we will burn very much," 5-year-old Assem told the team's doctors and psychologists.

"They come from above, from the air, and will kill and destroy us," said 5-year-old Sheima. "I can explain to you that we fear this every day and every night."

The children may not know that the hawks and militarists in the United States are bandying about the theories of "shock and awe," the idea being that they will pound Baghdad with 800 cruise missiles in the first two days of the war, one every four minutes, so that Iraq buckles to its knees in total devastation, presumably shocked and over-awed.

But the children know that they are helpless against the thundering onslaught.

Some of the youngest preschoolers cling, heartbreakingly, to magical comforts: one is sure that she is protected when her sister holds a blanket over their heads.

More than 5 million families face starvation if war disrupts the already tenuous food supply. Maternal mortality has more than doubled since the Gulf War – a "staggering increase" from 117 deaths to 294 per 100,000 live births, the report says.

Mothers who die in childbirth often leave behind multiple orphaned siblings. Household burdens fall on the little girls; orphaned or not, one-third of them are not even attending primary school.

Women have lost ground in every way, with declines in literacy, health and nutrition, life expectancy.

For the children, the report warns, there looms the risk of "avoidable pathological grief" at the loss of relatives, with lifelong mental health consequences.

Fear, grief, poverty, hunger, devastation in every aspect of everyday life – fertile ground for building democracy, or for creating another fanatical fundamentalism in the Middle East?

And if you are a mother or father in Toronto, what will you say to your children tonight, after the evening news?

Perhaps you'll be able to say that you did what you could to stop the war, by joining the millions who protested today, in cities and towns across North America....Around the world, there's a huge rising-up against the war: 100,000 Canadians marched in towns and cities last month in a hastily organized protest. Polls say that two-thirds of us are against an attack unless the United Nations agrees.

I'd be astounded if the Americans drew back from the brink, no matter how events unfold. But Canada does not have to follow them into what will amount to a bloody slaughter. Perhaps the most powerful moral lesson you can ever teach your children is to put your feet on the street today, and in the weeks to come, to say no to war.

• • • • • • • • •

WOMEN SPEAK FOR PEACE ABOVE THE DIN OF WAR
March 2003

Six days ago, on the brink of plunging the world into war, George W. Bush emerged from his Azores summit meeting with Britain, Spain, and Portugal and announced: "We have concluded that tomorrow is a moment of truth for the world."

How magisterial, how godlike, how far beyond correction, reproach, or persuasion: "We have concluded."

If you, like me, choked on the supreme arrogance of those words, perhaps you, too, are ready to question the structures of this world that lead inexorably, again and again, to spilled blood, burnt human flesh, whirlwinds of destruction.

One of those structures is the international arms trade. Sum it up this way, in the words of a current joke: "We know the Iraqis have weapons of mass destruction," said the American official. "We know because we have the receipts."

Another of those structures is male supremacy. A mere two years ago, the United Nations Security Council took an unprecedented stand on women's exclusion from world power. In Resolution 1325, it called on all nations to include women at the highest levels of decision-making, especially in peace negotiations. And it insisted on an end to the impunity enjoyed by warriors who rape and torture women and children in the course of combat.

Only in the past decade has the world begun to tally up the suffering of women in war. Now, everyone from the International Red Cross to the United Nations Fund for Women is documenting the cascading horrors: millions raped and left mutilated, homeless, and starving; tens of thousands of unwanted infants born from rape; hundreds of thousands of impoverished women and girls trafficked in an escalating global sex trade; an inexorable spread of domestic violence as demobilized soldiers bring their wounds, their rage, and their weapons home with them.

It's not that women are born more peace-oriented than men. A quick glance at the clique of right-wing women who enjoy favour in conservative times should disabuse you of that illusion. No, it's a question of circumstance. Shoved to the sidelines of power, the majority of women have the luxury of looking at the world from a different perspective....

• • • • • • • • •

THAT SPRING, I spoke to four toughly feminist Iraqi women who were on their way back to their homeland to resume their anti-violence work.

IRAQI WOMEN ARE CONSPICUOUS BY THEIR ABSENCE
April 2003

Iraqi women are said to be the most empowered and educated in the Arab world. They are free, unlike many of their sisters elsewhere, to learn and practice a profession, drive, and go forth unveiled.

Why, then, have you seen only moustaches, guns, and truncheons in the post-war news? Every crowd is all male, and all the "opposition members" who are currently meeting to plan Iraq's future are thoroughly steeped in contempt for and ignorance of women's equality.

The American conquerors have obviously not given a moment's thought to Resolution 1325 of the Security Council, which demanded that women be present at the highest decision-making levels in every situation of peacemaking and post-war reconstruction.

What a disgrace, because this is a pivotal moment of history, a moment in which an Arab country could remake itself as an egalitarian trail-blazer in the Middle East.

Instead, a corrupt bunch of power-mongers will huddle to divide the spoils. Human rights will not be on their agenda.

Last week, I met with four eloquent, passionate Iraqi feminists, front-line fighters against violence, who are living in Toronto but doing their best to demonstrate and militate against a new and vicious patriarchy now poised to seize power. They know about the old patriarchy. They pitted their lives against it to defend other women from beatings, mutilations, and murder.

In 1991, after the first Bush war on Iraq, Saddam Hussein tried to curry favour with Islamists by passed a law permitting "honour killing": Any man had the right to kill his sister, mother, wife or daughter if she threatened to besmirch his almighty honour. Even the faintest breath of irrational suspicion could mark a woman – or girls as young as 11 or 12 – for death.

...In a country with such an overwhelming tradition of male abuse of women, it would take a revolutionary effort of will to change directions.

But does anyone really believe that government by Halliburton, Bechtel, and their hand-picked puppets will have the slightest

interest in honouring Resolution 1325 and empowering the women
of Iraq?

• • • • • • • • •

IN THE HORROR that drags on and on, years after the sophomoric
George Bush dressed up in military costume to grin "Mission
accomplished!" nearly 5,000 American soldiers have died – and, at
the very least, 100,000 Iraqi civilians (though some estimates go as
high as 650,000). Hundreds of tanks have rolled over the crushed
remains of Mesopotamia, the birthplace of civilization.

Writing columns about these horrors is a form of mental
torment; you can't distance yourself, as would an ordinary person
turning the page of the newspaper, if you have to spend all day
steeping yourself in the vivid details.

Everyone who confronts trauma and anguish has her or his own
remedy for the emotional pain. Mine, unlikely as it may seem, has
been the garden, the backyard oasis that I created when I struggled
through breast cancer in 1994 – and which grew into a delicious
distraction from the burdensome realities of international conflict.

TINY COMFORT OFFSETS STUPIDITY OF WAR
April 2003

The dahlia tubers – like skinny brown potatoes – are in the cellar, but
poking up into my consciousness every night now as my dormant
garden memory begins to reawaken. Is it time to pot them up? Are
they okay? Will they be rotten and useless when I unwrap them, or
bursting with vitality?

I don't like to think about the garden (or even look at it) in winter.
All its excitements and burdens become too much by late fall and
I'm glad to let it go under the snow and out of mind. Now that I've let
myself get seduced by dahlias, however, this winter forgetting may
be a luxury of the past.

Dahlias are the shameless dance-hall girls of the garden,
flamboyantly gorgeous. After I was hooked into growing them by

their layers of rich colours (rose, cream, raspberry, sunshine, wine, coral, peach), I also got stuck with all the fall and winter tasks of shepherding the tubers through until spring. As a recompense, though, I also acquired a new vocabulary of dahlia types (water lily, cactus, stellar) with which to while away the minutes at the dark edge of sleep.

Knowing a specialized language is one of the privileges of any private obsession. I've noticed this enthrallment to lingo in other, less benign contexts. Note how much pleasure the commentators on the U.S. war channels get from mouthing their newly acquired expertise in ordnance. How lovingly they repeat the names of weapons, planes, missiles, and troop divisions, especially if numbers are involved: "F-117s, Fighting Falcons, CentCom, 82nd Airborne, 7th Cavalry," they say, bobbing with eager, boyish deference to the retired generals who will explain everything. With each bit of jargon, they seem to swell with the thrill of borrowed importance.

But even worse was the homey language I heard last week. A U.S. expert was challenged about civilian deaths in Iraq. He gave a comfy little smile and said, "Well, you have to break some crockery...."

It's my age, I guess. At one time, I might have been caught up in the theoretical or historical arguments. This time around, I'm fighting against a tide of feeling that is probably way too simple, and it's this: The men who dreamed up this war and are pushing it forward and making the decisions that will affect us all, for decades to come, are stupid. They are so stupid that they think human lives are crockery to be broken. They are so stupid they thought their tanks would be greeted with roses.

They are so stupid that they seem to think it's a shocking breach of etiquette if people who are attacked respond with "terrorist" acts in their own defence against an army invading their country. They are so stupidly arrogant that they can't even bother to get the name of their enemy right: they call it Eye-rak. They think they can stand at lecterns and microphones and sternly scold Iran and Syria not to "interfere" while they themselves invade and occupy a sovereign nation.

They are so stupid that they choose to send their own young people to die in some distant desert, and think it good. They are so stupid that they think they can "win" a war, even after Vietnam, even after Afghanistan.

There's some basic human understanding of the world and its people that is simply absent from these men.

That's a dangerous thought, scarier than thinking they are evil or greedy, and riskier to say out loud in public than almost anything else. It opens a pit beneath our feet where once we thought was solid ground.

Last week, sleepless one night with my fifth or sixth virus of the winter, I resolutely turned my mind from the dragging sadness of the war spectacle and focused again on the dahlias. Now at last I understand my parents, who confounded me when I was a teenager because they wanted to see only those movies that made them happy. Once you get old enough to understand sadness – real sadness, sadness that doesn't go away after a good cry and some chocolate, sadness that has no cure – you want to keep away from it at all costs.

Well, you can't, if you're a good citizen: you have to pay attention in your waking, working, rational hours, and try to do what you can. But in the depth of night, I forgive myself for thinking about the real, small, distracting comfort of beauty, and the magic of taking something small and rooty from my basement and turning it into a soft, bright blaze of colour when the summer comes.

**The equal treatment of unequals
does not bring about equality.
It only perpetuates and strengthens
existing patterns of inequality.**

Chapter Seven
CHARTING EQUALITY:
FEMINIST ACTIVISM AND THE CHARTER OF RIGHTS

IT WAS A FIERY accusation at first, then a cliché, and now a wrung-out platitude: feminism is white and middle class. Second Wave feminism, in particular, is said to be fatally monochrome and repugnantly bourgeois. This accusation suffers from the same fallacy as the truism that "feminism is dead:" the media choose their angle on the news and, whatever our beliefs, we end up parroting the commonplace mantra. When the popular media tired of (i.e., failed to see the profit in) covering women's issues, it moved on to pronounce feminism dead, and that became the entirely false premise of countless "man bites dog" or "young women reject equality" stories. Similarly, when feminist activism began to stir into life earlier in the 1960s, it was the media spotlight that shone most easily on the articulate middle-class women who had the confidence, the education, and the time to take leadership roles.

Maybe, in our rushed and inattentive lives, we took in only the brief bold-face prominence of white women such as Laura Sabia and Doris Anderson, especially in feminism's early days, but no movement flourishes without the activist efforts of thousands of grassroots supporters and organizers. Behind the scenes, and throughout the twentieth century, women's activism was multi-ethnic and vigorous, beginning with the Jewish women garment workers who stood up from their factory sewing machines to strike in 1912 in Toronto and ranging all the way to the blossoming of hundreds of diverse feminist organizations in the 1970s and '80s. That there was racism and deep-seated indifference to disability within feminist groups is without question. But at least the feminist movement – unlike most of the wider society – struggled with these prejudices, questioned them, and forced itself to change. Women of colour, labour women, aboriginal women, the disabled, farm women, and immigrants were a vital part of the movement, even if they never enjoyed their fair share of leadership positions, media attention, or public acknowledgement.

Strangely, the most prominent feminist leaders to emerge after the Famous Five, who won our right to be "persons" in 1929, were Laura Sabia and Doris Anderson, a Conservative and a Liberal respectively. Although women were active and prominent in the CCF and its later incarnation, the NDP, they were not necessarily feminist. The two mainstream capitalist parties, the Conservatives and the Liberals, loose and baggy coveralls that they were, allowed for women in their ranks to be furiously impatient with their lack of progress and to speak up for the feminist cause. Within the political left, however, which understood itself as devoted to social justice for all, there was little tolerance for political feminism, which was seen as a "single-issue" deviation from the "greater good" – a view which I no longer shared by the 1970s, but which nevertheless crept into my coverage of a gathering that reflected the growing exasperation of feminists of all stripes with the major political parties.

WE'LL SEE THE REBIRTH OF FEMINISM
February 1979

The yellow handbill invited us to the debut of a "Women's Political Party," a proposition just wild-eyed enough to attract my interest. So last Sunday, a day of nose-nipping frost, I squeaked over the snow with about 100 other women to the formerly all-male Hart House to see what was up.

The honour guard of women's activism was there: Laura Sabia, Kay Macpherson, and Moira Armour, all of them skeptical, under their breath, about a woman's political party. "It was a woman-welding ploy," Moira confessed to me, "and it worked. See how many came today."

There were certainly a lot of new faces there, women from

universities, daycare co-ops, business, and the professions, all looking for a fresh and pragmatic outlet for their feminism.

Frustration buzzed in the air as palpably as static. In three hours of orderly discussion, the constant theme was impatience. Traditional parties were brusquely dismissed as irrelevant; the mere mention of "lobby" or "briefs" drew groans; a ripple of laughter greeted one woman who worried about "alienating men."

"I've worked hard to elect all sorts of people...now I want someone to represent *me*," said one voice.

"If I hear about Flora MacDonald or Margaret Thatcher one more time..."

"We need a grass-roots organization."

"I'm never going to stuff envelopes for another political party until I do it for a woman's party."

The concept of a woman's political party isn't new, though it may have seemed like a hot inspiration to some of the less seasoned feminists there. The Women for Political Action – the group which stimulated Sunday's meeting and half-heartedly floated the idea – tried it five years ago in a federal election. They fielded two independent women candidates in Toronto and flopped miserably.

A one-issue party – whether it's dedicated to feminism, annexing Alaska, or defending the gold standard – is doomed to fringy isolation and self-destruction. And feminism isn't even as cohesive an issue as the gold standard. One tough national issue (abortion? nationalizing resources? the seal hunt?) would have splintered Sunday's meeting into a dozen factions.

"The fact that we're all women," argued one lucid young woman, "is not politically...somehow...*enough*. There are real, profound divisions between women who have different political allegiances."

The idea of a women's party still roused some cheers for its aggressive simplicity, but you could already feel it drifting off into limbo.

Still, the meeting was far from a waste of time. On the contrary, it marked an important new stage in the evolution of the women's movement. Long gone is the single-minded crusade of the suffragettes; even the heady fervour and sisterhood of the early '70s is a fuzzy memory. The last five years have been hard slogging, as women buckled down to a hundred separate and urgent tasks, from rape crisis centres to equal-pay groups.

Somehow we lost the sense of focus and drifted out of touch with each other. The big coalitions, like the National Action Committee and Status of Women Councils, seem remote and inaccessible behind their unwieldy titles. Women call the newspapers to ask helplessly, "Where can I get in touch with the women's movement?"

All that's about to change. More than 20 representatives from Sunday's meeting will be going to Women for Political Action's annual meeting on Feb. 23, possibly to join forces. We learned that a new Ontario Federation of Women will be meeting on Feb. 24. Someone popped up to announce a women's forum on unemployment on Feb. 21. New groups are bubbling up everywhere.

It's not a coincidence. In this cold pre-election winter, with the economic thumbscrews tightening fiercely and more and more women being driven into poverty, the fragments of the women's movement are coming back together again.

The phrase "a woman's union" kept surfacing at Sunday's meeting. It's a more appropriate suggestion than a feminist party, implying, as it does, a pressure group with a common economic and social interest. I think a grass-roots resurgence of feminism is about to happen, with a crisp new sense of purpose. Praise the Lord and pass the ammunition.

• • • • • • • • •

AT THE SAME TIME as the short-lived Women's Political Party, international feminism was making itself felt in Canada like a refreshing breeze. Its main thrusts were electoral reform, environmental action, and nuclear disarmament.

FEMINISTS' VISION REFRESHING
November 1979

So often I've come away from a feminist meeting depressed and exhausted, dismayed by the political naiveté, the adolescent bickering between factions, the deafening clamour of neurotic fringes.

Saturday was different. The Feminist Vision Of The Future

conference at Bloor Collegiate, first in a series sponsored by the National Action Committee, was as briskly refreshing as a cold breeze in a smoke-filled room. More than 150 feminists were gathered to exchange new information and to turn a level, questioning gaze on our common future.

Berit, as the lucid and down-to-earth Norwegian MP…set the tone with her keynote speech in the morning. Her sheer scope is terrific; I settled back in my seat with the happy awareness that I would hear no rhetoric, no fund-raising, and no trendy burble about How To Get Ahead In Business. Berit, like the other speakers, focused instead on the tough adult stuff, the environmental and economic challenges ahead, and how women might understand and try to tackle them.

In Sweden, she said, 70 percent of the female population is adamantly opposed to the use of nuclear energy, though only 30 percent of the men object. "The response of the government is to commission 1,400 in-depth interviews by an advertising agency," she said wryly, "to find out why women have such deep-seated irrational anxieties about nuclear power." Meanwhile, 50,000 normally conventional Swedish women are quietly stitching anti-nuclear flags, which will soon flutter from their rooftops.

Dr. Ursula Franklin, University of Toronto metallurgist and respected author of *The Conserver Society* also zeroed in on nuclear energy. "We can't simply tinker with the edges of this nuclear issue," she said.

"We have to look at it fundamentally. Nuclear energy is the prime example of the ultimate structural madness, the fascist technology of our society."

Fascist technology? There was a time when phrases like that were an instant tip-off that you were listening to a crazy fanatic. Running dogs of imperialism and all that. But no more. This was serious, precise, and accurate.

Gerda Wekerle, York University professor of environmental studies, talked about urban planning as a feminist concern. "Transportation and zoning bylaws aren't very exciting, and they're not usually thought of as women's issues," she said.

"But did you ever think that cities and transit are planned almost exclusively by men, planned as though all women are full-time housewives, and that this planning actually creates greater handicaps and inequities for women?"

I hadn't thought about that. Not until Wekerle pointed out what should be obvious: two-thirds of all public transit users are female. Women are the poor; twice as many of them use transit to get to work; women operate under twice the time constraints that men do (rush rush to pick up the kids, make dinner, get the laundry going after work). Yet male planners continue to design idiotically as though all this didn't exist. They actually opened the St. Lawrence neighbourhood, supposedly for downtown working families, with no daycare centre. Single mothers are stuck in suburban high-rises, miles from jobs and daycare. And who ever discusses female poverty when they hike transit fares?...

Changing the world is just what the serious feminists at the conference have in mind....

• • • • • • • • •

WHAT A DIFFERENCE a decade makes! At the beginning of the 1970s, even the stately CBC couldn't resist openly mocking women's dreams of equality. By the late '70s, quirky feminist pioneer Laura Sabia could look back on a decade of stunning progress in which she had played a major role. Sabia, a Tory, a wealthy and tart-tongued matron, and an active feminist, used her position as chair of the Canadian Federation of University Women to lead other women's organizations in a push for a government Royal Commission on the Status of Women, which was finally established in 1967.

CBC TV began its report of the women's demand for equality with a lingering shot of an apple growing on a tree, while an avuncular voice-over intoned, "It all began in the Garden of Eden..." Among the announcer's derisive quips was this observation, "What do women want? Not even women know what they want!"

Feminists haven't changed much in the decades since, but the Conservatives have. In Laura's day, a feminist could be a Tory and raucously outspoken. Today, we have a Conservative government so oppressive that a true feminist Tory senator, Nancy Ruth, told a visiting delegation to "Shut the fuck up!" if we wanted to achieve anything. Vocal opposition, she said, would only provoke a backlash. Nancy Ruth knows her Tories.

In her heyday, Laura Sabia did not shut up.

MS SABIA JUST KEEPS SAILING ON

October 1978

Laura Sabia's husband died suddenly last spring, her four children are all grown, and last month she turned 62. After a tumultuous decade of the women's movement, during which Laura was frequently out on a limb and sawing energetically, you'd think she might welcome a comfy retirement.

Not at all. Even widowhood hasn't mellowed Laura's zest for saying the unthinkable out loud, to jolt others out of complacent hypocrisy or conventional niceness.

"After the first great sadness of parting...I don't quite know how to say this...there's almost a feeling of relief," she told me, reflecting about her husband's death. "For the first time, my life isn't circumscribed by my husband and children. I'm my own person at last.

"Oh yes, the evenings are lonely. But I prepared myself for this after his first heart attack. You learn to depend on yourself and whistle and laugh so you won't cry."

Laura Sabia, National President of the Canadian Federation of University Women, at "Women Speaking", a CFUW event, in Halifax, 1966.

Laura was an unlikely candidate for the role of feminist leader. South of the border 10 years ago, hip young women in granny glasses were picketing the Miss America pageant or making cool, tough intellectual arguments for the cause. Here in Ontario, our most audible spokeswoman was the fire-breathing Laura: convent-reared, married to an affluent St. Catharines surgeon, a devoted mother who delighted in intimidating cabinet ministers by surging into meetings in an enormous sable hat.

Laura, as an establishment matron, worked through establishment channels: she whipped up women's organizations to pressure for the Royal Commission on the Status of Women, convened conferences, and capped her career with her three-year leadership of the Ontario Council on the Status of Women.

Fellow feminists were often made uneasy by Laura's quicksilver convictions. In 1975, she both damned the provincial Tories and announced she'd vote for them. Hardly a week passed without another of Laura's wild witticisms (cross-my-heart jockstraps, or Laura as Pope) making headlines. I often worried that Laura's calculated outrageousness would only serve to distract from or even discredit the serious aims of the movement.

Yet, looking back on the decade, I can see that her most lasting achievement (aside from the catalytic Royal Commission) was the consciousness-raising she dealt out as briskly as a spanking to sheepish business and government officials.

A quick-draw artist who also poured enormous energies into the fundamental battles for equal pay and opportunity, she managed to sweep the unconverted off their feet with her boisterous humour and Italianate charm.

Even if she didn't convince them with her flow of colourful argument, she made it impossible for them to ignore the issues.

"Oh, we made mistakes during the militancy of the '60s," admits Laura without a trace of regret. "I think affirmative action was one of them; all we got was token appointments of very *safe* women. And government-funded councils are a waste of our time. What we need are women at the top rungs of political and corporate power."

The movement has changed. Laura is almost wistful as she remembers the solidarity of those days when it was one tiny band of women against the world. Her flamboyant brand of nose-thumbing at authority no longer makes them reel in shock.

But Laura is vigorously optimistic. "We'll never go back now," she exults. "Only the weakest men are frightened by feminism."

"Even marriage, a foul institution based on property, is being redefined in ways that don't depend on women's submission. Perhaps this generation of women is still torn between home and independence. But these same women are raising children who will accept each other as people."

Laura was a feminist firecracker in the days when we needed that spit and sulphur. It's good to see that she's not retiring to the bridge circuit but leaping feet-first into the future. "Test-tube babies," she muses aloud... "Maybe they're the way out of biological bondage?"

● ● ● ● ● ● ● ● ●

LAURA'S LEADERSHIP in forcing the creation of the Royal Commission changed the future for all Canadian women. By the time the Commission had toured the country, hearing hundreds of briefs and codifying the results (only one elected woman in the House of Commons; only fourteen women judges in all courts at every level, etc.), the Commission's 167 recommendations became the feminist action plan, laying out the legislative changes necessary to achieve greater equality in family life, education, and employment. At that time, feminist consciousness was so far from registering on the public mind that violence against women, racism, and sexual preference were not even mentioned in the report.

Nevertheless, dramatic progress lay nestled like a seedling in the workings and aftermath of the Commission – progress that sprouted, grew, and spread huge branches across the country. To respond to the recommendations, the government set up the Canadian Advisory Council on the Status of Women in 1973 as a quasi-governmental body. It was later to play an unexpected and explosive role in securing women's rights in the Charter.

The year before, twenty-two women's organizations had come together to create the National Action Committee on the Status of Women (NAC), an independent lobby group to press for the implementation of the Commission's report. NAC, as it came to be called, was the most important feminist group in Canada. By its peak in the 1980s, seven hundred groups had affiliated with it, and its vigorous leadership commanded public attention and influence far beyond its founders' dreams.

But back in the fall of 1978, when I had interviewed Laura Sabia, the coming crisis of the Charter of Rights, in which all these feminist leaders would play a starring role, was just over the horizon, and my old friend and mentor Doris Anderson was running in a by-election for the federal Liberals. Irreverent as ever, Doris didn't disagree with me about the essential void in Liberal principles. During the campaign she was interviewed on television and challenged by the program host to state the core values of the Liberal party. Doris grinned. "Power at any cost," she said mischievously.

Doris did lose the by-election, but she had been correct in her calculations of where the power was and how to tap into it. Not long after, she was appointed as chair of the Canadian Advisory Council on the Status of Women, the government-appointed council reporting to Lloyd Axworthy, the male Minister Responsible for the Status of Women. Under Doris's astute leadership, the Advisory Council soon gained substantial resources to research and publicize important women's issues. Though we didn't realize it at the time, she was about to have a galvanizing impact on the lives of all Canadian women.

Doris Anderson took over as editor of *Chatelaine* in 1956 when it catered to women who were homemakers. Within a short period of time she was tackling issues that no other women's magazines were touching. Her trusting readers numbered nearly two million by the late 1960s.

Years later, looking back, I seized on the publication of a book about *Chatelaine* to reminisce on the sweeping impact Doris – with whom I had worked for seven years as *Chatelaine*'s staff writer in the 1970s – had made on the feminist revolution and on our Canadian society.

RECOGNITION FOR A FEMINIST TRAILBLAZER
March 1996

Do you remember 1981, when Parliament was going to pass a Charter of Rights that drastically undermined women's equality? And do you remember how an extraordinary uprising occurred, with 1,300 determined women descending on Ottawa from every corner of the country to demand – and win – significant equality rights in our Constitution?

American women have often marvelled at the grassroots feminist consensus we achieved at that crucial moment. But I knew that one of our secret weapons was Doris Anderson, for 20 years the editor of *Chatelaine* and then, in the mid-'70s, the head of the Canadian Advisory Council on the Status of Women. At the very last moment in the Charter of Rights impasse, with male parliamentarians insisting that no further changes could be

considered, Doris resigned from the Advisory Council in protest and triggered the whole heady outburst of activism.

Now historian Valerie Korinek has written a doctoral thesis ("Roughing It in the Suburbs: Reading *Chatelaine* in the '50s and '60s") that meticulously documents the early years of *Chatelaine*'s glory – unglitzy, down-to-earth, earnest and wry by turns, and wearing sensible shoes – but glorious all the same. For me, it's easy to make the link between *Chatelaine*'s early crusade for equality (long before Betty Friedan appeared on the U.S. scene) and the amazing and powerful unity Canadian women achieved in '81.

Doris ascended to the editorship in 1956, a time of prosperous but stifling conformity. "Those were the days," recalls writer Sheila Kieran, "when a sophisticated recipe was one without miniature marshmallows." No kidding. One winning *Chatelaine* recipe of the '50s was a casserole of peas, carrots, sausage, potato, and hamburger. With maraschino cherries on top.

How did Doris break the Jell-O mould of '50s womanhood? "Well, I grew up in a matriarchy," drawls Doris, humorously but fondly recalling her tough Alberta childhood. Both her grandmother and mother were single moms who ran boarding houses. That example of strength, plus the harsh lessons of the Depression, made Doris into a non-ideological feminist. She's a tall, confident woman who radiates cheerful pragmatism. Her editorials in *Chatelaine* were models of the genre: crisp 500-word essays that captured in vivid, housewifely analogies all the key women's issues that no one else was tackling, from political under-representation to the stupidity of gender stereotypes.

With the '60s, the big, glossy, shallow American women's magazines began to flounder. But *Chatelaine* flourished because it saw women whole. Yes, there were recipes for Tuna Shortcake (argh) and pages of suburban fashion, but there were also fresh political ideas and bold forays into the new terrain of gender relations. By the late '60s, one out of three Canadian women (nearly 2 million) read *Chatelaine*. Those women trusted Doris Anderson – her friendly, undogmatic counsel, her shrewdness and self-deprecating humour, her uncompromising Prairie insistence on dignity and fairness.

And the articles! Incest, child battering, divorce, lesbians, and the Royal Family. Superb writers like Christina McCall tackled our unjust abortion laws. Barbara Frum named 104 women qualified and willing to run for office after the government of the day said it couldn't find female candidates; Erna Paris rated every cabinet minister (A,B,C and MCP) on his attitudes to women; Dr. Marion Hilliard and June Callwood co-authored zestful columns about women's sexuality; Sheila Kieran, mother of seven, wrote "I Ran Away to Paris." The feminist assignments – like the tight and efficient management of the magazine's finances – flowed from Doris. And because she never lost touch with what the readers wanted and cared about, she was able to carry them along.

I joined the staff in the early '70s. Doris was a generous and stimulating editor. We had great times: we sampled the recipes, argued over the most economy-minded contestant for the title of Ms *Chatelaine* (our managing editor was a tireless and judgmental proponent of cheap skimmed milk powder), groaned at the beauty makeovers, worked hard, laughed a lot. Of course, those were innocent, pre-factional days for feminism, and the male chauvinists who ran Maclean Hunter didn't take us seriously enough to try to stop us.

None of us really grasped, back then, that Doris was acting as a trailblazer for the Canadian feminist revolution to come....

• • • • • • • • •

REEL BACK TO the end of the tumultuous '70s: Pierre Trudeau was prime minister, and feminism's peak hour was about to happen. As Trudeau planned to "patriate the constitution" – bring it home from Britain – and create a Canadian Charter of Rights and Freedoms, feminist lawyers and leaders buckled down to pore over every clause and comma, determined to nail women's equality rights permanently in place.

It was Canada's good fortune that a cadre of bright young women, dedicated feminists, had graduated from law school, because most of us find these dense paragraphs of legalese, heaped with headers and underpinned with subsections, absolutely mind-numbing. But here were women who could parse these dry deserts of language for hours, exclaiming with pouncing intensity over "Section 15!" (the equality clause) as though speaking in the code of

FEMINIST VISIONS SERIES No. 3 October 18, 1980.

THE MOTHERS OF CONFEDERATION THINK IT'S TIME TO HEAR WOMEN'S VIEWS ON THE CONSTITUTIONAL DEBATE

THE NATIONAL ACTION COMMITTEE ON THE STATUS OF WOMEN INVITES YOU TO JOIN US
ON OCTOBER 18, 1980 * AT THE CITY HALL, SECOND FLOOR, FOR
PRESENTATIONS, WORKSHOPS AND DISCUSSIONS ON THE MANY ISSUES OF RELEVANCE
TO WOMEN IN THE CONSTITUTIONAL NEGOTIATIONS

WHERE: CITY HALL TORONTO, SECOND FLOOR

WHEN: OCTOBER 18, 1980. 9.30 - 5.00 p.m.
Registration: 8.45 a.m. Fee: $5.00 (includes lunch)
Daycare on request - Please reserve by October 14.

Simultaneous translation provided.

SPEAKERS INCLUDE:

Louise Harel, Vice-President of Parti Québecois
Carole Swan, Economist - Status of Women Canada
Mary Eberts, Lawyer with expertise on Constitutional Law
Lynn McDonald, President, National Action Committee
Sandra Lovelace, Indian Rights for Indian Women
Doris Anderson, Federal Advisory Council on the Status of Women

AS AN ADDED ATTRACTION THERE WILL BE A DINNER AT THE PLAZA II HOTEL JOINTLY HOSTED BY WOMEN FOR POLITICAL
ACTION AND THE NATIONAL ACTION COMMITTEE. THE GUEST SPEAKER WILL BE THE HON. LLOYD AXWORTHY,
MINISTER OF EMPLOYMENT AND IMMIGRATION AND MINISTER RESPONSIBLE FOR
THE STATUS OF WOMEN

DINNER: PLAZA II HOTEL AT BLOOR AND YONGE STREETS

WHEN: OCTOBER 18. Drinks 6 p.m. Dinner 7 p.m.
Ticket $12.00. Limited reservations please call 960 5860.

National Action Committee on the Status of Women
Phone No. 922 3246

* October 18 marks the 51st Anniversary of the Persons Case.

an esoteric cult.

When Doris Anderson, from her perch at the Canadian Advisory Council on the Status of Women in Ottawa, issued a summons to a constitutional study day, these women showed up. They heeded her cautions about the weakness in the equality wording of the proposed Charter of Rights. (Doris had been warned by lawyer Mary Eberts that the Charter looked as fatally flawed as the earlier Bill of Rights.)

Soon after, the executives of the National Action Committee on the Status of Women, flanked by their legal advisor Marilou McPhedran, appeared before a joint committee hearing on the proposed Charter.

The National Action Committee on the Status of Women used wry humour to invite women to a discussion of "issues of relevance" in the constitutional negotiations of 1980. The fathers of Confederation have become mothers, courtesy of Moira Armour.

They read their brief, and they met with their bonanza: the golden words of Senator Harry Hays of Calgary, who said – in full view of the cameras – "You should have a section on children and babies. You girls are gonna be out working, and there'll be nobody to look after them."

I will never forget seeing the NAC women on the evening news, with Marilou McPhedran looking precise, intellectually keen and absolutely gobsmacked as she was quizzed by the hay-seed Senator.

It was fun taking the Senator to task in my column, but, in truth, he did women a service: his retro remarks made headlines, launched a thousand jokes at his expense, and alerted Canadians that something significant for women was afoot in Ottawa.

Hays was not the only male to rush stumble-footedly into the fray. The minister responsible for women himself, handsome, articulate and "progressive" Lloyd Axworthy, was about to make a very big mistake. Doris had planned a national conference on the equality provisions of the Charter; it was postponed once, purportedly because of a translators' strike, and now, with the February 14, 1981, women's gathering planned, Axworthy let the loyal "Liberal ladies" on the Council know that the prime minister would be very embarrassed to have a bunch of women criticizing his Charter, just as it was about to be ratified by Parliament. Doris's executive team, Liberals all, fought with her and then went behind her back to try to cancel the February meeting.

"Now is the time for all good women to come to the aid of

A large group attended the Women's Constitution Conference in Ottawa on February 14, 1981. The gathering, in the Confederation Room of the West Block, was the first public conference ever held in the Parliament buildings.

the woman who defied the party," I wrote in January of '81, summoning readers to support Doris in her struggle to hold the February meeting. "Ironically, Anderson's courageous act of dissent is exactly what qualifies her as the gutsy, aggressive, independent leader the Council needs right now."

The minutes of a crucial meeting of the Council executive were leaked to me, and the hastily scribbled notes were mortifying. They remain, even now, a painfully edifying glimpse into the minds of co-opted insiders.

Lucie Pépin's remarks (she was subsequently rewarded by being made president of the Council, then was elected a Liberal MP, and later appointed a Senator) were among the most shaming: "I thought we are doing what we are told," she said. "I think it's about time we learn how to do things. We have a minister. We are supposed to advise him…We have to accept to do things the way

Ottawa wants things to be done....[Just] because the larger group like NAC [National Action Committee] knows what's going on, does this mean that the rest of the women of Canada know things? The government is very well aware that women don't know everything. I am voting against having our meeting in February. We must keep our mouths shut, no press releases...."

When it became clear that her craven executive would not back her, Doris Anderson dramatically resigned from her job as Chair of the Advisory Council. She went public immediately. "We just can't buckle under to government this way," she told me in a telephone interview. "I've worked darn hard to establish our independence. Otherwise, there's not a woman's group in the country that would trust us."

In 2006, on the 25th anniversary of the 1981 Ad Hoc Women's Constitution Conference, women again gathered in the Confederation Room on Parliament Hill. Front row, left to right: The Honourable Judy Erola, the Honourable Flora MacDonald, constitutional lawyer Mary Eberts, 1981 Co-Chair Linda Nye. Seated in the second row are women who have been instrumental in securing constitutional equality rights in their own countries: Mary Balikungeri and Justine Uvuza of Rwanda, Malalai Joya and Sima Samar of Afghanistan, and Gertrude Fester and Lerato Legoabe of South Africa. Michele Landsberg is on the right of the third row, with Doris Anderson and Shelagh Wilkinson to her left.

But the women of Canada now trusted Doris more than ever, and they responded with indignation and determination beyond our wildest imaginings. A group of key feminists met in Toronto at the Cow Café and decided to hold an informal –"Ad Hoc" – conference on women's equality under the Charter, in defiance of the government. "Sometimes silence is golden and sometimes it is just plain yellow," said the Ad Hoc Committee, commenting on the cancelled conference.

A group of Ad Hoc activists rushed to Ottawa, camped out with friends, or triple-bunked in hotel rooms, and began working around the clock to pull off a conference, in a matter of weeks, with no government backing. Feminist M Ps from all three parties loaned their offices, telephone lines – and their influence. Conference rooms on Parliament Hill were booked, research papers prepared, briefs drawn up.

Meanwhile, I continued to write columns agitating for more women to attend the Ad Hoc Conference. Grassroots groups across the country raised money and made their plans. No one knew, in those days before the Internet, just how intense the interest was. In fact, nobody knew what to expect until February 14 – when 1,300 feminists streamed into Ottawa from every corner of Canada, all at their own expense, determined to have a say in their country's constitution.

AXWORTHY SULKED WHILE WOMEN FOUGHT
February 1981

...There's absolutely no doubt that the Ad Hoc Committee's Feb. 14 conference on women and the Constitution was a brilliant and heady triumph.

The timing was perfect. At the very moment when Parliament is debating the Constitution, and before the Charter of Rights undergoes clause-by-clause analysis in committee – a moment when there's one last real possibility for amendments – Canadian women have met, pored over the Charter, come up with detailed and sensible proposals for change, and set in motion a powerful lobby.

The sense of purpose, drive, and camaraderie was, by all

accounts, exhilarating. I've come back from vacation to hear the excited stories about Ottawa being ready to receive 200 women, and then the astonishment when 1,300 women streamed into the capital from every province, and from as far away as the Yukon and the Northwest Territories…

The press was ho-hum; *Maclean's* magazine didn't even bother to run a story.

No matter. The momentum was with the women at the conference.

"We were serious about pinpointing weaknesses in the Charter," said Linda Ryan-Nye, a conference leader. "It was fabulous to have so much expertise among the women.

"We'd be sitting in small groups, studying some clause, and we'd say 'Hey, we need a lawyer. And a constitutional lawyer would come over, settle our questions, and we'd say 'Okay, that's all.'"

The conference was democratic and flexible (some male reporters said it was "chaotic") and the women joked that they had invented Roberta's rules of procedure, less cumbersome and more down-to-earth than Robert's rules.

The best part, though, came afterward, when a core of women stayed on in Ottawa to lobby all three parties with their proposed amendments.

Cabinet ministers and leading members of all parties gave a respectful hearing to the women's proposals for strengthening women's rights in the Charter. "Jean Chrétien said he himself hadn't realized some of the flaws we were pointing out," Ryan-Nye told me.

There's a hard-edged realism about all this that is enormously encouraging. The 24 Ad Hoc lobbyists in Ottawa are keeping up the pressure on all three parties and are refusing to be tucked into anyone's pocket. Across the country, a telephone lobby of MPs is being organized.

Just a few weeks ago, prominent Liberal women were telling us that women should wait until May to discuss the Constitution. If Canadian women had listened to that advice, we would not now have a fighting chance at winning amendments to the Charter of Rights. Some of the proposals clearly are not going to be considered (like the reproductive freedom clause) but a specific guarantee of equality rights would be an excellent change.

• • • • • • • • •

LATER THAT SPRING, the two key amendments proposed by the
Ad Hoc Conference – known as Section 15 and Section 28 – were
passed by Parliament after endless federal-provincial arm wrestling
and intense effort by women's groups.

By fall, the Supreme Court proclaimed its view that provinces
should agree to the changes. The provinces, eager to assert their
control over the new provisions in the Charter of Rights, geared
up for yet another federal-provincial conference in November.
Women's groups, exhausted from the year's struggles, but even
more determined to defend their gains, got ready to fight again.

Meanwhile, Judy Erola had stepped into the hastily vacated
spot formerly held by Lloyd Axworthy.

LETTER TO EROLA: USE SKILLS OF TOUGH, HONEST WOMEN
September 1981

To: Hon. Judy Erola, minister of mines and minister responsible for
the status of women
Dear Mme. Minister,
Congratulations on your new portfolio. I know there are those
who say that Prime Minister Pierre Trudeau has coupled mines and
women this way not to honour women but to bury them – and as far
underground as possible. I hope, Mme. Minister, you won't be upset
by such cynicism.

I'm really writing you this public letter to offer some friendly
advice from the Women Out Here for whose status you are now
responsible.

First tip: What you do with a hot potato is to break it wide
open and let the steam out. The former minister-responsible, Lloyd
Axworthy, thought he could stick the hot potato in his back pocket
and keep it there. But what happened is that he got a burned
posterior.

Maybe you, Mme. Minister, will be the first one in your cabinet
to recognize that openness is the best policy. That Advisory
Council on the Status of Women you've got there – all of Canada

has twigged that it's just a twitter of Liberal ladies who last year disgraced themselves by racing around frantically covering for their culpable minister....

If Axworthy had been seriously listening to women's concerns, he wouldn't have dared meddle with the timing of that conference on women and the Constitution.

Speaking about the Constitution: Just supposing we do get our Bill of Rights, could you lean on some of the provinces to get the bill working in one year, not three? Human rights have waited long enough.

While you're leaning on them, give them a good sharp prod of the elbow about daycare, would you? The feds give out chunks of daycare money to the provinces, and the provinces spend it on warble fly posters. If we women are going to have a minister responsible for us, daycare is one of the best things about which to be responsible. And tough.

Affirmative action in the civil service is so overdue it's embarrassing. A third of the civil servants are women, but only about 3 percent of them make it to executive level. You should argue powerfully in the cabinet that it's shockingly wrong for the government itself to discriminate.

I wonder whether it might occur to you, Mme. Minister, that our cabinet colleagues have been remarkably mum about the fact that only 300 of Canada's 1,300 hospitals will perform abortions.

Your law says that any woman whose health or life is endangered is entitled to an abortion. Why isn't your government enforcing the law? If the law *forbade* all abortions, and 300 hospitals were doing them, wouldn't you be a little more upset at all that law-breaking?...

One last thing: The civil servants in your new department are going to pounce on you with their covetous proposal to scrap the Advisory Council [on the Status of Women] and move all its functions into their safe, secretive, territory-building little bureaucratic domain. Don't do it. Too many of us are watching – and an awful lot of us would think it was a political axe-murder.

The Advisory Council on the Status of Women is in a mess, but we're hoping you'll give it the kiss of life. We need it working right out there in the open where we can all see it....

Here's looking at you, Mme. Minister.

• • • • • • • • •

EROLA, AS IT turned out, didn't need gimlet-eyed scrutiny. She was one of the many women, from all parties, who supported and materially aided the Ad Hockers, as they came to be known, in their frantic efforts to stop the slide toward an "over-ride" – an added clause that would give the provincial legislatures permission to over-ride the equality clauses.

In early November, the premiers met in private and concocted their deal. Sure enough, it emerged the next day that they had written in a handy over-ride. Not only that, but a long-promised aboriginal rights clause was swept away altogether in the late-night "compromise."

After the exhaustingly strenuous year of intense lobbying, the Ad Hoc Committee felt it had to begin all over again.

CHARTER A CYNICAL SELL-OUT
November 1981

A year ago, many of us had the pie-eyed idea that human rights – and the equality of women – would be gloriously enshrined in the Charter of Rights.

Today, I'm sick and tired of their damned Constitution with its gross betrayal of the native people and its weasely evasion of principle.

Who can possibly care about a Charter of Rights that doesn't charter any rights? The thing is virtually meaningless now that the provinces can over-ride any "fundamental freedoms" or equality rights.

You can bet that at least some provinces will try. Those who have scoffed most crudely at women's claims of discrimination will be the first to protest, of course, that equal rights will mean equal pay and will therefore cost too much extra.

Worst of all, those backroom boys with their cynical deals, trading off everyone's rights but their own, have set us up for an exhausting ERA-style round of province-by-province battles. We'll have to wear ourselves out fighting for a simple guarantee of equality.

One gleam of hope: Women's advocates in Ottawa have pounced on a delicious oversight by the provinces. In their haste to sign an agreement in which they could over-ride fundamental freedoms, equality and mobility rights in the Charter, the provinces apparently overlooked a separate clause, section 28, that guarantees that men and women should enjoy all rights equally.

Provincial functionaries are scrambling to persuade the feds that section 28 should be part of the optional package. If the feds have any concern for women's equality (a dubious assumption, I admit), they will stand firm and insist that the provinces signed what they signed and, sorry, it's too late for second thoughts....

● ● ● ● ● ● ● ● ●

UNBELIEVABLY, women rallied yet again, gathering in Ottawa and phoning activists from coast to coast. It worked. Women's intense lobbying of the premiers made them grudgingly back off. As Penney Kome documents in her book *The Taking of Twenty-Eight*, mainstream women's groups – like the Federation of Women's Institutes, coming to the battle fired up and relatively unwearied – took up the struggle with zest and helped carry the day.

Winning our equality rights in the Charter – threatened twice more in the 1980s by Brian Mulroney's ultimately failed attempts to bring Québec into the Constitution – was the great legal triumph for women in the 1980's, an increasingly conservative era when we were lucky to have a mechanism to protect us (a little) from conservative governments.

But the Charter itself also proved to be sharply two-edged. It wasn't very long before a greedy group of men, fronted by one ambitious woman, used the Charter to destroy the single most powerful and dedicated women's organization ever to exist in Canada: the Federation of Women Teachers' Associations of Ontario.

The FW was a lively source of money and support for feminist causes. It helped raise money for LEAF, the legal fund that took important cases to the Supreme Court; it backed the lobbying efforts around the Constitution; it funded hundreds of feminist meetings, conferences, films, books, and research reports; it produced sparkling materials for schools about women's rights and women's history; it supported gun control, gave women teachers scholarships to teach leadership skills abroad, fought for better pensions for women, and promoted the careers and interests of tens of thousands of women teachers, helping crash through barriers erected by the men in power.

The FW was a pioneer in fighting for equity and social justice issues; it was out front in its ten-year struggle for better child care; another decade of effort went into naming and battling violence against women. FW, as it was affectionately known, gave all of us confidence and courage – it was so big, so intelligent, and so strong.

When people talk about why the National Action Committee on the Status of Women finally lapsed into insignificance, or why the women's movement began to lose steam, the crushing of FW is one of the reasons that remains largely unremarked.

THE CHARTER: HERALD OF FAIRNESS OR WEAPON AGAINST WOMEN?
May 1987

As our Charter of Rights and Freedoms wends its way through the courts, its shape and meaning becoming clearer with each new decision, a fearful suspicion grows. What if the Charter is a cheat, a weapon to be used against the women and minorities who most ardently welcomed it?

An alarming case coming before the Supreme Court of Ontario will be a crucial indicator.

This week, the men teachers' federation in Ontario launches an assault on the right of the women teachers' federation to exist in its traditional, time-honoured form. They mount their attack under the banner of the Charter's "equal rights" clause, a twist that may embitter but should not surprise us.

For the past two years, hundreds of men have rushed to court, under that same banner, and aggressively attacked women's tenuous rights and hard-won legal protections. In shock, women have watched while men use the Charter to assail a rape victim's right to anonymity, a single mother's right to family benefits, a divorced mother's right to child support.

Like most of the other "male rights" cases, the men teachers' suit presents itself in the guise of equality, fairness, and freedom. Those are words to which Canadians respond viscerally. But look again: is it really fair to treat two radically unequal contenders with strict evenhandedness? We would not dream of doing that in a foot race. Men and women are not yet equal in our society. To insist on a lofty gender neutrality in law, when gender bias still handicaps women in real life, is to enshrine an unjust status quo. The Charter itself, in fact, in protecting affirmative action programs, recognizes that the disadvantaged need special tools.

The Federation of Women Teachers' Associations of Ontario is among the more powerful of those tools. It has fought doggedly and often brilliantly for fairness for women since 1918 and, despite much progress, has a long way to go: women are 68.4 percent of the primary school teachers in Ontario, but only 10.6 percent of the principals. And even that number was achieved only through the FW's persistent lobbying.

The current case involves Margaret Toman, an Ontario public-school principal, who wants to have the "freedom of choice" to join the Ontario Public School Teachers' Federation, formerly known as the Ontario Public School Men Teachers' Federation.

fw
ta
o

The Abused And Battered Child

A COMMITTEE REPORT
PREPARED BY
PATRICIA CARSON, CHAIRPERSON
ELIZABETH BULMER
PATRICIA CHAPMAN
RITA CRAIGEN
RUBY DUNS
PHYLLIS IVANOFF

FOR

Federation of Women Teachers' Associations of Ontario
AUGUST 1976

The Federation of Women Teachers' Associations of Ontario was a leader in the struggle for justice and equity for women and children. In 1976, the FW produced this hard-hitting report on child abuse.

Under Ontario law, teachers are automatically assigned membership in one of five teachers' federations...women's, men's, Catholic, secondary, and French.

Now the men's federation, the OPSTF, is going to court to argue, under the Charter, that women teachers should not have to belong to the FW. Mrs. Toman, they say, should be "unshackled" from the women's federation – and so should all other women teachers – and be free to join the men teachers.

The men say the Ontario law discriminates against women by assigning them to a federation on the basis of gender. Note the hypocrisy: the men do not object to men being assigned to OPSTF on the basis of gender.

Should they win, their own union would remain intact.

Mrs. Toman, as it happens, is perfectly free to join the men's OPSTF as a "voluntary member," which she has done. Furthermore, as a woman principal, she continues to enjoy the fruits of 60 years of struggle by the FW.

The OPSTF is no noble champion of women. As recently as 1985, the men vowed openly to fight "in the strongest possible manner" any recognition or recompense of past discrimination against women, a vow they hastily dropped when they launched this case.

Even more revealingly, the men have always campaigned to amalgamate with the much larger women teachers' federation, and, just as adamantly, the women have refused. What the men are doing now is trying to force on the women, through legal action, what the women have always democratically voted against.

What is the OPSTF after? I think it is cynical of them to present themselves as passionate crusaders for freedom; to me, it looks more like a good old-fashioned case of union-raiding. The women's federation has 32,000 members to the OPSTF's 14,000. That is a lot of dues money. And, as the men must know, women would be swallowed up in the OPSTF. Numerous studies show that in existing mixed-sex teacher unions, the men dominate discussion, policy-making and executive posts; women's issues get ignored. An amalgamation, in this case, would amount to a takeover.

The FW has fought for equal pay, equal opportunities, maternity leave, non-sexist curricula...all the burning issues that only a women's organization takes seriously on behalf of its members. Gradually, they are gaining ground. In the next five years, 300 to 400 principals will retire. Thanks to the FW's leadership training programs and its affirmative action plans – bitterly opposed by the men for years – women will be in a position to step into a fair number of those jobs.

Except. Except if the FW suddenly has its statutory legs cut out from under it. Which is exactly what will happen if the OPSTF is successful in its court case.

The truth is, the men's federation is made up largely of principals, vice-principals and would-be principals – at the very least, men with a stake in keeping principalships clear for men. The women's federation is made up of classroom and kindergarten teachers, and has very different interests and goals for its members, including pension bridging rights (opposed by the men) that are important for women teachers who take time out for maternity.

The case of the men teachers versus the women will help define our country's progress. If the Charter can really be used to strengthen those who already have unfair advantages, it will be a knife in the heart of women's hope for equality.

• • • • • • • • •

THE BATTLE TO devour FW dragged through tribunals and courts for a decade until the men finally won. Facing the possibility of draconian new labour laws that the union-hostile government of Mike Harris might impose, FW finally voted to merge with the men teachers and become the Elementary Teachers' Federation of Ontario. Although the agreement between the two unions required that a certain number of leadership roles and program funding be set aside for women, the outcome was exactly what was predicted. The men in the union continue to control a disproportionate number of the top positions, and although equity and social justice programs continue, there is not the same powerful energy, imagination, and motivation behind them. The women have to face resentful annual attacks from male members who challenge their right to the percent set-aside for women's programming. Tellingly, although 81 percent of ETFO members are women, one report noted that only 71 percent of the executive is female, and of that number, only 58 percent spoke at meetings.

By the end of the '80s, women – led by Judy Rebick, president of NAC at that time – had to fight yet another bewilderingly complex constitutional issue, this time the Meech Lake Accord, designed by Brian Mulroney to bring Québec into the Constitution. He offered Québec the status of a "distinct society," as well as a general provincial opt–out from federal social programmes. NAC saw Meech as a direct threat to federal guarantees of equality; Québec feminists, who were nationalists first, vehemently disagreed. In a classic diversionary skirmish ("Let's you and her fight"), columnist (and non-feminist) Lysianne Gagnon accused Anglo feminists of being anti-Québec in their efforts to safeguard equality rights.

MACHO SMARM DOMINATED MEECH TV GIG

June 1990

MuchMeech.

Much too much Meech, in fact.

I don't want to play bad fairy at the christening, but I've never seen television so thoroughly emetic as the three-hour signing conference.

If we were going to have to sit through such a queasy wallow of self-congratulation, CBC ought to have issued barf bags right at the start of the trip. You'd think those "first ministers," as they constantly called themselves, had just emerged from a week-long encounter group in a sauna, all pink and hot and quivering with emotion.

Well, on second thought, not pink, but white. Eleven men, all looking white, white, white as Wonder Bread, buttoned into their navy or charcoal suits and bursting with smugness about the multicultural mosaic.

Somewhere along the path of the past decade or so in the women's movement, it stopped looking normal to me to see 11 men on a platform and not a single woman in sight. Now it looks downright peculiar. Unbalanced, unseemly and unfair.

There's surely never been an occasion so soaked in male bonding. We heard about the Fathers of Confederation and God the Father and how Don Getty is a terrific quarterback; we heard about fellow ministers and fellow Canadians and these wonderful 11 men in the room, and we heard them sing "In all thy sons' command" and it all seemed ludicrous.

New Brunswick's Frank McKenna took the cake when he praised his deputy premier: "Not only a woman, but a Canadian, too."

Gosh, wow. You mean, you can be both?

And where did they learn their style, from watching too many late-night talk shows? What a scene: 11 men slathering each other in smarm like so much marmalade. "And Gary, you were just terrific." "David, what a statesman, what a guy." The Johnny Carson School of Mutual Hype: "Honestly, Bri, I think you're just the funniest guy in show biz...no, really, folks, wait a minute, I mean it..."

Premier Vander Zalm gave us a soppy, interminable, account of his first meeting with Canadian soldiers, how his mother washed the guy's laundry, how all the Vander Zalms came to Canada and drove across it in a station wagon until they got to B.C. – where, I reflected, he was going to grow up and get a God-given chance to kick the bejeezus out of welfare mothers.

Clyde Wells spoke with forked tongue, mentioning the word "sincere" about 14 times before flying home to Newfoundland and telling the world that he didn't actually sign the thing after all.

They all looked very satisfied with themselves, thinking how this TV gig was going to wrap up the next election for them.

And they all told each other that they stood tall. Oh boy, were they tall. What's with this tall business? Is being tall a condition of writing a constitution? Or have they caught the John Wayne virus?...

• • • • • • • • •

THE MEECH LAKE ACCORD required unanimous ratification by each province in order to pass. The country was ferociously divided; according to polls, a majority of Canadians opposed it. NAC furiously rejected not only the high-handed, closed door, all-male process of such major reform, but also the prioritizing of Québec over aboriginal rights.

How shocking, how deeply satisfying, it was when, in June of 1990, MLA Elijah Harper, in Manitoba, stood holding an eagle feather to vote against the Meech Lake Accord – a constitutional pact drawn up with no contribution from aboriginal groups. After all that drawn-out wrangling and palaver, Elijah Harper put Meech out of its misery with quiet dignity.

Within two years, however, Brian Mulroney was back at it with his Charlottetown Accord, fancying himself a new Father of

Confederation. This time, too, women (especially aboriginal women, as represented by the Native Women's Association of Canada) were entirely excluded from the process. From the outside, NAC fought a sturdy battle against the "hierarchy of rights" and the provincial control over social programs, proposed by the Accord. This time, the Charlottetown Accord would be voted on by the people of Canada in a referendum.

SON OF MEECH SENATE DEAL LEAVES WOMEN OUT IN THE COLD
July 1992

We fought, argued, pleaded, lobbied. We spent thousands of woman-hours making the case for equality at those inspiring constitutional conferences last winter. Women – including aboriginal women – forged innovative proposals for keeping Québec in Canada while advancing the equality rights of more than half the Canadian population.

And then, as though all that good "inclusive" stuff had never happened, the nine premiers went into their private room, closed the doors, and made a deal – again.

We've been Meeched and re-Meeched.

Women's representatives were given exactly 20 minutes to enter the sacred chamber of the men to make their arguments. (The National Action Committee on the Status of Women, the Native Women's Association of Canada and the National Organization of Immigrant and Visible Minority Women shared that precious one-third of an hour.)

"Who's at the table determines what is decided," summed up a weary Judy Rebick, chair of the National Action Committee, as we began to hear the details of the preposterous Triple-E Senate deal.

Native men were promised the right to self-government and the right to opt out of the Charter of Rights. Native women got nothing, despite the stark evidence of massive inequality.

Provinces got the right to opt out of any new national social programs. Can you think of any possible new national program aside from child care? No, neither can I. The new deal, then, is the final nail in the coffin of a desperately needed national child care plan.

We should have tied a boulder around the Senate and sunk it once and for all. Instead, a new and ridiculously undemocratic Senate rises from the ashes, more powerful than before and, by the very terms of the deal, unchangeable. Fixed. Written in stone. If this deal passes, each province will have a veto over institutional change forever. That means that the 100,000-odd voters of Prince Edward Island (about 1 percent the size of Ontario) will be able to kill any proposal for Senate reform in the future.

What possessed the premiers? Was it folie à neuf, mass self-hypnosis, the fever of insularity that happens behind closed doors? How could Canadians accept a Senate in which, as a *Star* editorial pointed out, a mere 13 percent of the population may one day thwart the will of the House of Commons, leaving Ontario, Québec, and British Columbia paralyzed?

If we were going to be saddled with a Senate (and who needs two elected bodies?), the very least we should have had was a truly representative upper house, one that would give women and minorities a strong voice.

Judy Rebick, on behalf of the National Action Committee, had pressed for a commitment that the Senate would be 50 percent women. This was brushed off by most of the guys as "undemocratic." Words fail me.

If women had been at the table, we might have ended up with a sensible system of proportional voting in which each party would be required to present a gender-balanced list of candidates. (That's how Norway ended up with one of the most representative governments in the world.)

Instead, the premiers picked the one "proportional" system which can't possibly help women overcome our political disadvantage. There will be no party lists, said Joe Clark, thus eliminating the hope of putting pressure on the political parties to run more women. When we go to vote for our silly Senate, we'll have to vote for eight province-wide candidates (out of a welter of at least 25 or 30 names) and rank them in order of preference...

...the final wording was a terse mention of the "equality of women and men" in the Canada clause. As women's groups tried to explain again and again to the obviously distracted and indifferent premiers, such a bald statement could actually harm women's fight for equality. As the Supreme Court has pointed out, "same treatment" equality for unequal parties can work to women's disadvantage.

There's a further bitter irony in this Son of Meech mess. Just a couple of weeks ago, an Angus Reid poll determined that 56 percent of Canadians and 70 percent of Québecers thought women's views on the Constitution (as represented by the National Action Committee) were important. That's higher than even the highest-ranked politicians.

But women weren't at the table. So Alberta, the poor little rich province, got to turn Canada upside down to give itself more power. And women, more than half the population, got nothing.

• • • • • • • • • •

AS THE CONSTITUTIONAL waters roiled, yet again, a new snag loomed larger and larger. It became clear that the leading native women's organization had been completely sidelined from the discussions, while new rights and powers were being granted to the all-male native associations. NAC – and, surprise, the Federal Court of Appeal – insisted on the Native Women's Association's right to be included. The Supreme Court, sadly, over-turned that ruling.

At least it's a lovely symmetry that the final nail in the coffin of the Charlottetown Accord was public indignation about the raw, naked injustice being dealt to aboriginal women. After all, some of the first constitutional issues that alarmed Canadian women concerned Indian women and the harms done them under the Indian Act. Sandra Lovelace, Karen Perley, and Mary Two-Axe Early had joined a march of other Indian women to Ottawa in 1979, protesting the section of the Indian Act that extinguished their Indian status if they married non-Indians – while the same rule did not apply to Indian men.

PREMIERS FEAST WHILE WOMEN ARE TREATED TO THE SCRAPS

August 1992

Okay, I get it. Québec is going to have 25 percent of the power in Parliament and the Senate "for all eternity," as Robert Bourassa puts it, because that's how much of the population they represent.

Fine. Terrific. I'm led to understand that this is historically justified and morally correct.

But women can't have a guarantee of representation by population because that would be a quota. Unfair. Discriminatory. That's what the honourable dignitaries said.

Is there something wrong with this picture? Is there something out of focus about a bunch of guys carving up the golden goose of rights and powers, serving up the goodies to each other and crowing about the wonders of the New Canada – while overlooking (whoops) half the population?

We're out here in the kitchen, boys. Hope you're enjoying the banquet.

Oh, you say that we haven't really been left out because, after all, you represent us? Tell that to your granny. She was so well represented that she had to go to the British Privy Council to be acknowledged as a "person."

We're not doing that much better today. Premier Bob Rae did promise to reserve half of Ontario's Senate seats for women – but a verbal promise is a long way from a constitutional agreement to remedy inequality (16 women in the 104-seat Senate; 37 women out of 295 MPs). It seems the only way to nail down your rights and secure your privileges is to have your elbows on the table and be arguing for your own interests. And we women weren't invited.

Speaking of not being invited, what an extraordinary coincidence that was. On the very day that the premiers concluded their constitutional deal, the Federal Court of Appeal ruled that the Canadian government had discriminated against aboriginal women by denying them a place at the table.

The Court said that the government had given unfair privilege to "the male-dominated aboriginal self-governments" and had thereby restricted the aboriginal women's freedom of speech "in a manner offensive to the Charter of Rights."

Nice timing. Just when the party's over, the ticket of admission arrives.

Undaunted, the leaders of the Native Women's Association of Canada (NWAC), who had taken the case to court, flew off to Charlottetown to demand their rightful place at the talks.

Their position is iron-clad. The Court agreed that NWAC, and not the Assembly of First Nations, truly represents aboriginal women. Sure, the media made much of the fact that three Inuit "mothers of confederation" were included in the talks.

That was wonderful. But that still leaves 52 percent of the population unrepresented. NWAC should have been there, along with the National Action Committee on the Status of Women, which speaks for millions of Canadian women.

• • • • • • • • •

THE CONSTITUTIONAL DEBATE did have a light side. It was fun to mock the Tories' revealingly bigoted banter. In October, I recorded the following witticism from one of Mulroney's ministers:

John Crosbie blithely told Judy Rebick that women couldn't be at the negotiating table because then all the other 'special interest groups' – like 'coloureds and cripples' would have to be there, too.

Coloureds and cripples?

And this gang of ethically challenged mooks (a special interest group if ever there was one) makes fun of the 'No' side? Have we gone through the looking-glass here?"

In the October 1992 referendum, Canadians voted to reject the Charlottetown Accord. The exhaustion, the tedium, the blatant unfairness of the various constitutional processes that soaked up so much energy during the 1980s, left Canadians – both women and men – with a groaning reluctance ever to hear the word "constitution" again. It's also a humiliating footnote to women's heroic efforts in the referendum to point out that most of the historic overviews of the vote completely ignore the contribution made by NAC and by women.

In the end, our victory in securing and protecting the Charter of Rights' equality provisions was significant and salutary. Without it, we might not have had the joyful moment in 1988 when the

Supreme Court, in the Morgentaler decision, struck down the laws against abortion, because they violated women's Charter rights. In a way, though, the Charter fight was also a negative victory. We had to expend that much energy, because a Charter was going to be foisted on the country whether we liked it or not, and if we didn't enshrine women's equality rights, we would have been left with the injuriously feeble "equality for all" promise that had previously worked against women in the earlier Bill of Rights. (For example, in 1979 under the Bill of Rights, the Supreme Court ruled that it was not discrimination when Stella Bliss was denied unemployment benefits since it was only because she was pregnant, not because she was female. A decade later, under the Charter, the Supremes had to reverse that absurdity.)

The Charter of Rights was also a rallying call for Canadian women to be more active in the public life of our country. When men alone make and enforce the laws, women are constantly and severely discriminated against.

Toward the end of the original Charter struggle, I paused to reflect on some of the sharp political lessons we had absorbed through our strenuous and sometimes maddening efforts.

HELP WAGE WAR FOR WOMEN'S EQUALITY
November 1981

It's been an extraordinary two weeks. Never before in Canada's history has the moral authority of women stood so high. Never before have so few women accomplished so much on behalf of so many. Never before have the political lessons we must learn been so starkly clear.

Lesson Number One: We can't rely on men of any party to safeguard our rights. The Kitchen Constitution, concocted by amateur chefs Jean Chrétien (Liberal), Roy Romanow (NDP), and Roy McMurtry (Tory) showed that all three parties were capable of brushing off equality rights as casually as they might swat a fly.

The Charter of Rights came out of that kitchen looking as shrunken and useless as a boiled wool sock, yet the potboy premiers didn't hesitate to endorse it.

Lesson Number Two: It really does help, despite my long-standing cynical conviction to the contrary, to have women in every political caucus.

It was Flora MacDonald (Tory) and Pauline Jewett (NDP) who sounded the alarm about Section 28, and Judy Erola, the new minister responsible for the status of women, showed herself a thousand times more responsive to the emergency than her predecessor, Lloyd Axworthy, would have been.

It's particularly worth noting that there is not a single woman in the legislative caucus of the Saskatchewan New Democrats. I have no doubt whatever that this helps to account for Premier Allan Blakeney's obtuse inability to see that women's equality is not a chip in a poker game, to be traded or gambled away.

Lesson Number Three: Every protest counts. The Ad Hoc Committee has clout now because of Doris Anderson's resignation-on-principle last fall, the triumphant Ad Hoc conference on the Constitution, and then the brilliant coup of getting women's equality clauses into the proposed charter. All year, women's rights have enjoyed a snowballing legitimacy.

Just as instructive was the stinging humiliation dealt out last winter to Axworthy in his tangle with Anderson. Male politicians across the country took note and remembered: men who get caught patronizing women may suffer a severe pain in their political ambitions.

A Fourth Lesson: This whole astounding reversal that had the premiers backpedalling so fast that they nearly fell off their tricycles was engineered by a mere handful of women who took unpaid time off their jobs to do it.

No limos, no flunkies, no Telex machines for them. Linda Ryan-Nye, former teacher and now working for a non-profit foundation, simply flew to Ottawa as soon as she heard about the accord.

She was joined there by Marilou McPhedran, Toronto lawyer, and a handful of Ottawa members of the Ad Hoc Committee. These women, working with no funds, and digging into their own pockets for long-distance calls and telegrams, swung public and press against the accord.

Ryan-Nye assures me that all major women's groups took part in the national lobby effort. Still, the most visible, the most dogged

From left to right, Linda Silver Dranoff, Michele, and Marilou McPhedran at the 2006 25th anniversary of the Ad Hoc Conference.

and the most effective has been the Ad Hoc Committee, which must surely now be seen as the natural leadership of the Canadian women's movement.

But Canadian women have to snap out of their apathy. Because the Ad Hoc [committee] had to work on a shoestring, there was neither time nor research depth to prepare for battle. Had there been more time, we might have concentrated our fire on the provincial over-ride of Section 15 (anti-discrimination clause) instead of solely on Section 28 (general equality). As it is, we may have irretrievably lost an important legal protection.

In the next week or so, we will probably win back Section 28. But we've been burned three times by now and we should have learned **Lesson Number Five**: In the coming days of constitutional wrangle, we must have a women's watchdog in Ottawa to protect our equality rights....

And here's **Lesson Number Six** for right now. Never before have we needed a women's rights watchdog more than we do today.

Our Roll of Honor

Containing all the
Signatures to the "Declaration of Sentiments"
Set Forth by the First

Woman's Rights Convention,

held at
Seneca Falls, New York
July 19-20, 1848

LADIES:

Lucretia Mott
Harriet Cady Eaton
Margaret Pryor
Elizabeth Cady Stanton
Eunice Newton Foote
Mary Ann M'Clintock
Margaret Schooley
Martha C. Wright
Jane C. Hunt
Amy Post
Catherine F. Stebbins
Mary Ann Frink
Lydia Mount
Delia Mathews
Catherine C. Paine
Elizabeth W. M'Clintock
Malvina Seymour
Phebe Mosher
Catherine Shaw
Deborah Scott
Sarah Hallowell
Mary M'Clintock
Mary Gilbert

Sophronia Taylor
Cynthia Davis
Hannah Plant
Lucy Jones
Sarah Whitney
Mary H. Hallowell
Elizabeth Conklin
Sally Pitcher
Mary Conklin
Susan Quinn
Mary S. Mirror
Phebe King
Julia Ann Drake
Charlotte Woodward
Martha Underhill
Dorothy Mathews
Eunice Barker
Sarah R. Woods
Lydia Gild
Sarah Hoffman
Elizabeth Leslie
Martha Ridley

Rachel D. Bonnel
Betsey Tewksbury
Rhoda Palmer
Margaret Jenkins
Cynthia Fuller
Mary Martin
P. A. Culvert
Susan R. Doty
Rebecca Race
Sarah A. Mosher
Mary E. Vail
Lucy Spalding
Lovina Latham
Sarah Smith
Eliza Martin
Maria E. Wilbur
Elizabeth D. Smith
Caroline Barker
Ann Porter
Experience Gibbs
Antoinette E. Segur
Hannah J. Latham
Sarah Sisson

GENTLEMEN:

Richard P. Hunt
Samuel D. Tillman
Justin Williams
Elisha Foote
Frederick Douglass
Henry W. Seymour
Henry Seymour
David Spalding
William G. Barker
Elias J. Doty
John Jones

William S. Dell
James Mott
William Burroughs
Robert Smallbridge
Jacob Mathews
Charles L. Hoskins
Thomas M'Clintock
Saron Phillips
Jacob P. Chamberlain
Jonathan Metcalf

Nathan J. Milliken
S. E. Woodworth
Edward F. Underhill
George W. Pryor
Joel Bunker
Isaac VanTassel
Thomas Dell
E. W. Capron
Stephen Shear
Henry Hatley
Azaliah Schooley

Chapter Eight
FEMINISM FORWARD

THE SHOCK IS a recurring one. I believe it happens to sentient women in every generation; it is happening right now to young women in Canada.

Twenty years ago, I stood reading the "Declaration of Sentiments" drawn up by Elizabeth Cady Stanton, Susan B. Anthony, and their sister feminists, inscribed on a waterwall in Seneca Falls at the National Historic Women's Rights Park in New York State. I couldn't tell if the words were blurred by the screen of water that fell continuously over them or the tears of astonishment and gratitude that filled my eyes. I was shocked, shamed, and astounded that I had never read these world-shaking words before, and shocked again that they so exactly prefigured the sentiments that would fire up the energies of the Second Wave of feminists in the mid-twentieth century.

The Sentiments, framed in the round and ringing language of 1848, were a bill of "abuses and usurpations" of women by men. Far from being solely devoted to winning the vote, the suffragists had deeply understood the ways in which women were subjugated and "fraudulently deprived of their most sacred rights" by law, marriage, custom, and religion.

Why had I never been taught about these extraordinary revolutionaries, at any stage of my education?

In 1983, Australian feminist author Dale Spender interviewed Rebecca West, ninety-one, author and intrepid suffragist, and was taken aback by her hurricane-force intellect and scimitar

Kathleen Wynne, then Ontario's Minister of Education, read from her favourite feminist literature at a 2006 Miss G Read-In at Queen's Park, Toronto.

wit. West's writings of the past seventy years were, writes Spender, "a revelation... entertaining, enjoyable, inspiring...they represent a form of *permission*. They show me it is all right to abandon the male-approval-device (MAD) that has been so carefully cultivated within us as women..."

In 2005, a group of young women at the University of Western Ontario were talking about their "eye-opening and life-changing" Women's Studies and Gender Studies classes. They were shocked that they had never been exposed in high school to these ideas. They vowed to change the deep silence that engulfs women's history. Under the defiant banner of "The Miss G Project," they have campaigned ever since, with wit, invention, and growing impact, to institute gender studies in Ontario high schools. The name they chose, Miss G, honours a brilliant young Harvard scholar of that sobriquet; she died in mid-studies and was said, by Dr. Edward Clarke of Harvard Medical School, writing about her case in 1873, to have perished because "she ignored her woman's make" and tried to "compass man's intellectual attainment."

In 2011, I received a touchingly earnest letter from a young Swedish academic who had stumbled across my earlier books and was amazed to discover that, as long ago as 1982 (!), I was writing about "gender and language," "battered women," and "internalized guilt." She felt, she said, as though she were reinventing the wheel.

We have all been shocked to discover that our feminist insights, so fresh and bold to us, were common parlance in a generation before ours. Because our history is constantly overwritten and blanked out (consider the way women's participation in the Charter fight has been utterly ignored in the history books), we are always reinventing the wheel when we fight for equality. The shock (and thrill) of each generation of young feminists, suddenly discovering its foremothers, is instructive. We need to know our past, to mine it for its riches, to benefit from our foremothers' insights, as we launch into the future. From my childhood, long before I knew the word "feminist," I was deeply moved to discover sister-spirits – bold, critical, questioning women – in the books I read outside of school. Later in my life I came to know Canadian women who made a difference in my own home town.

FEMINIST REBELS OPENED DOORS
November 2002

They're as spicy and surprising as cinnamon hearts sprinkled through the stodgy porridge of Ontario history: women so unconventional in their thinking and tactics that they actually managed to change the world. They fought (and still fight) for women's equality, and even though many of them are almost lost from sight – a mere tantalizing footnote in the history books, a mention of a name in dusty archives – their thoughts and deeds go on after them, touching our lives even though we may be utterly unaware of them. They are like kindly ghosts, invisibly pushing aside the curtains or opening the doors as we move blithely forward.

...Women's liberation, like the great and ongoing struggle for racial justice, is one of the ground-shaking triumphs of the last 100 years. For you and me to pull on a pair of pants and go out to work, confident that the law is on our side in asserting our right to be free from assault, harassment, and discrimination, is the victory of thousands, tens of thousands, of women who went before us.

It wasn't easy. Toronto was the puritanical and conservative heart of colonial Canada.

Women were freer, bolder, and feistier almost everywhere else – certainly in Britain and the U.S. – and Toronto's Toryism forced many a rebellious woman's heart into sullen conformity or even exile.

By 1892, when the *Star* was born, fiery African-American Mary Ann Shadd was long gone. She had emigrated to Canada from Delaware, opened her own school, published and edited the *Provincial Freeman*, an abolitionist and pro-woman's suffrage newspaper in Toronto, and finally returned to the U.S. to enter law school at the age of 60. "In Toronto, with the strong attachment to antiquated notions respecting woman and her sphere...," she wrote once, covering a speech by U.S. feminist Lucy Stone.

Emily Stowe was Canada's first woman doctor and the founder of Women's College Hospital in 1883.

Susan B. Anthony, the brilliant American suffragist, also campaigned in Canada. She lambasted local women in British Columbia as "meek, milk and water [who] had no rights of their own."

The ones who rebelled still captivate me. Dr. Emily Stowe is revered now as Canada's first woman doctor and founder, in 1883, of what was to become Women's College Hospital, but she was both quirkier and braver than that pat description suggests. A farm girl, raised a Quaker with a strong belief in equality, she was undaunted in her quest for a medical education. The University of Toronto, implacably hostile to women, turned her away. She married and had three children before she seized the chance to study homeopathy in New York. Back in Toronto, she opened a practice serving women and children – and endured a lengthy trial for performing an abortion. (She was acquitted.)

Wish I'd been there in the court to cheer her bravery. I'd have signed up in a flash when she transformed her Toronto Women's Literary Club into a hotbed of political discussion and suffrage organizing.

Gloriously, Dr. Stowe's daughter, Augusta Stowe-Gullen, became the first woman to graduate in medicine in Canada and a staunch fighter for votes for women. In 1892...Augusta was one of the first three women elected to the Toronto school board.

How I would have loved to meet one of Augusta's friends, the sparky Flora MacDonald Denison, who came originally from Picton, escaping a genteel family fallen on hard times because of her father's alcoholism. Flora, when not dabbling in journalism, was a fashionable seamstress. Her life was transformed by Dr. Emily Stowe, who drew her into the women's movement.

Augusta Stowe-Gullen, Dr. Emily Stowe's daughter, became the first woman to graduate in medicine in Canada.

Unlike some more conformist and conservative Toronto suffragists, who sought the vote in the service of temperance or morality, Flora was an impassioned justice-seeker who admired the more militant British suffragists. From 1906 to 1914, Flora wrote weekly feminist columns, agitated for saner dress for women, paid for the suffrage movement's headquarters, opened a "vegetarian suffrage restaurant," brought Emmeline Pankhurst to speak in Toronto, and argued that housework, especially "meal-getting," should be made a "social industry" to free women from domestic slavery.

Flora Denison's daring may not seem like much to us today – but I love her free spirit, her socialism, her boldness in writing about women's need for sexual pleasure, for birth control, for access to divorce. Possibly because of her vocal disdain for mainstream religion (as a Rational Sunday member, she was in favour of Sunday tobogganing), she split with the stuffier mainstream women's movement. But even later, in 1916, when she opened a wilderness Ontario resort called Bon Echo, she served dinner on "Votes for Women" plates.

From the late 19th to the early 20th century, poor and working-class women also struggled for a fairer deal, usually without much success. My heart goes out to the "hello girls," the 400 Bell operators who went on strike over unequal pay and arbitrary work conditions (sound familiar?) in 1907. Their manager sneered that they were well paid for girls who worked only for "pin money or to buy a fur coat," and a government commission managed to patronize the women right back into their unfair wages.

With the First World War, the women's movement splintered into pro-Empire and anti-war factions. Much later, Nellie McClung wrote nostalgically: "The old crowd began to break up, and our good times were over."

But within a few years of the end of the war, Canadian women had not only won the vote (in 1917) but had transformed Canada's social fabric, fighting for, and winning, mother's allowances, Children's Aid Societies, kindergartens, home and school associations, juvenile courts, and separate women's prisons.

The ground had shifted forever.

Colourful characters and inspired leaders emerged again with the so-called Second Wave of the women's movement, struggling up out of the stifling conformity and gender straitjackets of the 1950s.

One of them was Laura Sabia of St. Catharines, an irrepressibly outspoken iconoclast who was politically Conservative and emotionally insubordinate (a state of defiance she ascribed to her convent schooling). Sabia, as an activist in the Canadian Status of Women Council, led the demand for a Royal Commission on the Status of Women, and when Doris Anderson backed her with a campaign in the pages of *Chatelaine* magazine, Canada was poised for a seismic shift.

There were so many others, stubborn, resilient, and imaginative women who wouldn't settle for second place. In the exhausting two-year battle to enshrine women's equality in the Charter of Rights and Freedoms, adopted in 1982, one name bobs up repeatedly: Toronto lawyer Marilou McPhedran, who spent tireless months lobbying on Parliament Hill, drawing up legal briefs, rallying the troops for one more try, testifying in committee, persuading the media, and doggedly coming back to fight again and again when the male political leaders tried to pull off last-minute double-crosses.

I remember when Dr. Ursula Franklin, professor of metallurgy at the University of Toronto, roused thousands of women to nuclear protest when she analysed the amount of radioactive fallout in their children's baby teeth. Pat Kelly, breast cancer activist, began fighting for more research money – and a cure – when merely to speak the word "cancer" (let alone "breast") was a social taboo. She started an avalanche of attitudinal and medical change.

Hundreds of women struggled, at considerable risk, for our reproductive freedoms. The fearless and toughly logical Judy Rebick, later the highly visible leader of the National Action Committee on the Status of Women, was an abortion rights activist. I also fondly recall the soft-spoken Dr. Marion Powell, whom I first met in the early '70s when she proposed a radical sex education curriculum for Scarborough primary schools. Later she founded the Bay Centre for Birth Control at Women's College Hospital. Her advocacy on behalf of women was polite, firm, and totally startling in the context of prudish Ontario.

Justice Bertha Wilson, the first woman on the Supreme Court of Canada, was brave enough to think as an egalitarian; male supremacists have been bashing her for it ever since, but she made Canada a better, fairer place, and a more sophisticated country in its grasp of what equality meant.

Justice Rosalie Abella decisively enlarged our understanding when she imagined the idea and the phrase "employment equity" in her groundbreaking 1984 report. Nancy Ruth (formerly Jackman) helped fund LEAF, the feminist legal action fund that pioneered dozens of breakthroughs in the law at the Supreme Court of Canada level – as well as many other feminist causes that would have shrivelled on the vine but for her generosity.

No, we didn't have (especially in our earliest history) very many brilliant orators and impassioned political stars of the kind

The National Action Committee on the Status of Women presented the first "Women are Persons" medallion, designed by Dora de Pédery-Hunt, to Justice Bertha Wilson, soon after her appointment as the first woman justice to the Supreme Court of Canada in 1982. At the Ottawa event were (left to right) Wendy Lawrence, Rosemary Billings, Doris Anderson, Justice Wilson, Pat Hacker, and Michelle Swenarchuk.

that glittered in the United States and Britain. Maybe that's why I cherish these names, and hundreds more, as the ones who defied the conventions, sacrificed leisure, thought more daringly, shrugged off lucrative rewards, and risked comfort and respectability in the name of a blazing ideal: justice, justice, justice, and freedom for women.

• • • • • • • • •

WHAT A RUN we had! All through the 1970s, the excitement, argument, intensity, and passion ran high. In every city and town in Canada, there was some high-spirited manifestation of the new feminism that moved women to self-creation in defiance of old norms.

Organizations sprang into existence, official and unofficial. At the National Film Board, Studio D began making award-winning women's documentaries in 1974; women's studies came alive in the universities; women's publishing, sports, satire, stand-up – all of it was new and drew instant adherents. Women's drop-in centres, newspapers, theatre groups, rock bands, magazines, impromptu libraries, counselling clinics, rape crisis centres, consciousness-raising groups, fund-raisers, book clubs, take back the night marches...Budding feminists tore into every accepted convention and conventional teaching, reinterpreting, rejecting, and re-making.

I doubt there was anything like it in Canada's last century: the Feminist Revolution, which stimulated a surge of creative enrichment and enhancement of freedoms, transformed every cranny of our culture. Of course there were individuals and institutions that remained wilfully untouched by the revolution, and the

Then Judge Rosalie Abella delivered her report on Equality in Employment in November of 1984.

groundwork of shifting entrenched prejudices is far from over. But for those of us who recognized feminism as the truth of our lives, it was a time like no other.

We had an intense sense of camaraderie and sisterhood, regularly shredded by internecine squabbles and schisms, then re-knitted at the next threat from the outside. National organizations grew to represent native women, black women, immigrant women, women with disabilities. By the early 1980s, white feminists were forced to recognize how unconsciously and damagingly they had assumed dominance and centrality. Our dawning awareness only served to enrich us and the movement. The joyousness of the movement – the sense of discovery, community, and new power – buoyed us through days and nights of tedious meetings or arduous volunteerism.

No part of a woman's life was untouched by the spirit of newness. Those of us with children jumped into becoming new kinds of mothers, creating new forms of schooling, or at the very least, working to reform the local public schools.

Frieda Forman, who created and ran the innovative Women's Resource Centre at the Ontario Institute for Studies in Education (OSIE), looked back in nostalgia at the end of her reign in 1998 when her unique library was about to be closed by the powers that be. Recalling its origins in the 1970s, she told me in an interview: "We began in the wildly enthusiastic days of the mid-'70s. Everything mattered: the toys we gave to children, the courses offered in grad school. We women were going to remake the world. There was jubilation every time a woman refused to make coffee for her boss. Every high school girl who wandered in here to find out about women's history was treated like a queen."

Riffling through the resource centre's riches, I found and used this snippet from Napoleon Bonaparte: "Nature intended women to be our slaves...they are our property...just as a tree that bears fruit belongs to a gardener. What a mad idea to demand equality for women! Women are nothing but machines for producing children."

Our care for children, of course, made us hostages to men (before women were able to earn their own way) and to the family law that ruled over the dissolution of marriages and the distribution of goods – including children. As we became more independent, we were more vulnerable in court.

Family law reform had been pushed into motion after women's rage was provoked by the raw injustice done to Irene Murdoch in 1975 by the Supreme Court of Canada. Ontario reformed its family law in 1978, and it wasn't long before feminist lawyer Linda Silver Dranoff was testing its utility.

WILL FAMILY LAW REFORM LET US DOWN?
March 1981

Despite the starched white shirt and the formal swirl of black robes, Toronto lawyer Linda Silver Dranoff could have kicked up her heels with glee last week when the Supreme Court of Canada agreed – as a matter of national importance – to hear her appeal of the Leatherdale decision.

Last fall, in a shocking reversal of an earlier court ruling, the Ontario Supreme Court said that Barbara Leatherdale, a 43-year-old part-time bank teller was not entitled to half her husband's retirement nest egg, $40,000 worth of Bell Canada shares.

Lawyers and their clients will be holding their breath until the appeal is heard, possibly next fall. If Barbara Leatherdale is again denied her half of the family's savings, it will be a nasty setback for women who counted on the Family Law Reform Act to redress some old wrongs.

The Leatherdales' financial quarrel has been battled back and forth in Ontario courts since 1978, when their marriage broke up. The timing was exquisite. The Ontario Family Law Reform Act was in its infancy, so it was of enormous public interest when Ontario Supreme Court Judge Mr. Justice Holland ruled last year that Barbara Leatherdale had made "a direct and substantial contribution" to her husband's ability to buy the stocks. Their marriage was "a true pooling of resources," the judge said, and Barbara was entitled to $20,000....

Gordon Leatherdale appealed. Last fall, the Ontario Court of Appeal said he was right, that Barbara was not entitled to that $20,000 because she hadn't contributed *directly* to the purchase of the stocks; because Gordon was the sole financial provider for 10 years; and because letting Gordon keep the savings "fairly reflected the joint contribution of each spouse."

This decision is strange and ominous. Wasn't it the whole point of Family Law Reform that a wife's work, in or out of the home, should weigh as heavily on the scales of justice as her husband's? Does it seem fair and right to anyone else that a couple's savings should go entirely to the husband?....

The law, I think, is like a coral reef. The bones of millions of tiny creatures – and millions of words, papers, arguments, moments – are required to build it up. It can't be pleasant for the Leatherdales to become, publicly, particles in the process. But if all goes well in the appeal, Barbara Leatherdale may have the comfort that her name will pass into the legal language of the country as a synonym for women's equality in marriage.

• • • • • • • • •

A YEAR LATER, the Supreme Court recognized Barbara Leatherdale's financial contribution while she worked for pay, but brushed aside as valueless her contribution in housework and mothering.

Family law pioneer Linda Silver Dranoff did not stop lobbying all three parties in the Ontario legislature until they endorsed a revised Family Law Reform Act that ensured that "all the financial products of a marriage" (including the value of the housewife's labour) be divided equally. Just one more example of feminists fighting for, and winning, greater justice for housewives and mothers – some of whom could always be counted on to complain loudly, in letters to the editor, that feminism "put them down."

If the law was like a coral reef, built of the bones of millions of tiny creatures, so indeed was the women's movement. The women who had marched in the streets for abortion rights at a time when the very word "abortion" could scarcely be uttered aloud, the women who committed outrageous acts of art and lesbian underground revelry, all of them led up to the huge shifts in law and public awareness that took place in the '70s.

Gradually, feminist lawyers beat back the prejudices that doomed women to poverty if they left a marriage (or the marriage left them). They won the battle for a much more equitable sharing of assets, for custody decided in the best interests of the child, for a "drop-out" provision in calculating the Canada Pension so that women were not financially penalized for staying out of the work force to raise children.

Other laws began to shift and change under the pressure of the women's movement and organized lobbying by women's organizations. Affirmative action was another one of those changes. Despite the right-wing governments that took hold in the English-speaking world in the 1980s, business independently adopted one of feminism's key demands for what we called "substantive equality." In the United Sates, of course, affirmative action was a necessary remedy for generations of anti-black discrimination. By the time Canadians began timidly to approach some legislation – at the same time as President Ronald Reagan was threatening to undo affirmative action – U.S. corporate business had long since embraced the idea as good business practice. The corporate world offered such stiff resistance that Reagan's administration backed off.

In September 1985, I was amazed to interview top American business executives and hear their lively defence of affirmative action: "There's no such thing as voluntary compliance with affirmative action laws. If voluntary compliance worked, Moses would have come down from the mountain with the Ten Guidelines," said William McEwen, chairman of the Resources and Equal Opportunity Committee of the U.S. National Association of Manufacturers. He snorted with laughter at the idea, being touted in Canada, of voluntary affirmative action. "We drive fifty-five miles per hour because we know there's a state employee around a corner somewhere who's going to make it economically advisable for us to do so. We were dragged kicking and screaming into setting targets for hiring women and minorities, and our entire work force has benefited....Forcing us to (change) our rules forced us to use all our human resources better."

For all the gains in equality law both north and south of the border, the era of the backlash was fully upon us by the 1990s. While Canadian feminists were exhausted by the onslaught of constitutional battles in which we were forced to take part, lest our newly-won rights be threatened, our U.S. counterparts were on the attack with glee. With my two-city life – shuttling between New York and Toronto – I enviously watched New Yorkers fight the backlash with wit, energy, and outrageous acts. They had been inspired by the street-level activism of Act Up, the militant AIDS organization. "We've borrowed the method of direct action and just New Yorked it to death," said Tracy Essoglou, one of the leaders of WAC, the Women's Action Coalition.

WAC had been formed partly because American women were enraged at the dismissal of Anita Hill's harassment allegations against Clarence Thomas during his Senate confirmation hearing for the Supreme Court. Mere words cannot evoke the contempt, condescension, and dismissal with which Republican and Democratic senators alike treated the patently earnest Anita Hill, or the rigging of the hearing. (Strong supporting evidence for Hill's complaint was strenuously excluded.) As she described the ugly and demeaning sexual atmosphere in which she had been forced to work by her boss, Clarence Thomas, she was further insulted, disbelieved, and dismissed in the televised hearings. As was perfectly evident to women watching the hearings, she was telling the truth, and her denigration was painful to watch. Today, many years later, we have evidence that other African American women suffered the same ugliness at his hands. No wonder an angry collective of New York artists and writers formed WAC and staged weekly, electrifying meetings and street actions that stunned the public with their dark humour and incredible numbers.

At WAC demonstrations, you could hear the rat-a-tat-tat of the Lesbian Drum Corps long before it smartly stepped into sight, banners, signs ("WAC is here! Some are queer!") and emblems waving above, and at least a thousand high-energy protesters in their wake. "Get that gavel off my head/Pick on deadbeat dads instead!" shouted WACers in front of a courthouse. "Off our backs! On our feet! We refuse to be discreet!" WAC's innovative – intensely democratic – structure and inspired sloganeering were not only exciting, but often effective.

US FEMINISTS ARE FINDING CONFRONTATION GETS RESULTS
May 1992

Direct action – "in your face" confrontational street theatre – is raising the profile of U.S. feminism's drive for social change.

WAC, the Women's Action Coalition, is a ferociously organized group of downtown New York artists and activists, including celebrities like performance artist Laurie Anderson and painter Ida Appelbroog. WAC's telephone tree can mobilize 650 women within 24 hours for a phone, fax, or letter "zap" to a sexist company or a biased judge.

WHAM, Women's Health Action and Mobilization, filled New York's streets with 4,000 marchers, massively outnumbering Operation Rescue when it straggled into town to harass abortion clinics. Another morning, New York awoke to see the Statue of Liberty (neat symbolic choice) draped by WHAM with gigantic banners: "Abortion Is Health Care...and Health Care Is a Right."

WHAM gate-crashed a psychiatric conference devoted to "converting" lesbians to heterosexuality; they held the floor until security guards gave up and the psychiatrists decided they needed to hear WHAM's protest.

Direct action is dramatic – and far more American than Canadian. At the sexual harassment conference in New York a couple of weeks ago, I was fascinated to hear about the decisive impact that courageous American feminists can have by doing things their Canadian sisters wouldn't dream of.

"Silence keeps women as victims," said Heidi Herr of WHAM. "Silent women are ghosts...they allow the world to carry on as though nothing happened."

WAC and WHAM refused to be ghosts this winter when six white members of a university lacrosse team were being serially tried for gang rape of a student from Jamaica. Some of the men plea-bargained and were sentenced to six weeks of community service in a battered women's shelter. The protesters "zapped" the judge with letters, packed the courtroom, and found themselves being roughed up by court attendants. Result: WHAM and WAC were invited to meet with the chief justice and state officials to help draw up protocols for more sensitive handling of female witnesses and court observers. And the sentence was changed to mandatory attendance at a course for male batterers.

Direct action is frightening. "We were well brought up and want people to like us," admitted Temma Caplan of No More Nice Girls. "On the other hand, I'm committed to direct democracy."

"When we speak out, we're called bitches," Tracy Essoglou of WAC agreed. "But when we're nice, we only create rhetorical moments that are instantly forgotten."

Proof positive of WAC's effectiveness was provided, startlingly, right in the workshop. Essoglou described WAC's intervention in a recent New York rape trial. A jury convicted Ernesto Garay of raping and sodomizing a 24-year-old incest victim with a mental age of 11. Pondering the sentence, Judge Nicholas Figueroa said, "There's rape and there's rape...there was no violence..." He thought the impact of the rape would be minimal on someone who had already been attacked by her father and brother.

WAC "zapped" the judge and the media with angry letters and demonstrations. In an unprecedented move, the rattled Figueroa then asked a panel of judges to decide on the sentence. They handed down the maximum.

After the four panellists described this action, and how they had to train themselves to overcome feelings of embarrassment at being seen as "crazy people" in public, a dignified black woman rose at the back of the room.

"I was the prosecutor in the Garay case," she said. "I want to tell you that you said things I couldn't say, and you had an educational impact on the panel of judges...You weren't crazy."

WAC works with groups like the Gorilla Girls (art activists disguised in gorilla suits) to challenge sexist museum policies with witty poster and postcard campaigns. And now they're planning videotaped "feminist public service announcements" to distribute to television stations.

"We're media whores," wisecracked WHAM's Heidi Herr, referring to the direct action groups' high-octane publicity.

Meanwhile, a mainstream feminist organizing campaign has resulted in a record 150 women candidates in the forthcoming elections.

Ellie Smeal, founder of the Fund for a Feminist Majority, urged women at the conference to "Ignore the myths that women can't win. The more women who run, the more will win. When a lot of women run, it creates excitement that brings in campaign money. So what if you lose the first time – Bush lost and lost before he won." Polls now show that the electorate favours women, Smeal said, and any pro-choice candidate gains an automatic 9 percent over anti-choice opponents.

U.S. activists have always achieved political change through extra-political means like the civil rights movement and anti-war demonstrations. Although Canadian women's situation is less drastic and our methods more institutional, we would do well to absorb something of the determination and quick-witted, media-savvy dynamism that is driving the U.S. feminist movement forward.

• • • • • • • • •

THE BACKLASH tossed up some amusing flotsam during those agitated '90s: we all savoured the lunacy of American TV evangelist and ranting Republican Pat Robertson who declared that feminism "is a socialist, anti-family political movement that encourages women to leave their husbands, kill their children, destroy capitalism, and become lesbians."

"What incredibly sloppy reporting," I wrote. "Robertson completely overlooked the rest of our agenda: to subvert all teenagers by recording satanic messages backwards on rock and roll records and to take over world governments by fluoridating bottled mineral water. If he wants to indulge in fem-bashing, okay, but he could at least get his facts right."

Joking aside, most activists knew we were headed into an era that was unfriendly, at best, to real economic equality for women. The inspired innovations of the '70s had settled into stable institutions in the '80s and many successful women fighting to hold on to freshly established gains. Educated women put on corporate suits and aimed for the top, eager to gain the highest rewards. Advertisers, greedily eyeing this new market, strewed the path with designer shoes, diamond rings, and must-have cosmetic surgery.

Here we were in the last decade of the century. Yet when Bertha

Wilson, former member of the Supreme Court of Canada, did an in-depth study of women in the law profession, she found a wasteland.

LAW FIRMS WON'T ACCEPT HER JUDGEMENT
March 1994

...You can bet that the guys in the beautifully cut suits are not chatting among themselves about the desirability of longer maternity leaves, on-site daycare or a reduction in the "billable hours" demanded of lawyers who are also young parents.

Wilson's report was tough. She and her colleagues on the Canadian Bar Association's task force stripped away the law's veneer of egalitarianism to expose a "staggering" degree of discrimination, harassment, and inequality. In an interview, Wilson confided that she was also shaken by the "widespread horribleness in law schools, and the extreme cynicism of some faculty. Too many professors like to exercise their acerbic wit in ridiculing students' idealism."

The report reveals that a high percentage of female students suffer discrimination from other students, from potential employers, and from sexist or anti-feminist professors. A poisoned environment in the profession threatens to "kill the initiative of some of Canada's finest Aboriginal minds." Black women face especially painful bias and barriers – more a "brick wall" than a glass ceiling. Women lawyers are promoted less often, paid less – in one study, $20,000 less per year than men – and are often relegated to unglamorous and undemanding "pink files."

Even women who, by their own account, make it to a judgeship by "acting like one of the guys" often have to deal with slighting attitudes from male colleagues. "How is your little jury trial going, my dear?" oozed one chauvinist. And anyone who has been angered by a judge's prejudice in sexual assault, battering, or incest cases will be sickened to hear that some senior male judges are refusing to let female judges try such cases because women would automatically be "biased."

Evidently, these men cling to the thick-witted notion that their male viewpoint is "neutral" and universally valid....

• • • • • • • • •

THE CORPORATE LAW FIRMS were not the only place where progress for women lagged (or had never happened). By the time of the stunning Statistics Canada 1993 report on "violence against women," the resistance to the feminist message had set and hardened in concrete. The fathers' rights movement, viciously misogynist and sickeningly sentimental at the same time, had made terrific headway in the media. Opportunistic scribblers insisted, with joy, that girls were now proving as violent as boys.

FEMINISM NOT THE LINK BETWEEN GIRLS AND VIOLENCE
November 1999

There they go again!

The Southam newspapers, owned by Conrad Black, can't seem to stop hyperventilating about feminism and all its supposed catastrophic consequences – even when they have to twist and bend the facts to make their point.

At the end of October, several Southam papers, including the *Ottawa Citizen*, breathlessly announced that "feminism is driving girls to violence."

Supposedly, this shocking fact was revealed at an academic symposium held recently in Toronto.

Flip this story inside out.

"This is most disconcerting," exclaimed Dr. Sibylle Artz, director of the School for Child and Youth Care at the University of Victoria, in a telephone interview. "The stories are completely wrong; they're entirely backward. First of all, all the research shows that girls with a strong sense of feminism and female worth don't typically engage in violent behaviour."

Dr. Artz, an internationally respected authority on the subject and the author of *Sex, Power and the Violent Schoolgirl*, was a participant in the symposium.

So was Kathy Levene of the Earlscourt Child and Family Centre, who wrote to Southam to protest the "noxious reporting." In vain, as it turns out: her letter was neither acknowledged nor published.

Kirsten Madsen, another psychologist who attended the symposium, was equally indignant. "We didn't say anything about feminism being responsible. We didn't mention feminism at all," Madsen told Professor Jim Winter of *Flipside*, a muckraking Internet daily at the University of Windsor School of Communications.

Conrad Black owns more than half the newspapers in Canada. His newspapers' foaming-at-the-mouth diatribes about the evils of feminism are ridiculous, revealing – and purposefully dangerous.

At about the same time as the latest outbreak, I was approached by an aspiring film-maker who was "told by a vice-principal and a police task force member" that feminism was one of the causes of girls' violence. She thought she would base a documentary on this peachy insight. That's how urban myths and political lies get propagated: if "everyone is saying it," then it must be true.

But in this case, it isn't. I'm happy to claim many achievements for feminism, but offering "equal opportunity violence" to girls definitely isn't one of them.

The opposite is closer to the truth, according to Dr. Artz, who stresses the complexity of the issue. Girls with the most rigid, stereotypical, and negative attitudes about females are the most likely to engage in violence, Dr. Artz explained. Her current studies of girls in detention shows a sad pattern, she said: "When girls engage in girl-to-girl violence, it's because they're competing for male attention. This is true of oppressed groups: they commit violence 'horizontally' – that is, on people like themselves, in the name of people with more power."

Think, if you can bear to, of the repulsive Karla Homolka, so recently in the news again. [Homolka was the wife of serial rapist Paul Bernardo; together they engaged in the sadistic-sex murders of two schoolgirls.] Karla, in high school, was a crazed Retro Barbie – she actually belonged to the Diamond Club, a group of girls who passionately believed in marrying early and having babies as soon as possible. Homolka even sneered at higher education for women, calling it a waste of time. Studying might interfere with her man-hunt.

Soon, she was eagerly and without conscience abasing herself to Paul Bernardo. Only when she was caught did this young murderer embrace the feminist defence of the "battered wife" syndrome. Just one little hitch: That defence was an honest one for women so traumatized and trapped that they could escape death only by killing their abusers. Homolka's situation didn't even come close. Why should feminism take the rap for the cynical manoeuvrings of a psychopath and her lawyers?

It was the public's outrage at Homolka's light sentence, I believe, that lent force and credibility to the media frenzy about female violence. Obviously (who can forget the murder of Reena Virk?) girls and women, being human, are capable of violence. The stereotype of sweet, gentle women and bold, aggressive men was precisely the sexist belief system we feminists fought against. It wasn't feminism that created the Karlas of this world, and it wasn't feminists who denied the existence of female aggression.

Girls' violence is, because of social context and conditioning, less frequent than boys' violence. But where it exists, says Dr. Artz, look for underlying "family violence, poverty, power relationships, sexism, and consumerism. There's no one cause; these things are complex. We can't work on prevention until we explore and understand the causes."

Her exasperated conclusion about the constant misleading media prattle about girls and violence: "Silly and destructive."

· · · · · · · · ·

THE ASSAULT BY right-wing media never lets up. Most of the dominant misconceptions about feminism have flowed from media manipulation, ignorance, sloppiness, and/or outright propaganda. The *New York Times*, the most powerful media influence in North America, is pleased to run at least one magazine article a year on the way professional women are supposedly turning their backs on feminism and on their costly professional educations – a scenario completely constructed on the basis of anecdotes about a handful of highly privileged women who can afford to and wish to stay home with their children. And as for the generational war about feminism, what luscious media fodder! Weekly, we hear how young women hate the "f-word" – or, if they are indeed feminist, how they loathe their predecessors in the Second Wave.

This is "reality" news, scripted, honed, and polished to undermine a movement that might lure young women away from docile political views and the steady consumption of tight jeans and eyelash curlers. Feminism is not capitalism-friendly, no matter its political tint. It will always be in the interests of the mainstream media to distort what feminism means and how it is received.

As conservative governments busily dismantled feminist institutions over the next decade or so, the light-hearted confidence and optimistic exuberance of the '70s seemed to have vanished. It was more difficult to strike a note of fun as we felt the ground eroding beneath our feet.

There were occasional highlights: Dimwit U.S. vice-president Dan Quayle, declaring that "I stand by all my misstatements," tried to back out of his denunciation of the TV programme "Murphy Brown." The protagonist had "mocked fatherhood" by giving birth to a child "out of wedlock," he fulminated. I couldn't resist commenting: "Interesting word, wedlock."

When the federal government imposed the hated GST, mockery of their "menstrual tax" was likewise irresistible.

MENSTRUAL TAX NETS TORIES 20 MILLION DOLLARS
April 1991

When the most despised federal government in Canada's history sinks so low that it starts to tax women's bodily functions, you can almost hear the ping, snap, and sizzle of tempers fraying.

Ever since January, when the GST was slapped on pads, tampons, and panty-liners, women have been simmering with indignation. Calls complaining about the tax on pads rank among the top 10 subjects on the government's GST hotline.

Now, three Sarnia women are circulating a petition against the GST on "feminine sanitary products" and are learning that not only are women eager to sign, they want copies of the petition for themselves. A whole brigade of women is, evidently, ready to hit the streets and shopping malls to crusade.

"We started by leaving the petition in local stores, and already we have 5,000 names," Jackie Burnett, a Sarnia businesswoman, told me. She has joined forces with Sheridan Glenn and Denise McKinley to co-ordinate what they are calling the "Taboo" campaign.

Frankly, I'd blocked out the whole subject of the GST since we all had to bow to the inevitable in January. I didn't notice that previously untaxed sanitary supplies – and not just the Charmin' – were now being squeezed for big bucks by the feds.

An industry representative told me that the "feminine protection market" was worth $289 million in 1990. That adds up to a not inconsiderable $20 million a year in GST.

"Well, why not?" protested a calm, rational male of my acquaintance. "Everything is being taxed; that's the point."

"No taxation without representation!" I yelped. Women must be among the least represented people in Ottawa. We may be more than half the population, but we've been unfairly hammered and harmed by the Tories. They tried to pass a law that would make us criminals if we had abortions; they slashed funding to women's centres and women's publications; they refused to make good on their promises of a daycare plan; they cut back funding for women's prime social concerns, ranging from education to welfare to health; they spent buckets of money on the Gulf War, opposed by more Canadian women than men, and they have yet to pass even a relatively feeble gun control law.

And now they're collecting $20 million a year on our menstrual cycles.

But not, of course, on donated sperm. The exemption for that priceless commodity was just announced a couple of weeks ago, along with individual servings of yogurt.

Truth to tell, I think that the tax on books is far more serious, destructive, and essentially barbaric.

But even though it may cost each Canadian woman only a few hundred dollars in her lifetime, there's something specially galling, something maddeningly symbolic about the menstrual tax.

I ploughed through the GST legislation, searching for some rhyme or reason to the Tories' tax structure, and I could see the over-all pattern emerging.

Essential groceries and medical supplies are exempt. Okay, that's a start. But then the fine moral and social distinctions come into play. Read the list of groceries that are taxed and a vision swims into your mind: an army of clerks – desiccated Dickensian clerks, thin lips pursed in disapproval, scritching away with their quill pens as they viciously inscribe the list of "inessential" items to be taxed.

Among them: "Crisps" and "ice lollies." (Where do these guys come from, Liverpool?) (Addendum: probably. Looks in retrospect as though they lifted entire blocks of text from Maggie Thatcher's England.)

Still, it seems at first to have a certain holier-than-thou consistency. Pure living and home cooking will be rewarded. Potatoes will not be taxed, but potato puffs will. Salted nuts, taxed; unsalted nuts, no. "Brittle pretzels" will be taxed; no mention, however, of soggy pretzels. (You slipped up there, Bob Cratchit.)

All items intended for "the care of the human body or any part thereof, whether for cleansing, deodorizing, beautifying, preserving or restoring" are taxed.

So here we have it: the Tories' idea of the essential human being is a hairy, faintly malodorous creature, at home in the kitchen, laboriously salting her own peanuts. And, of course, pregnant – the only way a mature Canadian female can escape being taxed for her bodily cycles. (You understand now about that tax-free sperm?)

But if only the most bare-bones, essential, primal necessities are supposed to escape the tax, how did the following little anomalies slip, untaxed, past the steely gaze of the New Tory Order: chip dip, deposits on canoe rentals, frozen pizza, imported tourist pamphlets, and supplies of "dried and sorted tobacco leaves"?

Chip dip and canoe rides are essential, but pads and tampons aren't?....

• • • • • • • • •

IN THE MID-'90S, Mike Harris began to dismantle the entire $100 million structure that had been painstakingly built to protect women from male violence: training for police and prosecutors, public education programs, counselling and assistance for women moving out on their own, and most horrifically, the shelters themselves. First, eighteen of the twenty-three unionized staff in the Ontario Women's Directorate, which oversaw the anti-violence programs, were called in one by one and fired. Later that day, the fired workers were offered a Christian prayer service (most of them weren't Christian) to give them the "upbeat" message that "this could be a positive turning point in their lives."

News soon leaked out that Harris had contracted out a study of Ontario's women's shelters – with a brilliant idea: every battered woman in the province would get a free cell phone to call for help, but her stay in a shelter would be limited to forty-eight hours. The uproar in the women's movement, and an embarrassingly premature leak of the report's contents, fortunately kiboshed the whole piece of nonsense.

Less fortunately, women were still falling prey – and probably always will – to manipulation by the oldest ploy in the book: the good-mummy bad-mummy game.

WOMEN GETTING SUCKERED INTO DAYCARE WAR
May 1996

It's the biggest and most enduring shell game of the 20th century. Ever since the Industrial Revolution, when the extended family began to disappear in the urbanized West, there's been a permanent debate about child care.

In the last two weeks, we've seen a major CBC radio debate, a *Star* series, and a massive study published in the U.S. showing that daycare is not harmful to children. Yet every time this debate swells to a crescendo, women get deflected into a "Let's you and her fight" diversion, ferociously debating each other over the merits of daycare.

Invariably, we're suckered into believing that damaged children are always women's fault, or that it is women's burden to cope with all the pitfalls of human development, from thumb-sucking to psychopathy. Yes, most of us gladly take on the responsibility, but we're fooling ourselves if we think anyone can or should do it all alone.

Especially when jobs are scarce, it's women who are scolded not to be greedy, cold-hearted, and selfish enough to go out to work. (Of course, single mothers who are on welfare are always urged not to be so lazy, self-indulgent, and immoral as to stay home with their children.)

As reliably as goldfish rushing up to gobble the fish flakes, women rise to this debate with a chorus of mutual accusation. Some stay-at-home mothers can always summon up a frenzy of righteous resentment against public spending for daycare. Women who work outside the home can be counted on to lash back with equal fury. Or they'll agree about the need for daycare and quarrel about subsidies. Give half the population a very small wedge of the economic pie, and watch them savage each other over the crumbs.

Meanwhile, the male experts – from Freud to Spock to a gaggle of modern gurus, including the anti-daycare Calgarian Mark Genuis – loftily conduct the child care studies, collect the grants, establish the "family" institutes, publish the books, earn the bucks, take the tax breaks, and go to work every day, leaving the kids to the women. And they pontificate, pontificate, pontificate.

Why do women listen? Are we so haunted by guilt and angst because we've internalized the contempt in which mothering is held? After all, our society measures significance by money. Obviously, looking after children is the very lowest rung on the status ladder. Look at the proposal this week that teachers be forced to start work at 8 a.m. to look after the kids of working parents. Only those who work with children are held in such low regard that officials would dare suggest they be forced to work an extra unpaid five hours a week.

And so, embattled, we fight each other instead of fighting the power.

This is preposterous.

Nurturing the next generation ought to be one of our highest priorities. All child-rearing ought to be rewarded, supported, enriched, and enabled. A sane society would provide dozens of child care options – flexible, part-time, full-time, drop-in – for every parent, working or not working.

I stayed home for six years with our three children. Partly I did it because I grew up at a time when only mothers looked after children – and, given what my father was like, that seemed an excellent idea. Partly, I was lucky enough to have a portable kind of job – writing – that let me earn a few dollars while at home. And partly I did it because it was the most absorbing, intense, delightful, deeply rewarding work I've ever done, and learning to be a super, loving, responsive mom gave me a secret feeling of power and competence that I didn't want to share with anyone.

Staying home also made me stir-crazy, sapped my confidence to deal with the working world, and probably put a crimp in my little list of life accomplishments. I'm glad I had the chance to do it, but that doesn't mean it's the right thing for everyone.

The stay-home full-time mother, after all, is a historic anomaly; it's a condition that predominated for a brief 30 or 40 years out of all the millennia. Since when did it become sacred? Only since it suited the people who profit from our economic system.

Be wary of them. Challenge anyone who begins a sentence with "mothers should..." and doesn't say what "fathers should." What is sacred is not the role of mothers, but our collective responsibility to care for all the children.

• • • • • • • • •

WHILE THE MEDIA delighted in stirring up such meaningless debates with soul-deadening regularity, some of us watched with sadness the decline and eventual decimation of NAC. The National Action Committee on the Status of Women had been founded in the early 1970s to keep tabs on the implementation of recommendations by the Royal Commission on the Status of Women. By the '80s, it had become the biggest and most effective women's organization in Canadian history, with 650 member groups (ranging from the women's committee of the Communist Party to the Imperial Order of the Daughters of the Empire). Moreover, it had become impressively political and active, staging a televised leaders' debate on women's issues in the 1984 election campaign and fighting hard against free trade in the subsequent years. Forceful and formidable in its annual "lobby day" with key politicians on Parliament Hill, NAC won major attention for women's issues – and gradually antagonized and intimidated most of the leaders. (They were used to "ladies," not women.) All through the '90s, as NAC bravely struggled with racism in the movement, the successive federal governments were whittling away its funding, until national meetings and prompt communication had become all but impossible.

Antagonists like to say that the racism struggle destroyed NAC. (Little is now left of that redoubtable organization. Although it lists an office address, it has no website and no apparent activists.) I don't agree. The times were against NAC, the backlash had been rampant for more than a decade, and governments were hostile. Funding shrank away, and the popular energy and consensus on which movements float had dried up. Factionalism took its toll, of course: various kinds of feminists seemed angrier with each other than they had ever been at the powers that oppressed them all equally. On the whole, I think the hard and sometimes bitter anti-racism work that NAC, alongside the entire feminist movement, took on was essential, powerful, and a contribution to the larger society.

ANTI-IMMIGRANT BIGOTRY SPARKS ATTACK ON NEW WOMEN'S LEADER
April 1993

Sunera Thobani's entry on to the national political scene – on June 7, she'll become the new president of the National Action Committee on the Status of Women – provided a sharp moment of clarity for media-watchers.

Thobani is a PhD student, a single mother, and, as a Tanzanian of South Asian descent, the first person of colour to hold such a high post in the Canadian women's movement. Even before she took office, at a moment when parliamentarians of any dignity and intelligence would be extending a gracious welcome to her, she came under stinging attack by a Tory MP.

"She's an illegal immigrant!" spluttered John MacDougall in the House of Commons.

Since that was completely untrue, MacDougall had to cover his tracks, and fast. That night, CBC's Prime Time TV news caught him spewing a new line: "It's a slap to the women of this country…It's not fair to Canadians that we're being represented by someone who's not a Canadian citizen!" fumed MacDougall, his small moustache working furiously in indignation.

As It Happens, on CBC radio, pounced on MacDougall and caught him fudging again. "I asked two questions – she's not a Canadian citizen and she has no work permit," said MacDougall, somewhat incoherently.

Thobani was assured of landed immigrant status, entitling her to work, the day before MacDougall uttered his slander in the House. Not that he bothered to check.

MacDougall was angry that his remarks were called sexist and racist by infuriated NAC members. Referring to himself in the royal third person, he boasted: "John MacDougall is noted across the country as someone concerned with this country and with men and women..."

Wrong again, Mr. MacDougall. As far as I know, you're not even noted as far as Toronto; no one I spoke to had ever heard of you.

Then he flourished another fabrication. (Doesn't this guy ever do any research?) "Miss Rebick has a closed shop and appointed someone..."

Sunera Thobani, President of NAC, 1993-1996

I know MacDougall's speaking style is painfully obtuse, so I won't bother quoting any more of his ill-informed ramblings. What he was struggling to say was that Judy Rebick, NAC's vividly articulate outgoing president, had strong-armed her organization into accepting Sunera Thobani as president by acclamation.

This smear was eagerly picked up by several mindless editorial writers who ranted about the "undemocratic" Judy Rebick – their farewell salute to a national leader who could think, talk, and write rings around any of them.

Thobani was not "appointed" by Rebick, but was acclaimed president, through careful due process, because the only other candidate, Shelagh Day of Vancouver (an NAC vice-president) decided not to run. In fact, in the past 10 years, all but one of NAC's presidents has been acclaimed, mostly because it's such a demanding job that there are rarely many contenders. Day herself indignantly told me that the accusation about Rebick "appointing" Thobani was utterly without foundation.

And what of the deplorable John MacDougall, MP for Timiskaming? Did he ever ask if Judy Rebick (born in New York) was a Canadian citizen? Or does the question only occur to him when he sees a skin of a different colour?...

Last weekend, I had leafed through the newspapers and been struck by the suffocating number of pale male columnists and critics who bleated on and on about the intolerable burden of "political correctness." Gee, it's tough not being able to insult and demean women and racial minorities.

File their blathering under "B" for "backlash." Objectively, the truth is that white men just like them still overwhelmingly dominate every newsroom, legislature, and corporate headquarters.

And at the very moment these guys were whining about the demands of minorities, a small-minded member of Parliament was indulging himself in shameless immigrant-baiting. No retraction of falsehoods. No apology. No reproach from his Tory colleagues.

"I'm concerned," said Sunera Thobani, "about the chilling effect this will have on other immigrant women who choose to seek national office."

So am I. Because while over-privileged journalists sulk about a totally illusory "persecution" of white males, our country is starting to run a scary fever of anti-immigrant bigotry....

• • • • • • • • •

AFTER THE DEFEAT of the Charlottetown Accord in '92, some Conservative women had pinned on a badge that said "NAC Doesn't Speak for Me." That nasty slogan had a new life during the race debates in the mid-'90s, and this time, it smacked of bigotry.

YES, NAC SPEAKS FOR ME AND ALL WOMEN
June 1995

You know what? NAC *does* speak for me.

No matter how it is shunned by the media or denigrated by its very vocal enemies, NAC is growing, deepening its roots in Canada, flourishing in its diversity and strengthening its commitment to speak up for social justice and against the viciousness of the new conservative economic dogma. And every one of those qualities gives me heart and emboldens my faith in the courage and longevity of the women's movement.

This weekend, as the National Action Committee on the Status of Women, better known simply as NAC, stages its annual general meeting in Ottawa, I'm reminded of the drumbeat of reactionary sentiment that began to be heard several years ago.

"NAC Doesn't Speak for Me" buttons first sprouted on the tailored lapels of right-wing women who opposed NAC's eventually successful fight, led by Judy Rebick, against the Charlottetown Accord.

But the refrain didn't disappear when the Charlottetown debate faded into history. Instead, it became the slogan of those who resisted NAC's new anti-racist direction led by Sunera Thobani, its first non-white president. I understand the resistance. The women's movement surged from powerlessness to mainstream acceptability; many of its founders inevitably felt threatened, furious, and "blamed" when women of colour began to insist on sharing the platform.

Every one of us white feminists went through a period of angry denial that there was any racism in the women's movement. Slowly, and painfully, we began to realize that "racism" was no longer a question of personal prejudices, but rather of stubborn blindness, of refusal to see how privileges and advantages that flowed easily to us because of our white skin were denied to others who were equally talented.

NAC speaks for me because, almost alone of major Canadian organizations, it has profoundly struggled with the tough, often explosive debates required when white women are asked to stop hogging power. If there are more anguished contretemps ahead, I know the media will seize on them with spiteful glee, rather than giving NAC credit for having the guts to wrestle with the demon of racism.

A few months ago, I attended a NAC fund-raising banquet at a downtown Chinese restaurant. The place was packed with at least 500 high-spirited women (and men). As I looked around the room, I was astonished to see that at least a third of the faces were non-white – a huge difference from even five or six years ago. At least a third of the new member groups boisterously displaying their affiliation at every table had been left out, ignored or marginalized by the so-called "mainstream" women's movement in earlier decades.

In the last two years, NAC's membership has swelled with new recruits among union women, immigrants, community activists, wage earners of every kind, refugees, Asian and black women. These are the women who represent the great majority of Canada's population; from them will come the grass-roots energy, enthusiasm, and clout to move us forward.

Yes, they speak for me. The resolutions at NAC's general meeting take aim at the federal government's plan to abdicate responsibility for the social safety net and for Medicare. NAC argues that the deficit must be addressed by job creation, lower interest rates, and a fairer tax system. NAC insists that we must not accept the poverty of women and children as the price of balancing the budget.

Last week, the Québec Women's Federation marched from Montréal to Québec to protest women's poverty, their numbers swelling impressively to 15,000 by the time they reached the legislature. We have a steeper and longer road to march in the rest of Canada, but when the protest finally rises against the economic rubbish we've been fed by the Mike Harrises of this world, it will be women like the NAC members who lead the way.

Yes, NAC speaks for me, because I reject those smug middle-class types who contemptuously label feminists a "special interest group." From housewives to corporate executives, every woman in Canada today is enjoying the benefits won for her by the women's movement. (You thought REAL Women got you maternity leave?)

NAC speaks for me because it is the honourable heir to the suffragists of the past and the brave trailblazer to the inclusive feminism of the future.

• • • • • • • • •

NAC MAY HAVE SPOKEN for me and many others, but we were steering into stiff headwinds. The federal government had shifted decisively away from the expansive days of funding feminist organizations and making them near-partners in the forging of government policies.

The Conservative minority government elected in 2006, with

its strong base of fundamentalist and evangelical western support, was clearly anti-feminist and reactionary on women's, minorities', and gay rights. One of its first moves was to scrap the national child care programme proposed by the former prime minister Paul Martin. Then Bev Oda, the Conservative minister for Canadian Heritage, proclaimed that women had already achieved equality in Canada, and therefore the Status of Women Program was instructed to remove the word "equality" from its goals and its website.

That was the start of a determined dismantling of the feminist infrastructure, whatever was left of it after a decade of neoliberal economics. Stephen Harper's government promptly cut funding completely to fourteen different women's organizations, a list that later expanded to thirty-two. Among the most lamented targets were the National Association of Women and the Law, which had produced stellar research, and the Court Challenges Programme, an innovative and superbly productive organisation that enabled women and minorities to go to court to defend their rights under the Charter.

Some the Conservatives' anti-feminist moves were brazen (like the foreign policy initiative on maternal and child health, which excluded any funding for family planning), and some were surreptitious, like the backbencher bills to criminalize anyone who "coerces" a woman into having an abortion – which would have put at risk counsellors, medical practitioners, or partners.

In 2011, a Conservative majority government was elected. The outlook for Canadian women is bleak indeed, at least for the next four years. We are still at a major disadvantage, electorally and economically, in career advancement and in bearing the burden of both anti-woman violence and an unfair share of household tasks and child care. We face a time when government has washed its hands of equity and of the responsibility to prevent harm or to work toward the common good. Each man for himself is the cry of these extreme individualists.

Despite its unctuously hypocritical blandishments of being opposed to violence against women, the government will certainly augment the number of wife-murders by its determined abolition of the long-gun registry and by starving the shelter and anti-violence movement of funds. That money will no doubt go to various police forces and super-jails. The Conservatives prefer post-crime punishment to prevention.

Nothing except an aroused and infuriated public can stop a majority government from doing anything it wants to do. So far, despite a long list of blatant government misdeeds (cover-up of torture in Afghanistan, spending millions to bribe voters in Tory ridings, contempt of Parliament – the list is almost comically long), the public shows no sign of alarm or indignation.

And yet. And yet…we begin to see the signs that a new wave of feminism – mere ripples now, but the tide is coming – has begun, precisely because of the misogynist repression by government. The Internet – the new and intensely democratic commons – is alive with feminist blogs and feminist websites; the conversation is heated and intense. New organizations, like the Miss G Project, FemRebelles in Montréal, and FemRev in Winnipeg – youthful feminist collectives – have sprung to life and flourished.

In the last month, as I finished working on this book, three strikingly feminist, though seemingly unconnected, stories hit the front pages of the newspapers, a ratcheting up of attention that has not occurred since the beginning of the Second Wave. They were stories that quickly established a life of their own, snatching headlines and reams of comment, day after day. First came the Slut Walk, a defiant procession of women – two thousand of them – who marched in Toronto to protest a police officer's statement that if you wanted to avoid being raped, you shouldn't dress like a slut. Infuriated by this ancient calumny (evidently still alive and slithering), the women almost spontaneously rose up in colourful and defiant protest and, like wildfire, the idea leaped and flamed around the world. Women marched in the Arctic and in the Antipodes, and they are still marching and seizing headlines.

The second story, which generated more heated comment than any other story in some newspapers' history, was the tale of baby Storm, whose progressive Toronto parents refused to reveal the baby's sex. Furthermore, they had encouraged their two other children, boys ages five and two, to choose their own dress style (the older boy favoured flaming pink dresses) and hair styles (long). The creativity, care, and tenderness with which these enlightened parents chose to nurture their children, free of the straitjacket of pop culture gender stereotyping, caused so much panicked outrage and vile name-calling that I was delightfully reminded of the earliest days of the movement. These parents had touched a nerve. The reaction meant that the gender issue was coming back to life.

The third story was that of Brigette DePape, a page in the Senate of Canada and a high-achieving university student chosen for this privileged position on the basis of her accomplishments. On the day that Parliament opened, Brigette stood on the floor of the Senate and held up a homemade stop sign emblazoned with the slogan "Stop Harper." Explaining her actions, after she had been hustled out by the guards and promptly fired, DePape argued in a press conference that Harper had been elected to a majority by fewer than 40 percent of the electorate and that his reckless actions (ignoring climate change, spending billions on jet fighters, promoting the tar sands) demanded protest. Standing there in her prim uniform, her hair in braids, and her face earnest and innocent, Brigette was the perfect, civil, nonthreatening emblem of protest. Later, she explained that Canada needed an "Arab Spring," a reminder that the wave of change that began in Egypt was started by a young woman blogger who called for a peaceful demonstration in Tahrir Square.

These three stories appear to be an incoherent little concatenation of events; seen through the lens of feminist history, they may signify something powerful and new, a rising up of young women who will certainly forge their own style, their own vocabulary, their own way of framing issues. There is a common thread in these three disparate stories – a joy in defiance, in protest, in standing forth for feminist freedom with its passion for justice and equality.

The Revolution begins again.

Revolutions echo down through generations. Sometimes the voices fade and grow fainter, but then, when conditions ripen, the sound strengthens and the message is picked up by new, alert ears. Each wave of feminist resistance produces its own strategies, styles, and goals, but precedent also has deep lessons for us. One reason I undertook the writing of this book was to preserve some of the highlights, the successes, the byways, and the skirmishes of feminism's Second Wave.

Because history and memory have so much resonance for me, I want to finish with the following metaphorical note.

SPRY TREES ARE THE APPLE OF CITY'S CORE

February 1991

I never meant to write about the apple trees; I think they must have me under some kind of hypnotic spell. I met them four months ago in a public rose garden in North York. All this time later, I find I'm still thinking about them and about their imminent doom, so I went back up Yonge St. to say a proper farewell.

"Goodbye, dear fairy-tale trees," I told them, mildly unhinged by glorious sunshine. The three trees are old, old. They were planted by David Gibson in the 1850s, and are the last survivors of his orchard. There they stand, living pioneers, right across Yonge St. from Zippy Print and Original Pizza, at the corner of Park Home, a few blocks north of North York City Hall.

You think I've become a wing-nut, a tree-hugger? Ah, but these are Tolkien Ents, these are Brothers Grimm trees. They have a hoary antique presence. If they could speak (and their branches did, gently, creak at me), they'd speak Apple, the universal language of fragrance, ripeness, and harvest.

My favourite, a Tolman Sweet, is big and trunk-twisted, snugged into the earth with rooty bumps like elephant toes. I patted the friendly bark. There are smooth rounded holes in the bole: bijou residences for chipmunks. (Are there any chipmunks left?) There's even a green fuzz of moss on the tree's north side. The great limbs sweep welcomingly outward and upward, the smaller branches tangling in a magical thicket.

"Ah, those apple trees," said Bill Granger, now chief of urban design for North York. "I've climbed them and pruned them, and they're just wonderful. You know, as an arborist, I love to climb apple trees." I was amazed. A reporter's phone call rarely elicits such lyricism. "Apple trees cradle you," he continued. "It's like being held in someone's arms."

They are the oldest apple trees in North York. He sent the fruit off to an agricultural laboratory and verified that two of the trees are Tolman Sweet ("a yellow-tinged, very sweet apple") and the other a Snow ("intensely white").

"Yes, the trees are diseased, but they can easily survive that. In effect, they grow a complete new tree around themselves each year; just think of the annual rings. The Gibson House apple trees are good for another 50 years at least," Granger said.

Alas, it is not to be. North York sentenced them to the axe when it sold the little rose garden park to Penta Stolp Developments Inc. On the very site will soar up to the sky two glass and granite commercial towers, 29 and 31 stories respectively.

I have a special affection for Gibson House. It's a handsome brick Upper Canadian residence, just behind the tiny park and soon to be crouched, like a pea in the shadow of a pyramid, behind the Penta Stolpian towers. You'll still be able to visit Gibson House and the kindly costumed guides may give you a cookie, freshly baked from original "receets." I like the thought of David Gibson, too. He was a Scot from Glamis, a reformer, a rebel against the Family Compact (Hear! Hear!), and a supporter of William Lyon Mackenzie's rebellion. His laconic diary often mentions his hired men and the orchards: "Malcom drawing in apples and punkins [sic]" or "Jemmie picking apples." Even when he had to flee to New York State after the Montgomery Tavern battle, he kept up to date with his orchard in notes from his father: "Our apels [sic] are as good as any on the Street but there [sic] only offering a shilling with the bushel..."

I phoned the development's landscape architect, Bruce Corban, and told him I was interested in the apple trees. "Well, surely you don't want to change the whole course of history for the sake of a few apple trees!" he blurted, before I said another word.

Well, no, not really. I just wanted to commemorate them somehow. I didn't point out that Penta Stolp and "the whole course of history" were not synonymous to me.

Corban assured me that Penta Stolp planned an elegant indoor tea garden which will be filled with "foliage materials" (he meant plants), a lavish public park along Park Home, and a public conservatory too.

Thanks to Bill Granger, the real trees, as opposed to foliage materials, will not utterly vanish. He's grafting some smaller branches on to new root stock, to be planted in the Gibson House garden.

While there's time, and if you can stand it, take a drive up Yonge St. – from the 401 to Finch, it's an example of the silliest, most grotesque commercial architecture and crazy unplanned over-development anywhere on the continent – and commune with the trees.

Actually, before they go down, I think we ought to have a wild, witchy rite of lamentation. Bonfires and incantations. Failing that, at least go pay your respects. They're perfectly lovely. Remember them.

* * * * * * * * *

BUT A FUNNY and wonderful thing happened on the way out of the orchard.

Local park staff took cuttings of the trees soon after this column appeared and grafted the scions onto root stock. Five of the descendants are now growing and bearing fruit in a park near Gibson House, and one of the original trees survives at its original site.

There *is* continuity, there is resurgence, new growth, and new fruit to be plucked from the tree. It has been the great good luck of my lifetime that I could take part in the most exciting movement in Canada's past century, give meaning to my life by my participation, and watch the benefits flow to countless girls and women whose lives will be better because of our efforts.

Feminism dead? They said that from the beginning, and they were always wrong: Feminism is a passion for justice and equality, and that cannot die.

Acknowledgements

My thanks to the women of the Feminist History Society, who asked me to undertake this project and who were unfailingly supportive, and to Margie Wolfe, pioneer feminist publisher, who instantly agreed to co-publish;

My thanks to the *Toronto Star*, which owns copyright to all the columns I wrote for them, and which allowed me to use freely the columns in this book;

My thanks to my editor, Sarah Swartz, who has the patience and skills of organization that I so utterly lack, and who gave shape to an impossibly large amount of material;

My thanks to our son, Avi Lewis, who was never too busy to offer advice, support, inspiration, and editorial prowess;

And above all, my enduring gratitude and love for Colleen Pollreis, who was my indispensable assistant, colleague, and friend at the *Toronto Star* for fifteen years and who volunteered her intelligence and talents to help me think through this book, to assemble the materials, to research, and even to tidy the stacks of papers and books.

From a room full of feminist books, these are the ones I pulled most frequently from the shelf, for historical fact-checking, reminiscence, and inspiration, while writing this book:

Amin, Nuzhat, Frances Beer, Kathryn McPherson, Andrea Medovarski, Angela Miles and Goli Rezai-Rashti , eds. *Canadian Women's Studies: An Introductory Reader.* Toronto: Inanna Publications and Education Inc., 1999.

Backhouse, Constance and David H. Flaherty. *Challenging Times: The Women's Movement in Canada and the United States.* Montreal & Kingston: McGill-Queen's University Press, 1992.

Bashevkin, Sylvia. *Women on the Defensive: Living Through Conservative Times.* Toronto: University of Toronto Press, 1998.

Brodribb, Somer, ed. *Reclaiming the Future: Women's Strategies for the 21st Century.* Charlottetown: Gynergy Books, 1999.

Coontz, Stephanie. *The Way We Never Were: American Families and the Nostalgia Trap.* New York: Basic Books, 1992.

Dagg, Anne Innis and Patricia J. Thompson. *MisEducation: Women & Canadian Universities.* Toronto: The Ontario Institute for Studies in Education, 1988.

Doe, Jane. *The Story of Jane Doe: A book about rape.* Toronto: Vintage Canada, 2003.

Dworkin, Andrea. *Right-Wing Women.* New York: Perigee Books, 1978.

Fitzgerald, Maureen, Margie Wolfe and Connie Guberman. *Still Ain't Satisfied! Canadian Feminism Today.* Toronto: The Women's Press, 1982.

Hagan, Lee. *Fugitive Information, Essays from a Feminist Hothead.* San Francisco: Pandora, 1993.

Johnson, Holly and Myrna Dawson. *Violence Against Women in Canada, Research and Policy Perspectives.* Toronto: Oxford University Press, 2011.

Kome, Penney. *The Taking of Twenty-Eight: Women Challenge the Constitution.* Toronto: The Women's Press, 1983.

Korinek, Valerie. *Roughing It in the Suburbs: Reading* Chatelaine *Magazine in the Fifties and Sixties.* Toronto: University of Toronto Press, 2000.

Lahey, Kathleen A. *Are We 'Persons' Yet? Law and Sexuality in Canada.* Toronto: University of Toronto Press, 1999.

Leidholdt, Dorchen and Janice G. Raymond, eds. *The Sexual Liberals and the Attack on Feminism.* New York: Pergamon Press, 1990.

Mitchell, Margaret. *No Laughing Matter: Adventure, Activism & Politics.* Vancouver: Granville Island Publishing Ltd., 2008.

McKenna, Katherine M.J. and June Larkin, eds. *Violence Against Women: New Canadian Perspectives.* Toronto: Inanna Publications and Education Inc., 2002.

Morgan, Robin. *Sisterhood is Forever: the women's anthology for a new millennium*. New York: Washington Square Press, 2003.

Morrow, Eileen and Susan Wakeling. *"No More!" Women Speak Out Against Violence*. Toronto: Ontario Association of Interval and Transition Houses, 2000.

Rebick, Judy. *Ten Thousand Roses: The Making of a Feminist Revolution*. Toronto; Penguin, 2005.

Sharma, Nandita. *The National Action Committee on the Status of Women's Voters' Guide: A Women's Agenda for Social Justice*. Toronto: James Lorimer & Company, Publishers, 1997.

• • • • • • • • •

JOURNALS

Canadian Woman Studies, Vol. 18, No. 2 & 3, 1998.

Photo Credits

Thank you to Emelie Kozak, who undertook the photo research for this book with such thoughtfulness, diligence, and organization.

Page 12: Toronto Star / Ron Bull
Michele as she appeared in her first Toronto Star column in 1978

Page 15: Courtesy of Michele Landsberg

Page 16: QMI Agency

Page 21: QMI Agency

Page 23: Toronto Star / Dick Darrell

Page 25: Courtesy of Michele Landsberg

Page 26: Archives and Special Collections, University of Ottawa Library (NU-X10-118-33) / Amanda Bankier
A march at Toronto's Nathan Phillips Square on May 10, 1975

Page 28: Courtesy of Michele Landsberg

Page 29: Courtesy of Michele Landsberg

Page 31: Library and Archives Canada / PA-129344 / Dominion Wide Photographs Limited / Bill Olson

Page 34: Courtesy of Michele Landsberg

Page 39: Courtesy of Michele Landsberg

Page 40: Library and Archives Canada / PA-211613 / Duncan Cameron
Voice of Women meet Prime Minister Diefenbaker in his office, 1961

Page 42: Archives and Special Collections, University of Ottawa Library (NU-X10-118- 2) / Kay Macpherson Committee

Page 44: Courtesy of Schuster Gindin

Page 55: Archives and Special Collections, University of Ottawa Library (NU-X10-118-4) / Branching Out

Page 57: Archives and Special Collections, University of Ottawa Library (NU-X10-118-5) / Canadian Council on Social Development

Page 60: Archives and Special Collections, University of Ottawa Library (CWMA PC-X10-1-129) / Nancy Adamson

Page 69: Courtesy of Michele Landsberg

Page 70: Archives and Special Collections, University of Ottawa Library (NU-X10-118-7)

Page 73: Archives and Special Collections, University of Ottawa Library (NU-X10-118-8) / Johanne Pelletier

Page 76: Toronto Star / Jim Wilkes

Page 77: Archives and Special Collections, University of Ottawa Library (NU-X10-118-10) / Women for Political Action

Page 78: Archives and Special Collections, University of Ottawa Library (NU-X10-118-11)

Page 87: R v. Butler, [1992] 1 S.C.R. 452

Page 94: Library and Archives Canada / R5274-420X-E

Page 108: Archives and Special Collections, University of Ottawa Library (NU-X10-118-31)

Page 110: Courtesy of Constance Backhouse

Page 129: The Canadian Press / Fred Chartrand

Page 143: Archives and Special Collections, University of Ottawa Library (NU-X10-118-12) / Canada Post Corporation, Head Office Human Rights: Affirmative Action Division

Page 144: Archives and Special Collections, University of Ottawa Library (NU-X10-118-14) / Concept and art for poster, Joss Maclennan Design

Page 151: Archives and Special Collections, University of Ottawa Library (NU-X10-118-15) / Interval House

Page 160: Archives and Special Collections, University of Ottawa Library (NU-X10-118-18) / Adele Perron and Sarah Rashid

Page 167: Second Story Press / Joss Maclennan

Page 174: Archives and Special Collections, University of Ottawa Library (NU-X10-118-16) / Hestia House

Page 175: Archives and Special Collections, University of Ottawa Library (NU-X10-118-17) / Society Against Family Abuse

Page 176: Archives and Special Collections, University of Ottawa Library (NU-X10-118-19)

Page 182: Archives and Special Collections, University of Ottawa Library (NU-X10-118-22)

Page 185: Archives and Special Collections, University of Ottawa Library (NU-X10-118-1) / CARAL

Page 213: Courtesy of Michele Landsberg

Page 214: Archives and Special Collections, University of Ottawa Library (NU-X10-118-6)

Page 233: Courtesy of Avril Benoit

Page 234: Courtesy of CW4WAfghan / Oates

Page 250: Archives and Special Collections, University of Ottawa Library (NU-X10-118-30) / FWTAO

Page 257: Library and Archives Canada / E010753008 / Canadian Federation of University Women

Page 261: Archives and Special Collections, University of Ottawa Library (NU-X10-118-26)

Page 264: Archives and Special Collections, University of Ottawa Library (NU-X10-118-27) / NAC

Page 266: Archives and Special Collections, University of Ottawa Library (NU-X10-118-28) / Moira Armour

Page 267: Ela Kinowska

Page 275: Archives and Special Collections, University of Ottawa Library (NU-X10-118-29) / FWTAO

Page 287: Courtesy of Linda Silver Dranoff

Page 288: Library of Congress, Rare Book and Special Collections Division

Page 290: Courtesy of Alex Tang

Page 292: Archives of Ontario, S17839, Acc. 2802

Page 293: Victoria University Archives, Photography Collection

Page 296: Courtesy of Michele Landsberg

Page 297: The Canadian Press

Page 317: Courtesy of Fatima Jaffer